MILITARY OPERATIONS
1813 - 1814

* * * * *

BY
LORD BURGHERSH

The Naval & Military Press Ltd

Published by

The Naval & Military Press Ltd
Unit 5 Riverside, Brambleside,
Bellbrook Industrial Estate,
Uckfield, East Sussex,
TN22 1QQ England

Tel: +44 (0) 1825 749494
Fax: +44 (0) 1825 765701

www.naval-military-press.com
www.nmarchive.com

In reprinting in facsimile from the original, any imperfections are inevitably reproduced and the quality may fall short of modern type and cartographic standards.

MEMOIR

OF THE

OPERATIONS OF THE ALLIED ARMIES,

UNDER

PRINCE SCHWARZENBERG,

AND

MARSHAL BLUCHER,

DURING

THE LATTER END OF 1813, AND THE YEAR 1814.

BY MAJOR-GENERAL

THE RIGHT HONORABLE LORD BURGHERSH,

His Majesty's Envoy Extraordinary and Minister Plenipotentiary at the Central Courts of Italy; and, during the Years of 1813—14 accredited to the Head-Quarters of the Allied Army.

SECOND EDITION, WITH ADDITIONAL DOCUMENTS.

LONDON:

JOHN MURRAY, ALBEMARLE-STREET.

MDCCCXXII

PREFATORY ADDRESS.

Since the first publication of the present Memoir, a period of nearly four years has elapsed, during which time several works relating to the transactions of which it treats have been given to the public. Amongst them it is impossible not to distinguish the Narrative of Baron Fain, which, from the official situation (that of Secretary of the Cabinet of Bonaparte) held by its author, is calculated to excite a greater degree of interest, and hereafter to be more relied upon, as an authority, than any other publication which has appeared on the side of the French army. It has been a source of great satisfaction to the author of the present Memoir, to observe how entirely he has agreed in the detail of the leading transactions which he has described, with the work above mentioned. Some shades of difference will naturally be remarked, from the various appearance which the same circumstances assume, when seen from the Headquarters of opposing armies. But beyond the allowance to be made on this account, little or no discrepancy is to be observed between the two works. On the contrary, the opinions and statements given in the present Memoir are confirmed by the documents which could only be accurately known in the French army, and which have been brought to light in the work of Baron Fain.

Some documents, of which the substance only had been given before, have been added to the present publication. These are the Letters of the King of Bavaria to the Emperor Alexander, and the Emperor's answer, which are referred to in pages 11 and 12 of the Memoir; the Official Report made by Count Meerveldt, of his conversation with Bonaparte, on the 16th of October, 1813, referred to in page 53; the Note Verbale, transmitted through the Baron St. Aignan, referred to in page 58; the copies of Bonaparte's Letter to the Emperor of Austria, and the Emperor's answer, referred to in page 50; the copy of a Paper drawn up by the King of Prussia, and addressed to the Emperor Alexander, referred to in page 97; and a Note upon the Battle of Toulouse, which was produced by the preposterous statements made in some of the French military publications, and particularly in the *Annuaire de France*, Vol. I. pages 599 and 600, as regarding that battle.

CONTENTS.

Part I.

Comprises the period from the advance of Buonaparte into Germany, and the battle of Lutzen, to the retreat of the French Army across the Rhine, and the deliverance of Germany   1

Part II.

From the assembly of the Allied Armies on the banks of the Rhine, to the passage of that river on the frontiers of Switzerland, and the occupation of that Country   . 41

Part III.

From the invasion of France, to the establishment of Prince Schwarzenberg's army along the banks of the Seine, from Fontainbleau to Merry   . 71

Part IV.

Comprises the operations of the army of Marshal Blucher, from the battle of Brienne, to the junction of that Officer at Merry with the army of Prince Schwarzenberg, which had fallen back on Troyes . 127

Part V.

From the retreat of Prince Schwarzenberg from Troyes upon Bar-sur-Aube and Chaumont, to the re-establishment of his army in the positions along the Seine and Aube 153

Part VI.

Resumes the operations of Marshal Blucher since his separation from the army of Prince Schwarzenberg at Merry, to the battle of Laon, and the re-capture of Rheims by the French army, and its assembly on the banks of the Marne, near Chalons and Epernay . 186

Part VII.

Details the operations of Prince Schwarzenberg from the period of Buonaparte's advance upon him from the Marne, to his junction with Marshal Blucher's advance-guard near Vitry . . 206

Part VIII.

Details the movements of the French corps left upon the Aisne in observation of Marshal Blucher, the advance of the Allies upon Paris, the battle in front of that Capital, and its occupation . ., 226

Part IX.

Resumes the operations of Buonaparte, from St. Dizier, till the assembling of his Army at Fontainbleau; describes the general positions of the contending Armies throughout France, the negotiations at Paris, the consequent abdication of Buonaparte, and the termination of Hostilities . 260

Appendix 313

Addenda 343

ERRATA.

Page 1, line 11, *insert* one of.
" 4, " 10, *for* the French army was composed, *read* the French army was originally composed.
" 22, " 6, *for* the cavalry of the Gen. Arrighi, *read* the cavalry of Gen. Arrighi.
" 33, " 15, *omit* to each other.
" 76, " 1 and 5, *for* Droutte, *read* Durutte.
" 130, " 3, *for* division, *read* divisions.
" 156, " 4, *for* Russians, *read* Russian.
" 173, " 14, *for* Villigrue, *read* Villegrue.
" 181, " 2, *for* could, *read* would.
" 181, " 5, *for* could, *read* might.
" 185, " 1, *omit* hostility of the.
" 186, " 13, *after* 27th, *insert* of February.
" 188, " 9 and 10, *omit* the remainder of his army consisted of, *and also the bracket at the end of line* 10.
" 209, " 5, *for* and that the great army, *read* and that on the 20th the great army.
" 209, " 6, *omit* on the 20th.
" 215, " 19, *read* communicated.
" 234, " 19, *for* endeavoured, *read* endeavour.
" 265, " 9, *for* that officer, *read* General Tettenborn.
" 289, " 4, *for* summon, *read* summons.
" 294, " 2, *for* had unfurled, *read* had triumphantly unfurled.
" 294, " 3, *omit* triumphantly.
" 319, *read* Russian-German Legion.

MEMOIR

OF

THE OPERATIONS

OF THE

ALLIED ARMIES.

PART I.

So many publications exist relating to the transactions of the period comprised in this Memoir, that the author would hardly have ventured to commit to paper his own recollections of them, if he had not been encouraged by a feeling that on points so interesting to the history of the age, the views of all those who had the advantage of being actors in the scene, may conduce to a better understanding. and a clearer relation hereafter of the whole of those great events, which, together, will mark the era in which they took place as the most memorable in the history of the world.

Under these considerations, the following sheets have been written. They pretend only to give such information as may serve to elucidate transactions, many of which are but little known, or imperfectly appreciated.

Buonaparte having returned to Paris in the month of December, 1812, leaving on the frontiers of Russia the broken remains of the finest army that had ever been assembled, succeeded in engaging the French people, notwithstanding the tremendous disasters of which he had been the cause, in fresh exertions to support him. He was so successful in the application of the powers intrusted to him, that he was enabled to take the field in Germany with an army of 160,000 men, and on the 2d of May, on the plains of Lutzen, to gain a victory over the combined Russian and Prussian armies, by which he established himself in Saxony. By the battle of Bautzen he obliged his opponents to retire into Silesia, where he concluded an armistice, the terms of which were greatly in his favour, and which were submitted to by the Allies with the view of allowing time for Austria either to bring about an honourable peace, or to unite herself to the general cause in which they were engaged.

The cessation of military operations gave rise to negotiations, in which the Emperor of Austria, having previously disentangled himself from his engagements as allied with France, offered his mediation for the establishment of peace: in the mean time, he armed to support his own independence, and to increase his influence in the decision of the great points which, for the settlement of the world, seemed now about to be brought into discussion.

The conduct of Buonaparte, during this period, proves that, confiding in his own resources, he would not desist from the vast projects he entertained. He seems to have had but one object in the negotiations which preceded the assembly of the Plenipotentiaries at Prague, and which afterwards, for a short time, were carried on there, which was, to keep the Austrians separated from the Allied Powers; promising that, when he had terminated his quarrel with the latter, he would arrange every thing with Austria, as his father-in-law the emperor might desire.

He saw, however, the extermination of these hopes with calmness, and refusing the negotiation as it was offered, brought upon himself, with the expiration of the armistice, the declaration of war of Austria, and thus, the combined hostility of almost the whole of Europe.

The first results of the military operations consequent on these events, were of various success. The armies opposed to each other were not of equal force. The French army was composed of fourteen corps d'armée, and four corps of cavalry of reserve, besides a corps of observation under Marshal Augereau. Of these corps, three were at a distance from the great scene of operations, the ninth corps, which had been dissolved—the tenth, which was under General Count Rapp in garrison at Danzig—and the thirteenth, under Marshal Davoust at Hamburg.

Of the remaining part of the army, Buonaparte immediately opposed the fourth, seventh, and twelfth corps of infantry, and the third of cavalry, to the army of the Prince Royal of Sweden; the third, fifth, and eleventh of infantry, and the second of cavalry, to the army of Marshal Blucher; the fourteenth corps he destined to cover Dresden; and the rest of his troops, consisting of the guards, first, second, sixth, and eighth corps of infantry, together with the first and fourth of the reserve of cavalry, he retained to constitute the force which should act as occasion might require, and under his own immediate command.

The force of the Allies was divided into three great armies: the principal under Prince Schwarzenberg, composed of the Austrian troops, together with the Russian corps commanded by Count Wittgenstein, the Prussian corps under General Kleist, and the Russian and Prussian reserves under the Grand Duke Constantine, the whole of which was placed on the frontiers of Bohemia in front of Prague. The second army, under Marshal Blucher, was composed of the Prussian corps of General Yorck, and the two Russian corps of Generals Count Langeron and Baron Sacken, and was assembled in Silesia. The third army was commanded by the Prince Royal of Sweden, and was composed of the Prussian corps under Generals Bulow and Tauenzein, the army of Sweden, and the Russian corps under Baron Winzingerode, and was destined to operate in front of Berlin. The corps of General Walmoden, which was acting against Marshal Davoust, was also under the orders of the Prince Royal of Sweden.

The numbers of these different armies may be collected from a return* of their effective force, made previously to the rupture of the armistice (which will be found in the Appendix); and although the whole amount, as therein stated, may not actually have been present under arms, it would certainly be within the truth to estimate the Allies at 550,000 men: a vast superiority over the enemy, who never were rated at more than 357,107 †.

Marshal Blucher, in the battle of the Katzbach, greatly outnumbered the corps opposed to him, and the Prussians alone of the Prince Royal of Sweden's army obtained the victories of Gross-Beren and Denewitz. In the last of these actions, Marshal Ney, with considerable reinforcements, had been sent by Buonaparte to take the command of the force he had

---

* See Appendix, No. 1.   † Ibid., No. 2.

originally moved against the Prince Royal of Sweden; yet the result was disaster and defeat.

The remainder of Buonaparte's army when assembled at Dresden, was infinitely less numerous than the army of Prince Schwarzenberg; and when the latter in the end of the month of September, was reinforced by the corps of General Benningsen and the army of Bavaria, the disproportion became immense.

Under these circumstances, the efforts of Buonaparte were almost every where unsuccessful; the momentary advantage obtained by him in the repulse of the great Bohemian army from the walls of Dresden, was imbittered by the destruction of General Vandame's corps at Culm. Every other action was unfavourable to him, and the loss in consequence not less than from 130 to 160,000 men. This diminution of force, added to the increasing power of the Allies, forced Buonaparte, in the early part of October, to break up from Dresden, and concentrate his army at Leipzig.

In executing, however, this movement, he seems

not to have abandoned the expectation of a great and immediate success; in this view he left the first and fourteenth corps under Marshal St. Cyr, amounting to 35,000 men, as a garrison in Dresden; a point which could be interesting to him only for the future offensive operations he is supposed to have contemplated.

The Silesian army, pursuing the glorious career it had first opened to itself in the battle of the Katzbach, was established, after various brilliant and successful actions, in the end of September, at Elsterwerda. In the meantime, the Northern army had, after the battle of Denewitz, advanced upon the Elbe, and had thrown two bridges over it, at Roslau and Acken. The army of General Benningsen entered Bohemia in the early days of October, by Leutmeritz and Aussig, and occupied the positions in front of Töplitz, which had been given up to it by Prince Schwarzenberg, who had led his army by its left towards Chemnitz, Penig, and Altenburg.

The general object of the Allies was to enclose the French army. To effect this, the Prince Royal of

Sweden and Marshal Blucher were to operate from the Elbe, upon the Mulda and the Saal; the corps of Generals Bubna and Benningsen were to advance in concert, from the frontiers of Bohemia, on both banks of the Elbe, towards Dresden; and the army of Prince Schwarzenberg was to advance upon Lutzen.

In execution of these views, Marshal Blucher broke up from his position at Elsterwerda on the 1st of October, and moving through Herzberg and Jessen, established a bridge over the Elbe at Elster, and, passing his army across it on the morning of the 3rd, attacked the fourth corps of the French army, under Count Bertrand, in position at Wartenburg, and having completely defeated it, advanced on the 5th, to Duben, on the Mulda. Protected by this bold and decisive operation, the Prince Royal of Sweden moved his army over the Elbe on the 4th and 5th, and established it at Dessau, with its advance at Cöthen and Jessnitz.

Generals Benningsen and Bubna advanced on the 6th, having driven the enemy from Pirna, Dippoldiswalde, and Freyberg, to the environs of Dresden.

In the meantime, Prince Schwarzenberg had placed his army along the Elster and the Pleisse; his left at Zeitz, Pegau, and Lutzen; his right at Borna and Estenheim.

The Emperor Alexander broke up from Commotau on the 8th, and with his reserves arrived at Altenburg on the 12th.

During these marches, the treaty signed between Austria and Bavaria arrived at head-quarters, together with the decision, that the corps of Austrians under General Frimont, hitherto opposed to the Bavarians, should be united to the latter, under the orders of General Wrede; who was to lead the army, thus composed, from the Inn, on the 16th, and march upon Wurtzbourg.

The first opening to the negotiations, which terminated in these results, was a letter from the King of Bavaria, addressed to the Emperor of Russia, in answer to one from that sovereign, dated Nymphenbourg, the 10th of September, 1813; in which the King is reported to have declared, that, " A total stranger to the interests of the war, in which he had for too long a time been engaged—a war which was contrary to all his personal feelings, and which could only be a source of dangers and expense to him, he had, notwithstanding, fulfilled, with scrupulous fidelity, the engagements which, in other times and under other auspices, he had contracted; that now, when every circumstance concurred to disengage him from those obligations, he could only rejoice at the prospect of re-establishing those connexions, which he sincerely regretted had ever been interrupted. He had but one wish, which was, to see, as early as possible, the re-establishment of a general peace upon a solid and durable basis, and the preservation in their integrity of the states and territories submitted to his rule. He would concur, with zeal, with perseverance, and with all the means in his power, in every measure which would conduce to the attainment of this double object."

" He had already ordered General Raglawich to fall back on Bavaria; no act of hostility had been committed between his army and that of Austria, under the Prince of Reuss; General Wrede had long since had orders to abstain from all offensive movements, and this state of things might easily be prolonged till there could be some understanding upon the subject of the new relations he was ready to contract, and on which the intervention of his Imperial Majesty would have so powerful an influence."

The Emperor of Russia, from Töplitz, the 23d of September, is said to have answered this letter, by expressions of gratitude for the dispositions it announced, and the confidence it reposed in him, and by assuring the King of Bavaria—" That, united as he was by the most indissoluble ties to the Emperor of Austria, so he would not hesitate in acceding to the propositions that Sovereign was about to make to his Majesty, and in offering his guarantee to the arrangements which might be the results of them ; that the return to an order of things, which might assure to Europe a long continuance of peace and happiness, was the object towards which all his efforts tended ; and the independence of the intermediate powers he looked upon as the best means of obtaining it ; that the military frontiers of Austria must at the same time be better established—an advantage which could only be obtained by arrangements with his Majesty; that the king would himself be convinced of this, and that he (the Emperor) was too frank not at once to explain himself upon a matter of so much delicacy; the complete indemnification for the countries ceded, should, however, be formally guaranteed to his majesty, so that such an exchange could only prove an advantage to him. He would be called upon to give up those provinces only which did not amalgamate with his other states; and where the desire of returning to their former sovereign nursed a spirit of insurrection, which would at all times menace the Government with embarrassment. He declared his readiness, as soon as the preliminaries with Austria should be signed, to conclude, with any person his Majesty would send to his head-quarters, engagements founded upon the principles he had developed. In return, he felt himself authorized by the assurances he had received, to expect from his Majesty an active and immediate co-operation. In the contrary event, and if the brilliant prospect of the present deliverance of Europe should be lost, his Majesty must be aware that the Allies would no longer be in a situation to realize towards him those views which they now entertained, views dictated by friendship and the liberality of their policy."

The Emperor of Austria and the King of Prussia are understood to have written letters of a similar nature, and the Prince of Reuss was authorized to treat with General Wrede, the Bavarian negotiator. When the result of these different transactions, in the signature of the peace between the Allied Powers and Bavaria, was known to Buonaparte, connected as it was with so many other circumstances unfavourable to him, it would seem as if, clinging to the memory of his former glories, he was still unable to resolve on those measures which prudence would have dictated. By the movement of General Regnier, on the 11th and 12th from Wittemberg, upon Coswig and Roslau, combined with the advance of Marshal Ney towards Dessau, and the transfer of his own head-quarters to Duben, Buonaparte's intention appeared to have been either to pass to the right of the Elbe, and operate on Magdeburg, or to attack the Northern and Silesian armies, at this time collected between Halle and Bernberg, on the Saal: these his apparent objects, however, he abandoned on the 14th, assem-

* See the Manuscript de 1813, par le Baron Fain, vol. ii. page 370, and the following.

bling his whole army at Leipzig, where, notwithstanding the disadvantage of the position, he decided to accept a general battle *.

The Bohemian army having occupied the ground extending from Weissenfels to Rochlitz was destined to envelop the right of the French army; with this view, all the corps of which it was composed advanced on the 16th. The third under General Giulay, and the troops under P. Maurice Liechtenstein, from Kl. Zschocher attacked the fourth French corps under Count Bertrand, and for a short time took possession of the village of Lindenau which intercepted the only road to France left open to Buonaparte; but this communication was soon after re-established, General Giulay having been driven back to his original position, from whence he afterwards retired to Knauthayn. The corps of General Meerveldt was advanced upon Connewitz; that of General Wittgenstein formed into two columns, the right, under Prince Gorczakow, the left, under the Prince Eugene of Wurtemberg, was directed to attack the villages of Liebertwolkwitz and Wachau; whilst General Kleist advanced along

* See Appendix, No. 3.

the right bank of the Pleisse, from Gröbern upon Mark-Kleberg; these troops were to be supported by the Russian and Prussian reserves at Magdeborn, and the Austrian reserve at Zöbigker. General Klenau, forming the extreme right, was to direct his march upon Fuchshayn, Gross Pössna, and the right of Liebertwolkwitz. By these movements it was intended that Generals Meerveldt and Klenau should turn the enemy on both his flanks, while the corps of Generals Wittgenstein and Kleist, supported by the reserves, should force his centre.

General Meerveldt met with considerable difficulties in his advance upon Connewitz, and when by perseverance he at last forced a passage over the Pleisse, near Dölitz, in rear of the French position, he was taken prisoner, and the part of his corps which had crossed the river driven back and defeated. General Klenau was unable to advance against the corps of Marshal Macdonald and General Lauriston, which were opposed to him: and maintained himself with difficulty against their repeated attacks, in a position between Gross Pössna and Seyfartshayn. General Kleist, passing through Gosewitz, attacked and carried the village of Mark-Kleberg; in front of which, by a brilliant charge of the Russian cavalry, under General Lewachow, he established himself. The Prince Eugene of Wurtemberg succeeded for a time in gaining possession of the heights occupied by the enemy near Wachau; while Prince Gorczakow attempted to make himself master of Liebertwolkwitz. Marshal Victor, however, supported by the guards under Marshal Oudinot, and the reserve-artillery under General Drouot, re-took the ground which had been ceded, and drove back the Princes of Wurtemberg and Gorczakow upon the Russian grenadiers at the *bergerie* of Auenhayn and Gossa; and afterwards, aided by the cavalry of General Latour Maubourg under the immediate command of Marshal Murat, established himself in these places; while General Kellerman, with 6,000 cavalry, drove back the Russians under General Lewachow upon Gosewitz: the centre of the Allies was thus penetrated; the arrival, however, from Zöbigker, of the Austrian reserves, who crossed the Pleisse at Gröbern (the cavalry of which under Count Nostitz, checked the progress of General Kellerman, while General Bianchi, after occupying Mark-Kleberg, cannonaded the right and rear of the

French centre), together with the advance of the Russian and Prussian reserves, and the brilliant charges of the Cossacks of the guard under Count Orloff Denizoff, re-established the action :—at dark, the two armies occupied the positions they had held in the morning.

On the side of Marshal Blucher, the results of this day were far more favourable: this officer having learnt on the 15th that the great army was moving upon the enemy's position to the south of Leipzig, broke up immediately from Halle, and advanced to Gross-Kugel. It was hoped the Prince Royal of Sweden would, at the same time, have moved from Cöthen, either upon Bitterfeld, Duben, and Delitsch, or through Zörbig and Brehna, upon Skeuditz. In the night, however, he directed his army upon Sylbitz, taking up a position with the Swedes at Wittin and Petersberg, General Bulow at Oppin, and General Winzingerode at Zörbig.

On the morning of the 16th, Marshal Blucher formed his army in two columns: the left, under Count Langeron, supported by General Sacken, was destined for the attack of the enemy in the villages of Freyrode and Radefeld; the right, under General Yorck, was to advance upon Lindenthal, with a strong detachment composed of the Prussian guards which was to move along the Chaussee leading to Leipzig; the cavalry was concentrated in the rear ready to act whenever it should be required. The enemy, for a short time only, defended these advanced positions, but concentrated himself between Mökern, Eutritzsch, and Gross-Wetteritz. Count Langeron pursued his right, driving it before him, and was moving upon the Partha, with the intention of passing that river, when he was arrested by the arrival of a division of the third corps under General Delmas, on its return from Eilenburg, which attacked his left at the same time that the forces previously opposed to him (reinforced by the troops which Marshal Ney had sent in the morning to the assistance of Buonaparte, and which he now was bringing back), advanced upon his right. He was, in consequence, obliged to fall back to Klein-Wetteritz; from whence, he succeeded, however, at a later period, in re-taking the ground he had lost, and driving the troops opposed to him, through the wood of Podelwitz to near

Hohenheyde, in front of which place the Russian cavalry made a most successful charge, took 600 prisoners and 22 guns, and threw the enemy into complete confusion. The divisions of the French army which had been engaged in these actions, were in the night withdrawn across the Partha at Plaussig and Segeritz.

General **Yorck** had a more obstinate contest to maintain at Mökern: this village was five times taken and re-taken at the point of the bayonet; the obstinacy with which it was contested rendered this action one of the most sanguinary of the war; General **Yorck** at last carried the village, totally defeated the corps of Marshal Marmont, and drove it to the suburbs of Leipzig, having taken 1,500 prisoners, and 8 guns. If any part of the army of the Prince Royal had been present in this battle; if even the cavalry he was expected to lead to Delitsch and Eilenburg, in case Marshal Blucher should be engaged, had arrived there, the French corps employed in this action must have been destroyed. The Prince did not, however, break up from Sylbitz till the morning of the 17th, arriving in the course of that day at Breitenfeld.

On the morning of the 17th, at day-break, the opposing armies were close to each other, occupying the ground which, on the preceding day, had been the theatre of so much contention. Notwithstanding the losses, which on both sides had been considerable, no sufficient advantage had been obtained by Buonaparte or the Allies, to induce either, by renewing the action, to risk again their fortunes with the forces they possessed. The corps of Generals Benningsen and Bubna had been ordered to move from Dresden, by Meissen and Grimma, upon the right of Prince Schwarzenberg's position; and General Count Colloredo, by Chemnitz and Frohburg, was to form in rear of the Austrian reserves near Magdeborn. The whole of these troops having reported that they should enter the positions assigned to them, in the course of the day, and the army of the Prince Royal of Sweden being on its march to form on the left of Marshal Blucher, the Allies decided not to commence hostilities till the morning of the 18th. Buonaparte, perhaps induced to await the arrival of General Regnier, from Wittenberg, also remained throughout the day without attempting any offensive movement.

The only actions worthy of being recorded were when the enemy, having occupied Gohlis, was attacked and driven into the suburbs of Leipzig, and later in the day when General Wasiltschikoff, with four regiments of cavalry and the cossacks under his orders, charged the cavalry of the General Arrighi which had made a movement in advance near Eutritzsch, and completely routed it.

On the 18th Buonaparte had taken a more concentrated position, extending from the ground in front of Connewitz on his right, to Probstheide Stötteritz and Holzhausen, while the corps under Marshal Ney occupied Schönefeld and Neutsch, and the corps of General Regnier was posted at Paunsdorf. Count Bertrand was ordered to march upon Weissenfels, from whence he drove the Austrian brigade of Count Giulay's corps, under General Murray, and thus secured the passage of the Saale.

Prince Schwarzenberg, having observed the new position of the enemy, directed General Benningsen to take the command of the right wing, composed of the forces that officer had brought with him, of the corps of Generals Count Bubna and Klenau, and the brigade of General Ziethen, and to advance from Gross-Pössna, Seyfartshayn, and Klein-Pössna, upon Marshal Macdonald, who was opposed to him. The centre of the army, including the corps of Generals Wittgenstein and Kleist, and all the Russian and Prussian reserves, was intrusted to Field-Marshal Barclay de Tolly, who was directed to advance upon Probstheide. The left, composed of the divisions of General Bianchi, Prince Alois Liechtenstein, the Austrian grenadiers under Count Weissenwolf, and the cavalry of General Count Nostitz, together with the corps of Prince Colloredo, was placed under the Prince Philip of Hesse Hombourg, and was to move upon Dösen and Dölitz; while the division of General Læderer was to advance on the left of the Pleisse, upon Connewitz. The success of these operations was confined to the capture of Holzhausen, from whence Marshal Macdonald, finding his left turned by General Bubna, at Zweinaundorf, was obliged to retire upon Mölkau and Stötteritz, yielding his first position, after some contest, to the corps commanded by Count Klenaw, and the village of Zuckelhausen to the brigade of General Ziethen.

In the centre, the attacks made by the corps of Generals Kleist and Wittgenstein upon the second, and part of the fifth corps of the French army, supported by the guards posted at Probstheide, were unsuccessful, the enemy maintaining that position to the end of the action. On the left, after a very severe contest, which at one time was disadvantageous to the Allies, the Prince of Hesse Hombourg, being reinforced by a part of the troops under General Giulay, who advanced to Gautsch, obliged the French to fall back upon Connewitz.

The army of the Prince Royal of Sweden advanced from Breitenfeld upon Taucha, passing the Partha near Grasdorf, and between Plaussig and Segeritz. The corps of General Count Langeron, which for that day was placed under the Prince Royal, was directed to attack the left of Marshal Ney, and pass the Partha at Mockau, in which it entirely succeeded. Marshal Ney threw back his right and took up a new position, his left at Schönefeld, his right at Sellerhausen and Stünz. The corps of General Regnier, at Paunsdorf, formed the advance of this new position. At the moment however that this officer was attacked by the

Russians, the Saxon troops under his orders passed to the Allies, in consequence of which he was obliged to retire. Count Langeron, after a severe contest with the corps of Marshal Marmont, supported by a column of guards brought to its aid by Buonaparte, succeeded in possessing himself of Schönefeld, while General Bulow, assisted by the advanced guard of Count Bubna, under the orders of Lieutenant-General Count Neipperg who had moved from Zweinaundorf to near Stötteritz, and Mölkau, notwithstanding the efforts of Marshal Ney, supported by the cavalry of the guard under General Nansouty, took by assault the villages of Paunsdorf, Stünz and Sellerhausen. In one of these attacks Captain Bogue, of the British Royal Artillery, commanding a battery of rockets, was killed while leading his men with the greatest intrepidity.

Marshal Blucher, during these actions, directed General Sacken to attack the Faubourgs of Leipzig on the other side the Partha, and this officer for a time succeeded in occupying them; he was afterwards obliged to yield to superior numbers, and to retire into a wood in his rear. A considerable corps of the enemy, however, was kept throughout the day in observation of him; and when the general success of the battle became known, General Wasiltschikoff was detached to Skeuditz with orders to pass the Elster, to harass the retiring columns of the enemy, while General Yorck was ordered to move through Halle for the purpose of preceding them, if possible, at Merseburg and Weissenfels. Count Langeron was at the same time recalled from Schönefeld to replace General Yorck.

Buonaparte, discomfited on every side, withdrew his army during the night to a position immediately round Leipzig, from whence he directed the guards and the other corps in succession to retire upon Merseburg and Weissenfels, commencing their movement about midnight.

On the morning of the 19th, Marshal Macdonald and Prince Poniatowski, who were left in command of the rear-guard to defend the town, were attacked by the corps of General Sacken on the north, and the corps of General Count Langeron, Bulow and Benningsen on the east. In many of the actions which consequently took place, prolonged resistance was opposed by the French, and the assaults of the Allies cost them a considerable number of men.

Buonaparte quitted Leipzig about ten o'clock, and immediately after his passage of the Elster, the bridge over it, which was menaced by the advance of some sharp-shooters, belonging to the corps of General Langeron, was blown up by the enemy, under an impression that not a moment was to be lost in thus protecting the retreat of the army. Marshal Macdonald with the corps under his orders being thus left without the means of any organized retreat, each soldier sought to effect his own escape; the confusion attending such a state of things was necessarily disastrous. A vast number of officers and men, amongst whom were Prince Poniatowski and General Dumoustier, were drowned in attempting to pass the river.

The allied armies, about twelve o'clock, took possession of the town; the Emperor of Russia and King of Prussia established their quarters in it, and the population exulted with them in the successes of their arms.

Such was the termination of this memorable battle: the enemy was computed to have lost in it 50,000 men, including the sick abandoned in the hospitals of Leipzig, and 250 guns; Germany was freed by it; her independence established, and her whole power henceforth marshalled against him, who, till then, had so unfeelingly oppressed her. The tide of war was turned on France; her armies but lately carrying desolation to the extremities of Europe, were now obliged to return beaten and disheartened to defend their native soil.

The military conduct of Buonaparte, where interests of such magnitude were at stake, was very generally criticised; the difficulty of retreat from the position he had chosen, the great detachment he had left at Dresden, and the not having fallen back on the 17th, after his own failure in assuming the offensive on the 16th, when it was evident the Allies were receiving reinforcements, were the chief grounds on which these criticisms were founded.

On the side of the Allies, it was objected, that

the great army had not profited of the moment when the northern armies on the 18th, were forcing the whole of Buonaparte's position on the left, to make a general attack supported by the reserves, and thus endeavour effectively to assist in deciding the victory which was on the point of being gained ; and that Count Giulay, who, after the close of the action, had moved to Pegau and Naumburg, was not reinforced, and thus enabled to act with a decided superiority in the defile of Kœsen, and on the retiring columns of the French army.

The conduct of the Prince Royal of Sweden had latterly been marked by a system of so much caution, that it was only towards the conclusion of this great battle he was enabled to co-operate with effect in its successful termination ; the Swedish troops throughout the campaign had rarely been brought into action, and in the capture of Leipzig, they were but very partially engaged.

On the side of the French, as on that of the Allies, the basis of all their calculations, the leading pivot as it were upon which all the operations turned, seems to have been the formerly established reputation and fortune of Buonaparte. Trusting to that ground-work, he directed the movements of the French armies, while in perfect confidence they obeyed and vigorously seconded his views. On the part of the Allies, the same conviction of the superiority of his fortune and talents may be traced as the cause of the irresolution and hesitation which, notwithstanding a vast superiority of numbers, characterized their operations.

The composition of the opposing armies combined to fortify the feelings these circumstances were calculated to produce. The French generals were men brought up in fields of triumph; humble as the dust in obedience to Buonaparte, they confided implicitly in his talents, and were to enthusiasm attached to his cause; vigorous from character, impetuous in the attacks they led on against troops and officers they had been accustomed from success to look upon as their inferiors, they were the best instruments any commander was ever possessed of for the execution of his objects. The same feeling which actuated the superior officers, descended through every rank to the private soldiers, who, enthusiastic for their chief, with confidence foretold success whenever they were under his command.

A different sentiment was to be looked for in the allied army. The Austrians had, within a very few months created the force with which they were now embarked in this mighty contest. Their troops had been so reduced in numbers after the misfortunes of the preceding wars, that the corps which Prince Schwarzenberg commanded in Poland, in alliance with the French, was the chief ground-work upon which their present army had been formed. Their superior officers were impressed with recollections of the sad disasters they had experienced, and of the unavailing bravery and devotion with which they had struggled against the fortunes of Buonaparte. The soldiers, mostly recruits, and, in many cases, led on by regimental officers almost as lately appointed to the army as themselves, notwithstanding the high military character of the nations from which they were collected, could hardly be expected to be in a state of military organization fitted at once to oppose, upon equal terms, the hitherto victorious legions of France.

The Russian army was composed of older soldiers than the Austrians, although a considerable number of recruits were in its ranks; it was magnificent in its appearance, yet its officers were less accustomed to war; and it was generally less active, less vigorous in its movements, than the one it was opposed to.

The Prussians formed a most efficient portion of the allied army; their troops, though lately brought together, had secretly been trained for a considerable time; they had more hatred against the French, who had humbled their high character as a military nation; their officers were better instructed; and their army displayed, perhaps, more nerve and energy, adventured more, and reaped greater triumphs, than any other engaged in the same cause. The spirit of its great commander, Marshal Blucher, pervaded the whole, he was ever foremost in attack, decisive and resolute in his determinations; wherever in the course of the war offensive movements are to be traced, wherever the enemy is attacked and pursued, Marshal Blucher will almost always be found to have directed them. He was fortunate in the general officers who commanded under him: besides the Prussian Generals, Yorck, Kleist, and Bulow, the Russian Generals, Baron Sacken, Count Langeron, and Count Woronzoff, were all of them distinguished officers, and General Gneisnau, the chief of his staff, was of the greatest value.

Prince Schwarzenberg, who had a task imposed upon him far different from that which fell to the lot of Marshal Blucher, had fortunately the superior talents which could alone, perhaps, have conducted to so favourable an issue the great cause intrusted to his discretion. Directing in chief the movements of an army composed of troops which had all but lately been in hostility to each other; uniting in his headquarters, not only the respective sovereigns, but frequently the cabinets which had been engaged in the most violent opposition to each other, and still fostered jealousies, such as even general success was only calculated to increase; besieged by the contending interests of persons who, from deference to him alone, yielded submission to Austrian guidance and direction; nothing but the unimpeachable rectitude of Prince Schwarzenberg's character, the clearness and perspicuity of his talents, his bravery in the field, his amiability in his general converse with all, could have enabled him to keep together and direct successfully to one great object, the heterogeneous mass submitted to his guidance.

This sketch of the situation of the parties opposed to each other, would lead one to inquire which of the two had suffered most from allowing the established reputation and former successes of an individual to influence them in the conduct of their operations, or which in reposing most on such a ground-work, had more delayed or precipitated the success or disaster which, in the end, attended the establishment of German independence.

In deciding such a problem, it should be recollected, that though the Allies by more vigorous measures, might earlier have driven the French from their advanced position; yet, on the other hand, no defeat could have been more decisive, more disastrous, than that to which Buonaparte exposed himself *

The French army retired upon Erfurt where it was first assembled, and placed in position ; it was stated

* Appendix, No. 4.

to consist of about 80,000 men. On the 25th of October, being already aware of the approach of General Wrede to Wurzburg, and menaced by the arrival of Marshal Blucher at Langensalza, and of the army of Prince Schwarzenberg at Weimar, Buonaparte commenced his further retreat.

On the 26th, his rear-guard was attacked by General Rudczewicz at Gotha, where 2,000 men were taken, and at Eisenach by General Yorck, who carried the place by assault, and separated the fourth corps from the rest of the French army, obliging it to move by a circuitous road to re-establish its communication.

From this point it is to be lamented that Marshal Blucher was directed to move by the road to Giessen and Wetzlar, for the purpose of leaving the great road by Fulda and Gelnhausen open for the march of the right column of Prince Schwarzenberg's army, which was passing through the forest of Thuringen by Schmalkalden. He was thus prevented from following up the French army at a moment that he was in contact with its rear-guard, and when the promised vigour of his pursuit would have bid fair for the most fortunate results. The column for which he was obliged to make way did not arrive in time to overtake the enemy, so that Buonaparte without further molestation than he suffered from the cossacks under Generals Counts Platoff and Czerniczeff, was enabled to arrive opposite to the army of General Wrede at Hanau.

This officer having assembled his forces near Wurzburg on the 22d, succeeded, after a bombardment which lasted until the 26th, in taking possession of the town, the French officer having surrendered it, and retired into the citadel. On the 27th, General Wrede marched upon Aschaffenburg, from whence he directed the troops within his reach, amounting to about 36,000 men, to place themselves in position at Hanau. He was there attacked by Buonaparte with the greater part of his army on the 30th. General Wrede was posted in front of the Kinzig, his right near the village of Neuhof, flanked by the river, his left upon the great road leading to Gelnhausen. The cossacks under General Czerniczeff on the road to Friedberg. From this situation, after a resistance most gallantly maintained in spite of the inequality of numbers, the French cavalry under Generals Nansouty and Sebastiani, having made a successful charge on his left, General Wrede was obliged to retire behind the Kinzig, still occupying, however, the town of Hanau, but thus leaving open the great road to Frankfort and Mayence.

The French army, during the night, defiled along this road towards their own frontier, with the exception of the third, fourth, and sixth corps, under Marshal Marmont, who (with the view of protecting the retreat of Marshal Mortier from Gelnhausen), was directed to attack Hanau, from whence, after a short resistance, he obliged General Wrede to retire, taking up a position in rear of the town.

In this situation on the morning of the 31st, General Wrede was again attacked; the action which ensued was maintained with considerable obstinacy till about one o'clock, when the third and sixth corps having been directed to follow the rest of the French army upon Frankfort, and the fourth corps alone being left to oppose the Bavarians, they seized the opportunity and advanced against it. This effort was completely successful ; Hanau was retaken at the point of the bayonet, the bridge over the Kinzig, where the French made the last resistance, was carried, and the Allies established themselves on the other side of the river. In this last attack General Wrede was severely wounded while leading his troops, and was carried off the field of battle. The Austrian General Fresnel, who succeeded to his command, moved upon the French, who were in front of the bridge of Neuhoff, and, after a severe contest, obliged them to fall back. At dark the fourth corps retired on the road to Frankfort, its presence being no longer necessary to cover the march of Marshal Mortier, who had moved from Langenselbold, by a circuitous road, to Höchst. In the actions which were thus terminated, the loss of the Allies was estimated at 10,000 men, while that of the French was much less considerable.

The Bavarian corps, under Count Richberg, retired from Frankfort on Sachsenhausen upon the

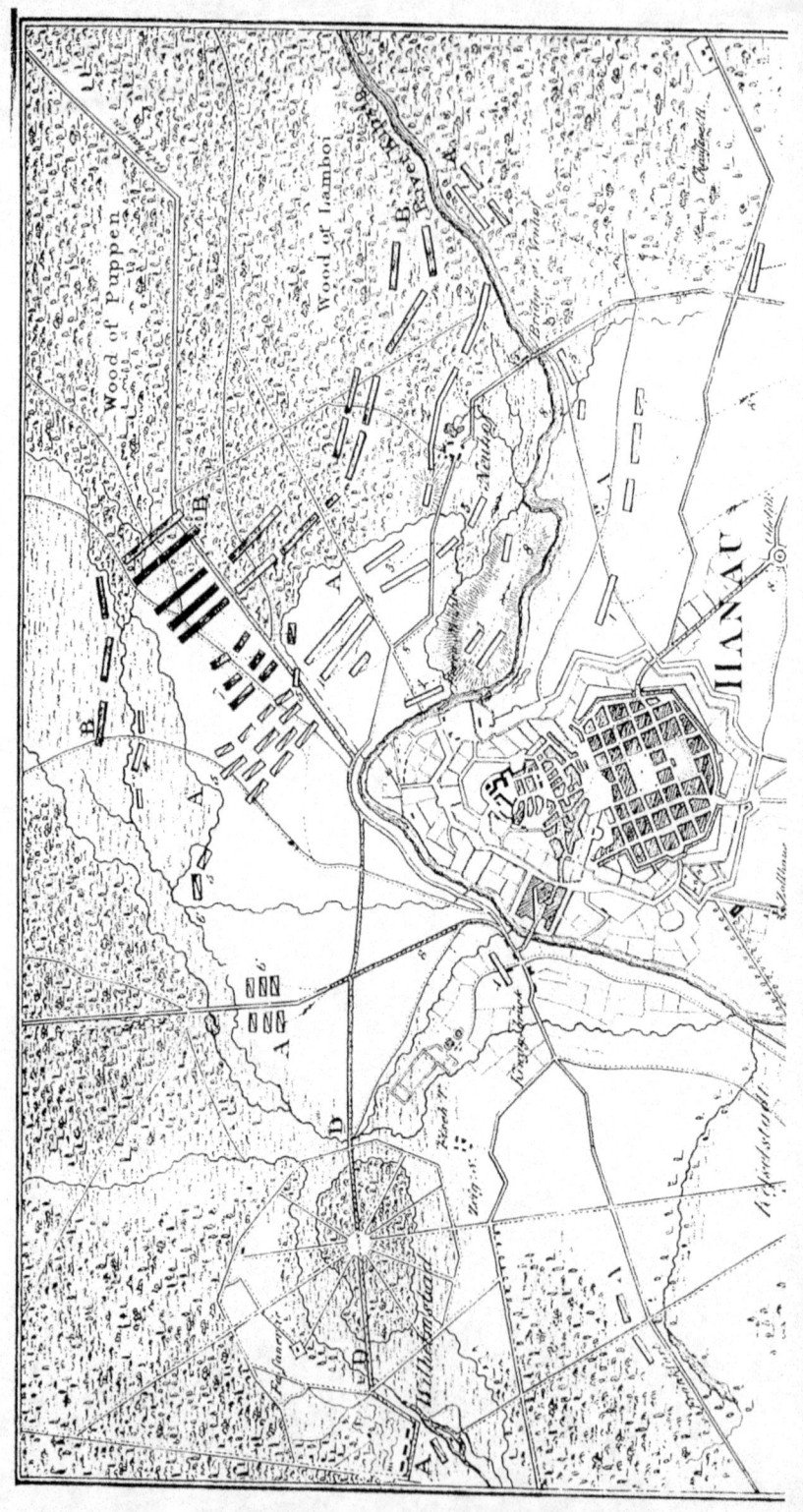

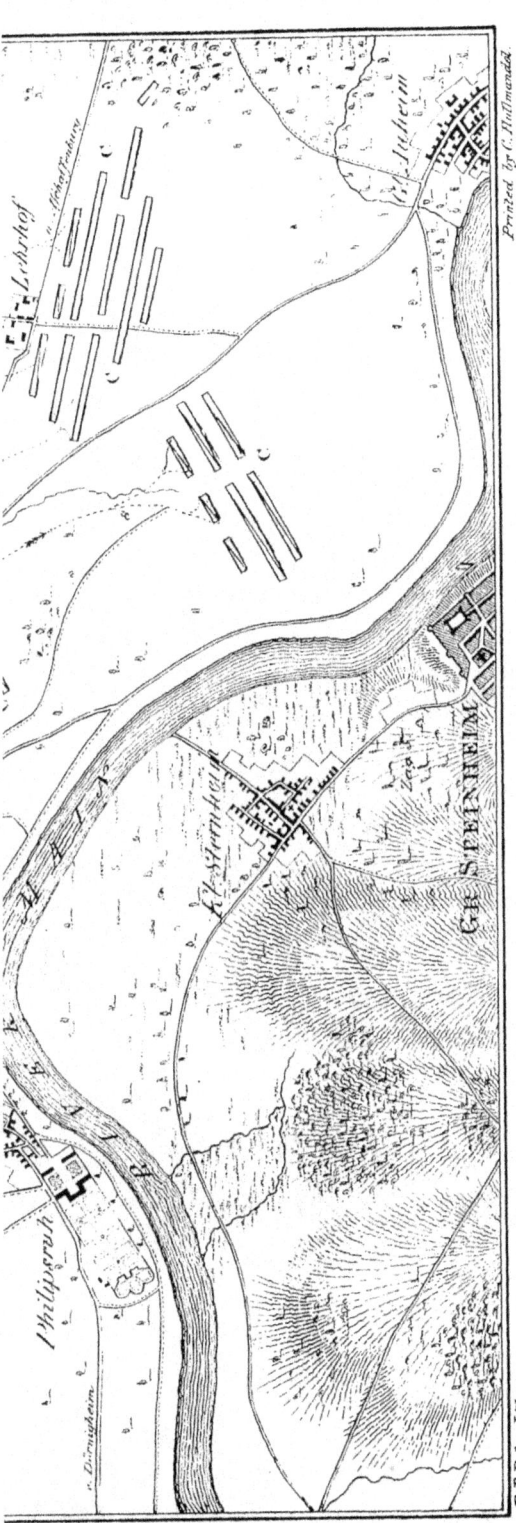

PLAN OF THE BATTLE OF HANAU.
Oct. 30th 1813.

A.A. First position of the Allies. B.B. Position of the French Army. C.C. The position to which the Allies retired. D.D. The march of the French Army towards Frankfort.

1. Division Delamotte. 2. Div.n Beckers. 3. Div.n Fresnelle. 4. Div.n Bach. 5. The Bavarian & Austrian Cavalry. 6. The Cossacks under Gen.l Czernicheff. 7. The attack of the French Cavalry under Gen.l Nansouty. 8. Direction of the retiring columns of the allied Army.

approach of the French army. Buonaparte entered it on the 31st, and on the following day continued his retreat upon the Rhine.

Frankfort was taken possession of by the Allies on the 2d, and on the 4th, the Emperor of Russia, the King of Prussia, and Prince Schwarzenberg, established their head-quarters in it. On the 9th, the enemy was attacked in the last post he attempted to maintain in Germany, at Hochheim. Buonaparte had left there 5,000 men in an entrenched position, destined to cover the approach to the *tête-de-pont* at Cassel, and to secure the occupation of a post on the right bank of the Rhine, which would facilitate any future offensive operations he might contemplate.

The corps of General Giulay, and the force lately under the orders of Count Meerveldt, and now commanded by Prince Louis Liechtenstein, together with the Austrian cavalry of reserve, and the division of light infantry under General Bubna, were destined to dislodge them. General Giulay moved upon the Chaussée from Höchst, Prince Liechtenstein by Massenheim and the Donner-Mühl. As soon as these columns had reached their destination, the enemy's entrenchments were stormed, and he was driven from them with the loss of four guns, and several hundred prisoners. Major-General Sir Robert Wilson was present in this action, and, at the head of one of the storming parties, particularly distinguished himself.

With this action, the campaign undertaken for the deliverance of Germany, was triumphantly closed.

PART II.

A NEW and totally different state of things commenced from this period. The whole of Germany was now combined in one general cause against France. The short time which was necessary to conclude the treaties of peace with those powers, who till then had been fighting in the ranks of Buonaparte, did not delay the universal enthusiasm. The troops and population ranged themselves at once on the side of the Allies. The Congress of Ministers, assembled at Frankfort, had therefore but to stipulate the amount of men each power was able to contribute to the general Alliance. These treaties were concluded upon the basis of twice the force of the contingent supplied to France by the treaty of the Confederation of the Rhine; so that the same arrangement which had been considered the master-piece of French finesse and diplomacy, the idea of which had been borrowed from the ambitious projects of Louis XIVth, but which had been carried into effect by Monsieur de Talleyrand, to an extent never contemplated by that Sovereign, became the groundwork of a combination which most contributed to destroy Buonaparte's empire, and to reduce France to the utmost extent of misery and distress. The sum total of the force to be raised was 145,560 men, troops of the line, besides the same number of Landwehr; the whole amounting to 291,120 *.

The contribution in money, to be paid by the German States, amounted to 84,970,000 francs †; the plan by which it was to be raised was, that the sovereign or governing authority of each state, which renounced the confederation of the Rhine, should sign an obligation for the whole amount of a year's revenue; all these obligations so signed were to be paid into the hands of the Allied Commissioners, of which

---

* See Appendix. No. 5. † Ibid., No. 6.

Baron Stein was appointed President. Each state was to liquidate the amount of the obligation it was bound for by the payment of one-24th of the whole at the expiration of every three months; so that at the end of six years the debt contracted would be paid off. The whole of these obligations, when received by the Allied Commissioners were to be divided into bills, signed by them, and bearing 5 per cent. interest, and to be issued as a paper currency. This contribution was to be divided into sixteenths, five of which were to be given to each of the three great powers, Austria, Russia, and Prussia, and one to Sweden. The obligations of Bavaria, Wurtemberg, and Hanover, in consideration of the great exertions they were making, were to be returned to them.

After the allied armies had taken their positions upon the Rhine, their corps were cantoned according to the following dislocation; the army of Prince Schwarzenberg, to which was added the corps under General Wrede and the Prince Royal of Wurtemberg, was in front of Frankfort, and extended to the southward as far as the fort of Kehl, which was observed by the Bavarians. The army of Marshal Blucher was opposite Cologne, its left being in contact with the great army. The Prince Royal of Sweden, who had marched from Leipzig through Sonderhausen to Mühlhausen, and was understood to be proceeding to Hesse Cassel, suddenly turned to the right, and passing through Heiligenstadt and Göttingen, reached Hanover on the 6th of November. The reason assigned for the adoption of this movement, in lieu of the apparently more natural one of conveying the greater part of his army in conjunction with the rest of the Allied Forces at once upon the Rhine, was the desire of operating against Marshal Davoust, and of preventing his retreat into Holland. With this view the Prince Royal directed the corps of General Winzingerode, which had occupied Hesse Cassel on the 28th of October, to march upon Bremen, detaching Count Worouzow with 6,000 men to Brunswick, while General Bulow was to move by Hameln to Minden. These officers were to unite upon the Weser, and operate against Marshal Davoust in case he should attempt to force his way through the countries occupied by them. In the alternative of the Marshal's remaining in Hamburg, General Bulow was authorized to advance to Osnaburg and Münster, and to detach a part of his force upon

Wesel, in the neighbourhood of which place General Czerniczeff was already arrived. General Winzingerode was also directed to push his advanced parties from Bremen on the frontiers of Holland.

The Prince Royal, having ascertained soon after his arrival in Hanover, that Marshal Davoust was maintaining himself, together with the Danes, in the positions north of the Elbe, directed the Swedish army to pass that river near Lauenburg, and connect itself with Count Walmoden; while the corps of Generals Counts Strogonoff and Woronzow occupied Stade, and were cantoned along the left of the Elbe opposite to Hamburg. The Prince Royal proceeded to take the command of the forces thus assembling on the frontiers of Holstein, and continued employed in operations against that country till the conclusion of the peace of Rendsburg.

While every thing remained in perfect tranquillity in the neighbourhood of Frankfort and Cologne, Generals Winzingerode and Bulow were rendering important services. The advanced guard of the first of these officers had followed General

Rigaud from Hesse Cassel to Dusseldorf, where it had driven the troops under his orders across the Rhine on the 12th of November; General Benkendorff commanding a detached corps belonging to the force under General Winzingerode, had repulsed General Cara St. Cyr, who had attempted, with a division of French troops assembled on the frontiers of Holland, to penetrate to Bremen. After these successes, General Winzingerode pushed forward his light troops upon Holland. Zwolle, Zoltkampt, Kampen, Deventer, Gröningen, Amersfoort, and Harderwyk, were all occupied by them, from the 12th to the 28th of November, while the division of General Oppen, detached from General Bulow's corps at Münster, took Doesburg and Zutphen.

Before these successes had been obtained, the spirit of insurrection against the French had universally shewn itself amongst the Dutch. Generals Arrighi and Le Brun perceiving this disposition, and feeling their total inability to resist it, gave orders for the retreat of the French Authorities, and they themselves abandoned Amsterdam on the 18th of November. The population of the town immediately rose, and, with one consent declaring their abhorrence of French dominion, proclaimed the Prince of Orange Stadtholder; a provisional government was formed to exercise the supreme authority until His Royal Highness's arrival, the president of which was Monsieur de Hogendorp. On the same day, in the towns of Dordrecht, Delft, Leyden, and Haarlem, a similar declaration of popular feeling took place.

On the 1st of December General Benkendorff crossed the Zuiderzee from Harderwyk, and entered Amsterdam, from whence he immediately advanced to take possession of the forts of Muiden and Halfweg. On the 2d the Prince of Orange arrived from England, and entered his capital amidst the universal joy of the inhabitants.

General Bulow having detached the brigade of General Borstel to form the blockade of Wesel, moved with the rest of the troops under his orders in support of General Oppen at Doesburg. Finding upon his arrival that Deventer had been evacuated by the enemy, he advanced upon Arnheim. General Oppen drove in the troops in front of it; and General Bulow deciding to carry the intrenchments which covered the place by assault, moved forward the brigades of Generals Krafft and Thumen, with the cavalry, and the brigade of the Prince Louis of Hesse Hombourg in reserve; and forming five columns of attack, stormed and carried them, together with the town, in the most brilliant manner. The two columns on the right were commanded by Colonel de Zastrow, the two on the left by General Krafft; the one in the centre by Major Colomb; the whole of these succeeded nearly at the same time in overpowering the troops opposed to them. The enemy having suffered considerable loss, was pursued by General Oppen, on the road to Nymegen. The brigade of General Krafft and the cavalry were pushed forward on the Whaal, to observe the fortresses of Nymegen and Bommel; while General Benkendorff established the blockade of Gorkum and Dordrecht,

General Thumen and the Prince of Hesse were advanced towards Utrecht, which surrendered. General Bulow, on the 17th of December, established his head-quarters at Bommel. The forts of Heusden,

Loevenstein, and Workum, were captured by General Krafft; St. André and Crevecœur, by General Oppen. General Benkendorff was relieved from the investment of Gorkum by a detachment of General Bulow's force, and his corps pushed forward upon Gertruydenberg and Breda, which he succeeded in taking possession of. General Sir Thomas Graham, with 6,000 British, landed at Schevelings, on the 6th of December, and moving upon Bergen-op-Zoom, occupied almost the whole of Zeeland.

The revolution in Holland, and the immediate recovery of that country from the forces of the enemy, was one of the most fortunate events that could at that moment have taken place. The rapidity with which the Dutch, from being obstacles to the invasion of France, became the instruments by which that undertaking was most facilitated, could only have been brought about through the detestable system of government which Buonaparte had pursued with regard to them.

The news of these events, while it was received with exultation at Frankfort, was the cause of some complaint against one of the members of the coalition. The Crown Prince of Sweden, by whose efforts the alliance had originally been so much benefitted, was now represented as pursuing only Swedish objects in Holstein, thereby preventing the immediate advance of the Allies into the Netherlands, and thus rendering them unable to take advantage of the great event which had occurred in Holland. It was strongly desired, by many persons belonging to the head-quarters of Frankfort, that the Russian, Prussian, and Hanoverian corps should be taken from his army: these counsels, however, were not listened to; but, in the anxiety to procure effective support to the Dutch, the King of Prussia wrote to the Prince Royal from Frankfort, on the 17th of December, congratulating him on the success he had obtained against the Danes, whom he had forced to agree to an armistice, and notifying to him, that, with the hope he would soon give a favourable account of Davoust, he had placed under his orders the corps of General Publitz and Colonel Marwitz. In the mean time, and until his Royal Highness should be able to march himself to the Netherlands, it was of the greatest importance that some reinforcements should be sent to Holland; the King, therefore, proposed that he should order General Winzingerode to move upon the Rhine in the neighbourhood of Dusseldorf, relieving with a part of his troops the brigade of General Borstel, which should proceed to join General Bulow: his Majesty recommended also that the Saxon troops should be directed to move upon Arnheim. The Emperor of Russia, from Carlsrhue, on the 21st. wrote to the same effect, communicating at once to the Duke of Weimar his wish that the Saxon corps under the orders of General Thielemann should commence the movement that was desired. Upon the receipt of these letters the Prince Royal gave orders for the immediate advance of General Winzingerode, recommending him, in case the enemy should present himself in force upon his left, when he should have arrived at his destination, to pass the Yssel, and connect himself with General Bulow. General Winzingerode received these orders on the 22d, at Bremen, having already detached the corps of General Orouch to relieve General Borstel; the remainder of the troops under his orders reached Munster on the 30th, and Dusseldorff on the 6th of January. The Saxons, under the Duke of Weimar, left Querfort, on the 2d of January, and arriving upon the Rhine at Arnheim, on the 2d of February, relieved General Bulow's corps, at Breda, on the 6th.

During the period in which these events were taking place, the garrison of Dresden, consisting of 1,759 officers and 33,744 non-commissioned officers and men, surrendered; Marshal St. Cyr capitulated upon the condition of returning to France without arms, and of not serving till exchanged. General Klenau is said to have informed him, that without Prince Schwarzenberg's ratification he could not answer that the capitulation would be observed, as he had not full powers to conclude it. Whether this was clearly understood on the side of the French, or not, the garrison marched out in six columns, the last on the 19th of November, and proceeded towards Altenburg, where the non-ratification of the convention was signified to it. Marshal St. Cyr was apprized that the troops under his orders might return to Dresden, receiving back the arms, ammunition, magazines, &c., such as they had left them at the moment of the capitulation*.

* See Appendix, No. 7.

He refused these terms, and his whole force was consequently marched prisoners into Bohemia. On the 30th of November, General Rapp capitulated for the fortress of Danzig, which he was to evacuate on the 1st of January. He was conducted to Russia with that part of his garrison which was composed of French, amounting to 9,000 men. Torgau was surrendered on the 26th of December, to the corps of General Tauenzein; 10,000 men were captured in it. General Count Narbonne, who commanded, had died there. The Governor of Erfurt capitulated for the evacuation of the town, on the 20th of December, not however, to take effect till the 6th of January, when the garrison was to retire into the citadel. Stettin had also, on the 5th of December been given up to the Prussians.

Having thus taken a general view of the state of affairs in rear of the Allies, till the beginning of the year 1814, it will be necessary to return to the transactions on the Rhine. The allied armies assembled there did not muster an effective force of more than 120,000 men. The Swedes, the corps of Counts Woronzoff and Tauenzein. the army of General Benningsen, the corps of Generals Klenau and Kleist, all of which had been in the battle of Leipzig, were now left in rear of the army. On the side of Buonaparte, his losses in the retreat having been immense, his effective force is stated to have been under 70,000 men. This force was distributed along the Rhine. Marshal Macdonald, with the 5th and 11th corps of infantry, and the 2d and 3d of cavalry, defended that river from Fort St. André, between Crevecœur and Thiel to Coblentz. Count Morand, with the 4th corps and other troops which were added to his command formed the garrison of Mayence, and observed the Rhine from Coblentz to that place; Marshal Marmont, with the 6th corps of infantry, and the 1st corps of cavalry, was placed between Mayence and Strasbourg; Marshal Victor, with the 2d corps of infantry, and 5th of cavalry, extended from that place to the frontiers of Switzerland. The reserves were to be formed at Metz under Marshal Kellerman, but their force was not at this time of any consideration. Count Maison, with the depôts of the 17th and 24th divisions, the skeletons of two divisions of the young guard, and 800 cavalry, was destined to protect Antwerp and the frontier of the Netherlands.

The first object of the Allied Sovereigns on their arrival at Frankfort, was to impress Buonaparte with a conviction, that they were ready to make peace with him, and upon terms such as the state of his remaining resources would in no way have warranted him to expect. There was, perhaps, to a certain degree, a want of energy in this proceeding; but the name of Buonaparte was still appalling, and the idea of attacking France, defended by his talents, considerably staggered many of those who were about to be called upon to execute it. Prince Metternich and Count Nesselrode were instructed, therefore, to communicate to the French government, through the medium of the Baron St. Aignan (who, having been taken prisoner at Gotha on the 22d of September, was allowed to return to France), an answer to the various projects for negotiation which had been held out by Buonaparte, in a conversation with Count Meerveldt, when that officer was brought to him, after having been made prisoner at Connewitz. At this meeting, Buonaparte stated to General Meerveldt, that, as a proof of his esteem for him, he would send him back to the Austrian army on parole; and, after some questions as to the force of the allied armies, and the effect which the knowledge of his presence with the army would have upon their operations, he inquired, " if this war was to last for ever ? He then declared that the propositions for a negotiation at Prague were not sincere; that so great a concern could not be settled where a fixed time was named to do it in; that Austria had lost the opportunity of playing a distinguished part. He would have done all she desired; and, in concert with him, she might have dictated to the rest of Europe; but that she had listened to Russia, who was under the influence of England; that this latter power, when she talked of the equilibrium of Europe, meant to confine the French to a given number of ships of war; if she meant otherwise, let her give up the colonies she had taken, and he would return Hanover and the Hanseatic towns. With regard to the independence of Holland, provided England relinquished her maritime pretensions, it was a question on which there might be some understanding. His honour was, however, engaged in adhering to the protectorship of the Rhine; the Sovereigns belonging to the confederation, who had deserted him, might shift for themselves—they would repent it; but he would adhere to those who were faithful to him. He might listen to a proposition of separating Italy from France; the establishment of that country united under one sovereign, might combine with a general system of policy in Europe. The duchy of Warsaw he had given up; he had also been obliged to abandon Spain. If these ideas met those of the allies, let them make an armistice, by which the Russians and Prussians should go behind the Elbe, the Austrians into Bohemia, and himself behind the Saal; if they thought he ought to go behind the Rhine, he must lose a battle to be forced to it, that might happen, but as yet had not." Buonaparte referred in this conversation to the letter he had addressed, through General Count Bubna, on the 25th of September, to the Emperor of Austria; in which he had expressed a wish that the pacific sentiments he was disposed to entertain, and which would be stated by Count Flahaut, the bearer of that letter, might be attended to; and that a war which could only be profitable to England and Russia, might be brought to a conclusion. The answer he is said to have received, was, that the Emperor of Austria, who, in a reign of twenty-one years, had seen ten of them miserably spent in war, could not but be desirous of peace, but that it was no longer possible to think of a partial pacification, it was better to fathom every chance in a war already begun, than to end it with the fear of new and inevitable convulsions;—that, actuated by these feelings, he would not in the present instance lose a moment in communicating with his allies, as to the pacific disposition which had been manifested.

In reference to this conversation, the conditions transmitted through the Baron St. Aignan, were, that France should return to her natural limits, the Rhine, the Alps, and the Pyrenees; Spain to independence under her former dynasty; Italy, Germany, and Holland, to be re-established as states independent of France, or of any other preponderating power. Some expressions with regard to maritime rights were made use of, which Lord Aberdeen (who had been invited to meet Baron St. Aignan) was stated to have sanctioned, and which were misrepresented as an engagement to renounce a part of the maritime code of England.

When these propositions were made, the question whether the establishment of Louis Buonaparte as King of Holland, and of Eugene Beauharnois in Italy, would be considered as securing the independence of those countries, was not explained. There certainly were some persons in official situations about the sovereigns who would have agreed to both; many of them would have yielded on the establishment of the kingdom of Italy with Eugene at its head. Buonaparte, fortunately, was not at once tempted by those offers. The tide of events soon after set so strongly against him, that the most cautious of his enemies would have refused to sacrifice their country's interest by adhering to such conditions; and the independence of Holland under its ancient form of government, and the revolution in the Netherlands, put an end to all question respecting that frontier of France, which unfortunately had been designated as natural.

The Duke of Bassano, by a letter dated the 16th of November, from Paris, invited the Allies to open a congress at Manheim, to treat for peace on the basis of the independence of all nations, with a view both to their continental and maritime relations; but this having been rejected, as an evasion of the basis which had been proposed, Mons. de Caulincourt, on the 2d of December, declared the adhesion of France to the general conditions demanded. This answer was immediately sent to London by the Count Pozzo di Borgo, who, being in the service of the Emperor of Russia, was fixed upon from his character and reputation, not only with those in whose service he was, but also in England, as the fittest person to explain the sentiments of the Allies, at this momentous period, to the British cabinet, and to obtain from it a corresponding manifestation of its views.

The decision taken in England, upon this communication, was to depute one of the cabinet ministers, to represent Great Britain in the Congress, which appeared now likely to be held for the final arrangement of a secure and lasting peace. Lord Harrowby is understood to have been first thought of for this mission; Lord Castlereagh, however, undertook the charge, and in the beginning of January joined the head-quarters of the sovereigns at Basle. No measure was ever wiser, or productive of greater benefits. Lord Castlereagh, by the manliness of his conduct, by the talent which he displayed under the most difficult circumstances, secured more solid advantages not only to England but to Europe, than perhaps will ever be generally known or acknowledged. In the various changes of fortune which attended the operations of the campaign of 1814, the steady course with which he pursued the general objects of the alliance, being never led aside from them either by reverses or success, placed him in triumphant contrast with others, who, elated or depressed by the events of each succeeding period, would have ruined their cause, as much by overstrained pretensions in one alternative, as by a conduct totally the reverse in the other. Lord Castlereagh is understood to have left England with instructions to negotiate for peace upon conditions honourable to France, but differing from those proposed at Frankfort, which the change of circumstances had rendered totally inapplicable. Buonaparte put an end to the chance of thus consolidating his power, by terminating at a later period the Congress of Chatillon, notwithstanding the urgent entreaties of his plenipotentiary. At the moment he did so, fortune had abandoned him, and the Allies were in a situation to refuse any longer to acknowledge him the ruler of France.

From the banks of the Rhine a new system of operations was to be combined for the future prosecution of the war. France was now to be attacked; the dreadful scourge which she had for so long a time inflicted on other nations by her invading armies, was now to be turned against her; yet her former glories seemed in their shade still to hold out to her a protecting hand, and to shield her from the menaced evil. There was a general fear and hesitation at the prospect of attacking this nation, which had put forth such resources, and which, for the defence of its own soil, appeared in the early part of its revolutionary career, invincible. The blow, however, was to be struck; the only means of offence remaining to the Allies was war upon the territory of France. The plan which was to be adopted for this object became the question of the greatest importance to decide. The barrier of the Rhine, the fortresses which protected it, and the mountains of Switzerland, alike opposed obstacles of considerable difficulty to overcome. The extent of Buonaparte's means to defend them was not correctly known; there was a degree of apprehension as to the resources he would be able to create, which constantly counterbalanced the credit due to the information which was received, and which, although obtained through channels at all times of doubtful authority, yet, to a greater degree, might have been depended upon. A vast superiority of numbers on the side of the Allies could not however be disputed, and upon such a basis it was necessary to commence the discussions of the system to be proceeded on. The natural line of operation was for each army to pass into France from the position it occupied. Thus an attack, concentrated between Strasbourg and Coblentz, would be made by the armies of Prince Schwarzenberg and Marshal Blucher, while the corps of Generals Bulow and Winzingerode would advance into Holland and the Netherlands. To oppose this system, the difficulties to be overcome in the protecting fortresses were set forth and insisted upon. It was in vain reiterated that the 140 fortresses, by which France was surrounded, and which in other times had been of essential service to her defence, were in her present reduced state of military resources, become a burthen to her: she was utterly unable to garrison and provision them; the Allies therefore instead of avoiding, should move immediately in the midst of them; and thus, by menacing the whole, oblige the enemy either by abandoning them to enable the Allies to establish themselves on a solid basis in the French empire, or, by sacrificing his active army to their defence, give up all hopes of any prolonged resistance in the field. These arguments were of no avail: a plan was proposed at the head-quarters of Frankfort, and afterwards adopted, by which Prince Schwarzenberg was to move to the neighbourhood of Basle, and from thence (passing into Switzerland, and forcing the neutrality of that country) to enter France, operating on the line of Befort, Vesoul, and Langres. The army of Marshal Blucher was in the mean time to occupy the positions left by the great army near Frankfort, and afterwards passing the Rhine at Manheim and Coblentz, to operate in the direction of Nancy. This plan was strongly objected to; first, because it would delay the invasion of France till the month of January, thus giving Buonaparte time for preparation; next, that in the extended movement proposed for the great army, if its progress should be arrested, or its supplies delayed by the snows, or other accidents of weather incident to the climate of Switzerland, it might be exposed to considerable danger: lastly, that if Buonaparte, assembling an army of 60 or 65,000 men, should attack Marshal Blucher while separated from Prince Schwarzenberg, and force him to fall back, and afterwards collecting the French garrisons as far as the Elbe, should fall upon the flank and rear of the army engaged in Switzerland, it was impossible to foretel the disasters which might happen.

On the other hand, it was urged, that the weakest point of the French frontier had always been acknowledged to be on the side of Switzerland; that by occupying that country, a strong basis, from whence offensive movements might be undertaken, would be established; that Austria had too much suffered in the first years of the revolutionary war by operating from the Netherlands and Lower Rhine; that the natural line for her to adopt was the one proposed, receiving her supplies from her own provinces by the Danube, and the direct communications through Bavaria; that great assistance to the Austrian-Italian army would be afforded by the proposed operation; and, lastly, that the object of the Allies should be to reach the important position of Langres, from whence, commanding the entry into the plains of Champagne and Burgundy, they might dictate the conclusion of peace on the terms proposed by them.

In addition to what was stated in this reasoning, it was an evident advantage to the Austrians to place their army in a situation, from whence, even in case of defeat, they could pour their forces into Italy, overwhelming the troops of the enemy defending that country; and thus securing for themselves an extension of territory, which was become almost necessary for the prosperity of their empire*.

The first serious obstacle, which presented itself to this plan, was the objection of the Emperor of Russia to any interference with the neutrality of Switzerland.

* See in the Appendix the different Plans proposed. Nos. 8, 9, and 10.

The difficulties of the return of the Austrian troops, who had already been marched to the southward, and the influence of the commander-in-chief, induced his Majesty, however, to listen to some proposals upon the subject, and to consent to their being transmitted to the government of that country. Although these propositions were not agreed to by the Diet, yet no considerable opposition to the progress of the Allies appeared to be intended by it. In the mean time the severest orders were issued to the different commanders of the allied troops, in the neighbourhood of Switzerland, forbidding them, on any account, from entering that territory, and rendering each responsible for the strict observance of these directions.

Prince Schwarzenberg left Frankfort on the 9th of December, and proceeded to Freyburg. The Diet of Switzerland had placed a corps of 12,000 men under the orders of General Watteville, to defend the neutrality which it had proclaimed, and which Buonaparte, as most beneficial to himself, had accepted. These troops were cantoned along the left bank of the Rhine, from Basle to Schaffhausen.

It appeared, however, upon further examination into the conduct of the Swiss, that a body of 300 conscripts had lately been sent from that country to France; palisades had been furnished from Basle for the fortress of Huningen; an Austrian officer, who had escaped from France, where he had been detained prisoner of war, had been delivered to the French authorities; and, as far back as the month of August preceding, the French division of General Boudet had been permitted to pass through Basle: these cases were now cited in a correspondence between the Austrians and General Watteville, proving, at least, that the neutrality of the Swiss territory had not been maintained with any great severity.

During this period the town of Berne, proud of the distinguished part it had formerly held in the Swiss Republic, and anxious to recover from its fallen state, took a decided measure in blaming, through the means of its provincial Diet, the conduct of its deputies at the general assembly, in having consented to the maintenance of the government as then established, and in having agreed to a system of neutrality to which they were unauthorized. The provincial Diet refused to publish the decree of neutrality, and thus separated itself from the general confederation. The head of the government, Monsieur de Freudenreich, offered to abdicate in favour of the commission of ten persons established in 1802, but upon condition that the Allies would guarantee the re-establishment of the former limits of the Canton. Count Senft Pilsach was sent by Prince Metternich from Freyburg, on the 14th of December, to Berne, to negotiate upon this basis, with instructions to communicate on his way with General Watteville, and, if possible, to engage him, either to take part with his troops in the cause of the Allies, or to retire from the line he was occupying, and permit the passage of the Austrian armies. The popular feeling in Switzerland was most decidedly in favour of this latter measure; there seemed but one exception, in the Pays de Vaud, where a spirit favourable to the French existed, and an aversion to the idea of returning to the dominion of Berne. Count Senft succeeded so far in his mission as to decide General Watteville to retire; he was accused of having gone somewhat beyond his instructions in his promises to the government of Berne, but it would be difficult precisely to determine how far that accusation was well founded.

In consequence of these arrangements, Prince Schwarzenberg moved his head-quarters, on the evening of the 20th, to *Loerach*, where he received a message from Monsieur de Watteville, stating his regret at being no longer able to defend the neutrality of his country, and that he should fall back, with the corps he commanded, behind the Aar. This movement having been effected the same evening, the Austrian troops, on the morning of the 21st, passed the Rhine in four columns; the 1st at Basle, the 2d at Crenknach the 3d at Lauffenburg, and the 4th at Schaffhausen. On the same day a proclamation to the Swiss was issued by the Allies, in which the causes of the entry of their troops were explained, and an assurance given, that the independence of Switzerland should be secured, and, at the termination of hostilities, its rights and interests fixed and guaranteed by all the powers of Europe.

PART III.

The march of the different corps composing the great army, and now engaged in offensive movements, was on the left, the corps of General Bubna, which having passed the Rhine at Crenknach, was ordered to advance through Berne to Lausanne, and endeavour to make itself master of Geneva, it was followed by the 2d corps, under Prince Aloys Liechtenstein, who, marching by Neuchatel and Pontarlier, invested Besançon. The 3d corps, under General Giulay, was directed from Soleure upon Biel, Porentrui, and Montbeillard, from whence, on the 7th of January, it entered Vesoul. The 1st corps, under Prince Colloredo, the 2d light division, under Prince Morice Liechtenstein, and the Austrian reserves, were destined to move through Berne, by Pontarlier and Dole, to Auxonne.

During the time that these movements were executing, the 5th corps, under General Wrede, and the 4th, under the Prince Royal of Wurtemberg, were assembled in the neighbourhood of Basle, and were occupied in the bombardment of Huningen, while the 6th corps, under Count Wittgenstein, was blockading the fort of Kehl, and observing the garrison of Strasbourg. The Russian and Prussian reserves were moving at the same time from the Necker towards Basle, where they arrived on the 5th of January.

Nothing could more singularly mark the caution which was observed on the invasion of France, than the movements of the offensive armies at this moment. The object of the Allies was to establish themselves at Langres, a distance, by the direct road, of five days' march from Basle. At the end of December not a single French soldier could have opposed their advance in this direction; yet complicated marches, turning the flanks of positions, inch by inch overcoming obstacles of rivers and chains of hills, all these scientific manœuvres were resorted to; so that, instead of being in possession of the place on the 26th or 27th of December, it was not occupied till the 17th of January.

Soon after the Austrian corps had passed into Switzerland, a report was received at Prince Schwarzenberg's head-quarters, that Buonaparte was at Strasbourg with a considerable army, and that his intentions were to cross the Rhine, and assume the offensive against the troops assembled near Basle. It is singular that credit should have been given to this statement, and that considerable apprehensions should have been excited by it; yet Buonaparte's means were totally unequal to such an operation. With his utmost exertions he was only able, in the end of January, and in the centre of France, to collect a force which could merit the appellation of an army.

General Bubna entered Geneva by capitulation on the 30th of December. The French officer in command there being destitute of the means of resistance, and dreading the hostility of the inhabitants, surrendered the place on being allowed to retire with his garrison. The people of Geneva immediately re-established their ancient form of government; and the inhabitants of Savoy, moved by the same spirit of hatred and aversion to the government of France, commenced an organization with the view of securing their independence. The Abbé Vauren, curé of Geneva, came to head-quarters to forward these objects. General Bubna detached a corps of troops to occupy the Valais and the posts on the Simplon and St. Bernard. He took possession also of Fort L'Ecluse. Prince Aloys Liechtenstein invested Besançon on the 9th, and was charged with the blockade of that place, and of the forts of Joux and Salins. The corps of General Bubna and the 2d corps thus formed the extreme left of the invading army. The division of General Bianchi formed the blockade of Befort, but being afterwards relieved, was united with the 1st and 3d corps, under Prince Colloredo and General Giulay, and was pushed forward, on the 15th of January, in front of Vesoul, for the purpose of attacking Langres.

The 5th corps under General Wrede, engaged in the attack of Huningen, opened its fire upon that place on the 29th of December; it was answered with considerable effect by the garrison, and the commandant having refused to capitulate, the siege was discontinued and the blockade decided upon. The same proceeding was adopted with regard to Neu Brisack. The 5th and 4th corps were then directed to advance upon Colmar, where a force of cavalry under General Milhaud had shewn itself, and had attacked and driven back an advanced party of Austrians under Colonel Scheibler. This movement was effected on the 3d of January, the enemy abandoning Colmar and General Wrede pushing forward his advance to Schlettstat which he blockaded, and from whence he communicated with the 6th corps, which, on the 3d, had passed the Rhine, taking possession of Fort Louis. General Wittgenstein, who commanded this corps, left a force of 10,000 men to observe Strasbourg, and with the rest of his troops advanced upon Saverne, to form the connecting link between the great army and the army of Silesia.

Marshal Blucher had distributed his troops in such positions, that on the 1st of January they passed the Rhine on four points. The right under General St. Priest, crossed, and surprising the enemy in a redoubt established opposite the Lahn, attacked the French division Drouette at Coblentz, and, driving it from the town, took a considerable number of prisoners, and 7 guns. The corps of General Yorck passed at Caub, and advanced upon Creutznach, from whence General Ricard, hearing that the division Drouette was attacked, had moved on Simmern upon the Hundsruck, to support it. General Yorck, therefore, entered that place without opposition, and the two French divisions, having formed their junction at Halzenbach, retired upon Laubach. General Yorck was enabled in consequence to push forward upon the Sarre, where he arrived on the 9th, at Sarrebruck, Sarre-Louis and Mertzig, detaching a corps under Colonel de Henckel, to take possession of Treves. General Count Langeron crossed at Bingen, and driving from that place a brigade under General Charoz, invested Mayence on the 3d; he then detached the corps of General Alsusieff to follow the operations of the Silesian army. Baron Sacken, passing a body of men from Manheim, succeeded (though with some loss) in carrying a redoubt, which had been erected on the left bank of the river. This obstacle removed, he pushed over his whole corps, and immediately advanced on Frankenthal, against Marshal Marmont, who was posted between Durkheim and Ellerstadt. This officer, being unable to form a junction with the divisions of Generals Durutte and Ricard, was obliged, after a sharp action, to fall back towards Kaiserslautern, where he arrived on the 5th, and the day following at Sarrebruck. General Sacken continued his advance, and on the 10th passed the Sarre at Sarreguemine. Marshal Marmont finding himself in danger of being attacked, both by the corps of Generals Yorck and Sacken, retired on the 10th, by St. Avold to Metz, which place he reached on the 12th. General Sacken advanced upon Nancy, where he established his head-quarters on the 15th, and detaching a division against Toul, immediately got possession of it. Pont-à-Mousson was taken by General Wassiltchicoff on the 13th.

General Yorck having established a bridge at Beking, passed the Sarre on the 10th, and arrived in front of Metz on the 13th. He was directed by Marshal Blucher to invest that place with a brigade, and to detach the rest of the troops under his orders to blockade the fortresses of Sarre-Louis, Luxembourg, and Thionville. The corps of General St. Priest was in the mean time advancing by Malmedy, and towards the end of the month was established at Dinant and Givet on the Meuse; from whence it became connected with the army of General Winzingerode.

The corps, commanded by this officer, arrived upon the Rhine opposite to Dusseldorff on the 6th of January. Marshal Macdonald who commanded on that frontier, being apprehensive for the safety of his left, menaced as it now became by the corps of Generals Bulow and Winzingerode, abandoned Cleves and Nymegen, and, leaving a garrison in Greve, retired to Gelders and Venlo : his right was in the vicinity of Cologne and Neuss, with a garrison in Juliers. On the 13th, the corps of General Winzingerode passed the Rhine, the cavalry under Generals Count Czerniczeff and Benkendorff, (the last having been recalled from Holland,) led the way, and on the 16th, entered Aix-la-Chapelle, and Liege on the 18th. Marshal Macdonald retired to Namur, at which place, on the 18th, he received orders from Buonaparte to march immediately upon Chalons-sur-Marne, where it was his intention to assemble his army. The Marshal in consequence put his corps in motion, leaving General Sebastiani with his cavalry to cover the movement. This officer abandoned Namur on the 24th, and reached Meziere on the 27th. General Benkendorff, on the road between Liege and St. Tron, met a corps of the enemy, commanded by General Castex, which had been detached by General Maison from Antwerp, to communicate with Marshal Macdonald. The cavalry of General Czerniczeff having come up to General Benkendorff's assistance, the enemy was beaten, and driven back with considerable loss. General Winzingerode established his headquarters at Namur, on the 2d of February. On the 6th, he marched by Sombref, Binch, and Beaumont, upon Avesnes, which he took possession of on the 9th, from whence he entered Laon on the 12th.

Having thus given the detail of the invasion of that part of the French frontier, which, according to the first plan of campaign proposed at Frankfort, might have been attacked in the end of November by the collected armies of Prince Schwarzenberg, Marshal Blucher, and General Winzingerode ; it is of interest to inquire what in reality proved to be the obstacles which should have deterred the Allies from adopting it. It has been seen that the corps, which entered by this frontier, met with no difficulties, except the detachments they were obliged to make for the blockade of the fortresses; to the force of the armies concentrated this would have been of no moment whatsoever. The same success would therefore have attended their advance. Marshal Blucher established his army at Nancy in fifteen days from the passage of the Rhine. What would have been the advantages, if in the same period the great armies had by the end of November advanced to the same position? This question having been put to Marshal Ney, he answered " Messieurs les Alliés auraient pû compter leur journées d'étapes jusqu' à Paris."

Before we return to the operations of the great army, it will be of advantage to consider the state of affairs on the frontiers of Holland. Buonaparte exasperated at the capture of Breda, recalled and disgraced General Decaen, whom he had sent to arrest the progress of the Allies in that quarter, and directed General Roguet to retake it. This officer, in pursuance of his orders, stormed the outworks on the 21st of December: he was however repulsed with considerable loss by General Benkendorff.

The French army then took up a position in front of Antwerp, extending from Turnhout and Hoogstraaten on the right to Wustwesel and Braaschaat on the left. General Bulow having invested Gorkum and Bois-le-Duc, placed his head-quarters at Breda, from whence in conjunction with General Graham, he determined to attack the enemy. With this view General Borstel was ordered to move on the 11th upon Hoogstraaten, General Tamar on Lönhout and Wustwesel, while General Oppen should endeavour to turn the enemy's left, and get upon the road from Wustwesel to Antwerp; these movements succeeded after a contest of some duration; the French retired to Wynegem, Deurne and Merxum. General Bulow made an attack on this new position on the 13th; General Graham, who had arrived with a division of 3,000 men under Major General M'Kenzie, from Rosendaal upon Calmhout, undertook to attack the enemy at Donck and Merxum; and after a most brilliant action, maintained by the brigade under the orders of Colonel M'Leod, he completely succeeded and advanced to Antwerp. The Prussians met with considerable resistance at Wynegem, which was taken and retaken. The result of this action not appearing to General Bulow to answer his expectations, and menaced as he conceived himself by a corps of the enemy at Lierre, he decided to fall back on the position of Hoogstraaten. The English returned to their cantonments.

General Maison, who had been appointed by Buonaparte to command in the Netherlands, established his head-quarters at Louvain on the 16th. On the 1st of February, General Bulow again attacked the position of the French in front of Antwerp. General Thumen, who was to have driven the enemy from Deurne, did not succeed in his attempt. General Graham at the point of the bayonet carried Braaschaat, and Merxum. General Krafft occupied Schoten. General Oppen, unable to advance across the canal of Herenthals, took no part in the action. The following day the Prussians succeeded in passing the canal of Herenthals, and General Graham advanced to the walls of Antwerp, the bombardment of which place was immediately commenced*. On the

---

* The detail of this operation is given in Colonel Carmichael Smyth's work upon the attacks of the enemy's fortresses by the British and Prussian armies in the campaigns of 1814 and 1815.

6th, however, the Allies, being unable to undertake the siege, and the bombardment appearing to make no impression, they retired to the positions they had before occupied. General Bulow put his troops in motion on the 13th, to join the great armies by the road to Genappe, Mons, and Laon. Brussels had been evacuated on the 1st of February by General Maison, who had retired to Tournay; it was taken possession of by the Allies on the same day; and the Duke of Saxe Weimar moved into it with a part of the Saxon troops on the 8th, when he assumed the chief command as Governor of the Low Countries. The 2d division of Saxons, under General Gablentz, was ordered from Sier to join General Sir T. Graham, who having his advance at Zundort, was intrusted with the blockade of Antwerp and Bergen-op-Zoom.

It has been of interest towards understanding the complicated movements of the campaign we are describing, thus far to carry the operations of the armies advancing upon the northern frontier of France. The corps of Generals Bulow and Winzingerode, both penetrating the ancient barrier of fortresses, which had covered that country against the Netherlands, were advancing upon Laon, from whence, in the future conduct of the campaign, we shall find their operations combined with the army of Silesia. It may be of service here to remark, that the Prince Royal of Sweden obliged Denmark to accept of the conditions of peace, which had been offered to her, and which were stipulated and agreed to at Rendsburg, on the 15th of January. The corps of Generals Count Woronzoff, Walmoden, and Strogonoff, together with the Swedish army, were in consequence directed to move upon the Rhine. The army of General Benningsen remained charged with the blockade of Hamburg.

We must now return to the movements of the great army. By the advance of General Wrede upon Schlettstat, General Milhaud had been obliged to retire by Ste. Marie-aux-Mines towards St. Diey, and Marshal Victor, menaced by the forces both of General Wrede and Wittgenstein, quitted the neighbourhood of Strasbourg, uniting himself by Mutzig with the corps of General Milhaud at Bacarat. This operation was effected without loss; Buonaparte is said, however, to have been displeased at it, and in consequence, to have directed Marshal Ney, with a division of 5,000 men and 400 horse, to move from Sarre Louis upon Nancy, and in conjunction with Marshal Victor to retake the debouches from the Vosges into the valley of the Rhine, which had been ceded. General Wrede did not allow the enemy time for this operation; he had directed his advanced guard under General De Roy to advance on the morning of the 10th upon St. Diey; at Ste. Marguerite it was met by the French division of General Duhesme, supported by the brigade of cavalry under General l'Heritier. General De Roy having had time to form his corps, in consequence of the good conduct of his advanced troops, who had considerably delayed the march of the enemy from St. Diey, attacked and drove the troops opposed to him to Raon l'Etape and took 500 prisoners. General De Roy was wounded in this affair, and the pursuit of the first advantages was directed by Colonel Freuberg.

The Prince Royal of Wurtemberg had in the mean time arrived, with the fourth corps, on the morning of the 10th at Remiremont, where learning that a detachment from Marshal Ney under General Rousseau, supported by the cavalry under General Davigneau, was assembled at Epinal, he decided to attack it. He moved forward to effect that object on the 12th, General Count Platow co-operating with him, and marching by the left of the enemy towards Charmes in his rear. The French retired on the advance of the Prince Royal. That officer, however, pursued with his cavalry and some artillery, and connecting himself near Thaon with the advance of General Platow, under General Grechow, he charged and dispersed the French, and pursued them to Charmes.

The results of these advantages were the obliging Marshals Ney and Victor to abandon Nancy, and the clearing the strong country upon the right of Prince Schwarzenberg of the presence of the enemy, thus enabling him to employ his whole force in the attack he projected upon Langres. The Prince Royal was therefore ordered to advance upon Bourbonne les Bains, Count Platow upon Neuf Chateau, and General Wrede, who had already taken possession of Luneville, upon Mirecourt.

To render the attack of Langres still more certain of success, the Austrian reserves were ordered to assemble at Gray, and those of Russia, which had been delayed a few days in the neighbourhood of Basle, (that they might pass the Rhine on the 13th* of January, the anniversary of their passage of the Niemen,) were ordered up by forced marches, to co-operate in the battle which was to be fought on the 17th.

By these arrangements the whole of Prince Schwarzenberg's effective army, amounting to 97,000 men, was brought to act against Langres, and every exertion was made to render the action expected there, decisive and successful; Marshal Mortier retired, however, on the night of the 16th, and General Giulay entered Langres on the morning of the 17th. It was with considerable surprise that Marshal Mortier was discovered to have had with him a force of but 10,000 men, mostly of the old guard, which, having originally been destined for the defence of the northern frontier of France, had been assembled at Namur, from whence it had been directed upon Langres, where it

* The 1st of January according to Russian style.

had arrived on the 10th of January. Marshal Mortier fell back upon Chaumont, to which place he was pursued by General Giulay, and by the Prince Royal of Wurtemberg, who established the corps under his command, on the 18th, upon the heights between Choignes and that place. The French, menaced by the forces thus advancing upon them, retired on the 19th to Bar-Sur-Aube, leaving an advanced corps at Colombé les deux Eglises.

The Austrian reserves under the Prince of Hesse, the first corps under Prince Colloredo, and the division under General Bianchi, were immediately marched from Langres on Dijon, which they took possession of on the 20th*. The corps of General Wrede occupied Neuf Chateau.

---

* To shew the facility with which the Allies took possession of the principal towns of France, the surrender of Dijon might be cited. Fifteen hussars arrived there demanding its submission; the authorities sent these men back to the corps they belonged to, with a message, stating that 30,000 inhabitants could not submit to 15 dragoons; but if their commanding officer would send a more respectable force, they were ready to give up the keys of their city.

The positions of the offensive armies of the Allies now extended from Dijon to Nancy, the strong country which defended the entry into France was passed, and the foreign armies were established and concentrated in the heart of it. The corps of Marshals Marmont, Ney, Victor, and Mortier, had been unable to oppose any serious resistance, and the people of the country had shewn perfect indifference in the contest. Some persons, indeed, professing to be attached to the royal family of France, had appeared at head-quarters and had made considerable offers of support. The insurrectional movements they proposed, however, were all to be made under the protection of the Allies; upon which a constant answer was returned, that no expression of the feeling of the French people could carry any weight with it, or in the face of Europe could be looked upon as a genuine declaration of its sentiments, unless it took place without the range of country occupied by the Allied armies. This declaration was not calculated to excite the ardour of the royalists; and it soon became evident, that although the French were beat down by the accumulated oppressions heaped upon them by Buonaparte's government, there was notwithstanding so general a dread of his power, that no national sentiment was strong enough to bring about a declaration of hostility against it. On the other hand, neither a feeling of national pride, nor the burthen of an hostile army, without magazines, and subsisting entirely upon the inhabitants, engaged the people in any effort to assist the government in expelling the invaders from their country. So far otherwise, that, in some places, the Allies were received with acclamations. The spirit of the nation seemed broken; the contending armies moved in the midst of the inhabitants without aid or resistance from them; all was suffering and obedience.

The conduct of the war, notwithstanding the great advantages of numbers on the side of the Allies, had not been pushed with any considerable vigour. The object in view, according to the original plan for the campaign, was already attained. Langres was the point from whence the Allies were to dictate the conditions of peace. No plan was combined for any advance beyond it; and throughout the succeeding operations, when want of success attended the Allied armies, it was not unfrequently attributed to the advance beyond that position, so far as which alone, a solid basis had been prepared to act upon.

The head-quarters of the great army had successively been moved from Basle, on the 3d to Altkirch, the 6th to Montbeillard, the 9th to Arcey, the 10th to Villersexel, the 11th to Vesoul, the 17th to Langres, where Prince Schwarzenberg determined to remain stationary for a short period, to allow his army to recruit from the fatigues it had undergone, and to give time for the opening the negotiations with Mons. de Caulincourt, who being named Plenipotentiary of France, and having been driven from Luneville, whither he had repaired from Paris to receive the propositions in answer to his letter of the 2d of December, was now requested to meet the Allied ministers appointed to treat with him at Chatillon.

Various opinions were expressed as to the military operations to be pursued from Langres; on one side it was declared, " that unless the grand object for which the Allied Powers had coalesced was to be promoted by penetrating further into France, the *éclat* of a march to Paris ought not to induce them to sacrifice to it, or even to put to hazard the great cause for which they were contending. The purpose of the Allies was the restoration of independence to the states of Europe by the reduction of the power of France; and they actually occupied the provinces of that empire which they had decided to take from her. The French government ought, therefore, now to be allowed to decide whether it would consent to yield to the determinations of the Allies; if it did, the war would cease; if not, it would be continued; but it should be directed against the government of Buonaparte as the only obstacle to peace.

" In a military point of view it should be recollected, that every day's advance would reduce the strength of the Allied army by sickness, by losses in actions, and by the extension of the line of operations; that, once beyond Troyes and Chalons there would be no stopping, the enemy must be pursued to the walls of Paris, or even beyond the capital. Hence there would be no means of calculating on the arrival of the reinforcements to the Allied army, nor would it be possible to fix upon any attainable object as the limit of its operations. Beyond Langres all the roads run towards Paris; none, passable in the winter season for an army, crossed that direction; the communication between the different corps of the Allies would, therefore, be extremely difficult, and all flank movements nearly impossible. On the side of the enemy all operations on the flanks of the Allies would be along the chaussées, and consequently easy; he might therefore turn the Allied armies, while it would be impossible for them to out-manœuvre him, being unable to operate but in advance, or in retreat. It was also to be remembered, that no army could be maintained for any length of time near Chalons and Troyes, on account of the poverty of that country; that if the Allies proceeded from Langres to Paris, they would have upon their left the most fertile country in France, which would be occupied by the enemy, and from whence he would draw his resources, while the French fortresses in Flanders would be on their right, and those on the Rhine, in Lorraine, and Franche Comté on their rear. Thus the Allies would have every disadvantage on their side, the enemy every advantage. If therefore the Allies had not considerable reserves at Dijon, Langres, and Joinville, the enemy would annoy them whensoever he chose, and this danger would be augmented if the force of the Allies did not allow them sufficiently to blockade the fortresses left in their rear, in which case the garrisons by joining together might produce the most fatal consequences. Such were the risks the Allies would have to encounter; those of the enemy might, perhaps, be considerable, but it should be remembered that Buonaparte would fight to the last, and that this war would become a war of extermination."

From another quarter a general view of the state of the Allied armies, and of the principles on which their operations ought to be conducted was produced, in which it was stated, " That the plan of campaign adopted at Frankfort, was founded, upon the conviction that the forces of the enemy, reduced as they then were, could in no way oppose the entry of the Allies into France. These advantages, the results of the battle of Leipzig, were to be turned to account as early as possible. It was necessary to begin by extending the Allied armies, which had been concentrated near Frankfort, and to place them on a new basis for their future operations: with this view a movement was undertaken to the left, the possibility of the execution of which existed only in the previous destruction of the enemy's army. In the conviction of the difficulty which the French frontier of the Rhine, defended by a triple line of fortresses, would oppose, it was necessary, with the greatest rapidity, to endeavour to gain in front of Switzerland, the only vulnerable point of the French empire, a point which was particularly so, from the circumstance of Buonaparte's considering himself safe in that quarter; for if he had occupied the débouchés from that country with 50,000 men, the obstacles he might have offered to the Allies would have been almost insurmountable. It was by the rapidity with which the operation was effected, that the Allied army was enabled to seize, almost without firing a shot, the whole of the defiles leading from Switzerland into France. The new basis of the great army was now firmly established; on its left by the occupation of Geneva and the fort of L'Ecluse, its centre upon the mountains of Switzerland, its right was molested only by the fortress of Huningen.

" It was necessary, after the acquisition of these advantages, that the Allies should still occupy a part of the Vosges, and the defiles which from Langres and Dijon, form the last rampart for the defence of the plains of France.

" To attain this object the march of the Allied armies was continued with rapidity. Success crowned their efforts. Those points were taken possession of, by the occupation of which all the French positions on the Saone, the Meuse, and the Moselle, were turned, and there remained to the enemy but the ground between Paris, Troyes, and Rheims, to form upon. The left flank of the Allied army which, at the commencement of its forward movement, seemed menaced, had since been secured by the position of General Count Bubna, between Bourg en Bresse and Macon, while the troops left to blockade Auxonne, Salins, and Besançon, together with the garrison of Dijon, would be strong enough to support General Bubna, if a French army should attack him from the south, till from Langres a sufficient corps might be detached to his assistance.

"The whole of the great army might, in five days be moved to Dijon, while from Macon, to the same place, the enemy would require eight; as long, therefore, as the Allies maintained the position of Langres, their left would be perfectly secure.

"The advantages obtained by the occupation of this position, justified the operations by which it had been secured, and were an answer even to those who were most unfavourable to the project of a winter campaign, since to occupy at a later season the ground now possessed by the Allied army, would have cost an infinitely greater number of lives from the more advanced state of preparation of the enemy than it had done at present*. The great army was now in a position where the first basis of its operations was Switzerland, the second the Saone, and the third the country between Langres and Dijon, its left and centre were secured, and its right was covered by the army of Marshal Blucher, the right of whose army was, however, liable to be

* This paragraph was in reply to a memoir, given in by a person of very high distinction at the head-quarters of Frankfort, recommending that the Allies should suspend all active operations during the winter.

attacked. Such was the situation of the Allies, they subsisted on the resources of the enemy, they were distributed so as to menace the great plain of France which lay open before them, and they might be moved in whatever direction was required.

" The enemy up to this time had shewn a force of from 40 to 50,000 men; he retired whenever he was seriously attacked, but there seemed lately a disposition on his part to defend himself with more vigour. Buonaparte seemed anxious to gain time, not being as yet in a state to meet the Allied armies, the consequence was that operations against him should be pushed forward, not to allow him to assemble his troops; the period during which it was possible to calculate on the non-existence of a French army was rapidly passing away. Buonaparte must be supposed to have profited by the three months he had had for preparation, and to have added at least 70,000 conscripts to the 50,000 old soldiers whom he had already brought forward; he must consequently be in a situation to oppose to the Allies an army of 120,000 men. The Allied army might be calculated according to the following rates:

The columns under General Bubna and Prince
Louis Liechtenstein, forming the left of the
army 25,000
The centre, composed of the
    3d corps . 12,000
    4th ,, . 10,000
    5th 30,000
    6th ,, . 15,000
    Guards and Reserve . 30,000
                                       97,000
The army of Marshal Blucher   40,000
Making a total of . . . 162,000

old soldiers, which gave it a vast physical superiority over the enemy.

" The probabilities of victory were therefore in favour of the Allies; they must not, however, put out of the question the possibility of a reverse, for a battle near Troyes, Chalons, or Paris, could not be brought to the same mathematical certainty as was the battle of Leipzig. The advantages of pushing forward at once, before the enemy had completed his means of resistance, were to be kept in view; yet the difficulties and disadvantages of continuing offensive operations must be duly weighed. Each step the

Allies now took in advance they separated themselves from the basis of their operations. The enemy would defend himself, the Allies must therefore fight to be able to advance. It must be remembered also, that up to the present time the Allies had been able, during their progress, to canton themselves in towns and villages; as they approached the enemy they would be forced to bivouac, in consequence of which their loss from sickness would be augmented. The corps of Marshal Mortier, which appeared destined, by the direction of its retreat, to occupy the attention of the Allies, might be intended to mislead them, while the enemy was forming his principal force at Chalons; Buonaparte might be leaving open the road to Paris for the purpose of falling upon the right flank of the Allied army while on its march to the capital. In such a case it would be impossible to advance, for the enemy, by moving from Chalons on the communications of the Allies, would force them from the basis of their operations.

" This movement would be of no inconvenience to the French, for their fortresses on every side would form a basis to their operations, while the situation of the

Allied army at Paris would be the counterpart of that of the French army at Leipzig. These, however, might not be the projects of the enemy; it was possible he might choose to run the risks of a general battle in the plains between Chalons and Troyes. If the Allies should gain a victory, Buonaparte's struggle would afterwards be for existence; he might hope for much from the Allies, before the loss of such a battle, afterwards for nothing; there would remain to him no hope but to continue to defend himself to the utmost extremity.

" In such a case what would be the situation of the Allies?—Their principal army would have lost so considerably, in the action it must be supposed to have fought, that the reinforcements it expected would hardly replace its former numbers. Marshal Suchet might advance in the south with 20,000 old soldiers and the same number of conscripts, forming together an army with which he would be able to relieve the fortresses of Auxonne and Besançon, since from Paris the Allied army could no longer detach in support of its left.

" The Austrian-Italian army being now upon the

Adige, could only be expected in the end of March at Turin; therefore the Allies, from their advanced position, could no longer hope to establish any communication with it, nor could they expect any assistance from their right, excepting from the corps of General Winzingerode, that of General Bulow being still supposed to be engaged in Holland.

" These considerations would lead to this conclusion, that the advance of the Allied army upon Paris, from its present position, would be to push forward the centre, leaving both the wings at the distance of 100 leagues in the rear. Another consideration must be, how, in such a march, and during the winter, to provide for the number of troops to be employed.

" The advantages and disadvantages of the continuation of military operations having thus been brought under consideration; it must be recollected since negotiations for peace were going forward, that the present was the last moment in which Buonaparte could agree to any reasonable conditions; beyond the present moment he must consider the struggle as for his existence;—he must oppose to the Allies every desperate means in his power, the Allies must do the same towards him ; to meet a general levy, which he might order, the Allies must promote a general insurrection. The activity of the French character would every day give proofs of the necessity of giving a direction to the national spirit ; when the Allies should determine to direct their efforts against the existence of the power of Buonaparte, their purpose must be avowed. At Chatillon, it would, however, soon be known whether the French government would listen to equitable terms. In any case it was of the greatest importance to the future prospects of Europe that the great question should maturely be weighed and considered, whether the Allied army should remain in its present position, give time for its reinforcements to reach it, and for its wings to draw closer to it; or if it should descend into the plain, and engage in a struggle, the result of which could not be calculated with certainty, but the advantages and inconveniences of which had thus undisguisedly been set forth."

A different view of the situation of the Allies, and of the most advantageous mode henceforth of conducting their affairs, was brought forward, in which it was stated, "* That to suspend or paralyze the operations of war from causes foreign to military considerations, would be to deprive oneself of the only decisive means of obtaining political advantages. The position of Langres was no otherwise of consideration than as a point it was necessary to pass to reach the ground on which the force of the enemy was to be combated. The movements of the Allied army in advance of that position could not be considered as the commencement of a new campaign, but as the consequence of plans already decided upon, and of the entry of the Allies into France. The determination to carry into effect this great invasion was not limited to a mere attempt, but was a great operation of war, tending to destroy the resources of the enemy, to take from him the means of re-organization, to diminish his power, and lastly, to do him all the injury which, while hostilities continued, it was lawful to occasion him.

" Till war had ceased, it was impossible to determine whether the objects of the Allies were obtained; while it continued, its results must depend on

* Extract from the Memoir drawn up at the head-quarters of the Emperor Alexander.

success. Upon this principle alone could the Allies look forward to the accomplishment of their views, they must seek to reduce the power of the enemy ; his present weakness was dependant on the demoralization of the greater part of his troops, on the inexperience of his new levies, and on the want of discipline which the disasters of the last fifteen months had occasioned, and which the want of time had prevented his re-establishing. These disadvantages were each day in progress towards being corrected, and the Allies might delay their operations till they had wholly disappeared. The only prudent determination, therefore, was to push the war with the utmost vigour while it lasted ; thus seeking to destroy the armies Buonaparte might bring forward, and to take from him the means of forming others."

Having thus given some account of the different views which existed at Langres, as to the future operations of the Allies, we will return to the detail of the military transactions.

The corps of Marshal Mortier, reinforced by the division of General Christiani, but totally unsupported by any other body of troops, having remained at Bar Sur Aube, the Prince Royal of Wurtemberg in conjunction with General Giulay determined to attack it; this operation was undertaken on the 24th, by the advance of the third corps by La Ferté Sur Aube, Clairvaux, and Fontaine, and of the 4th corps upon the great road leading from Chaumont. Marshal Mortier occupied a position from Fontaine on his right to the village of Rouvré on his left, thus covering the town of Bar. On the approach of the Austrians, observing a favourable opportunity, he detached General Michel across the Aube near Fontaine, to attack General Giulay: a severe engagement ensued; the Austrians, however, in the end prevailed, drove back the French corps, and carried by assault the bridge of Bondclaine. The Prince Royal of Wurtemberg in the mean time had driven the advance of the enemy from Colombé by Lignol to the high ground between Voigny and Rouvré, where in conjunction with the third corps he intended to make a general attack upon him on the following morning. Marshal Mortier, however, during the night, retired to Vandœuvres.

General Sacken, after the capture of Toul, on the

20th, had advanced on the 22d, and passed the Meuse in two columns, the right upon Ligny, which was taken on the 23d, by the divisions of Generals Wassiltschichoff and Czerbatoff; the left upon Joinville where Marshal Blucher established his head-quarters on the 25th: on the same day Prince Czerbatoff drove Marshal Victor from St. Dizier. In consequence of these movements, Prince Schwarzenberg advanced his army on a line with that of Marshal Blucher. His left under Prince Colloredo moved from Dijon to Chatillon, where it arrived on the 28th; on the same day, the Russian and Prussian reserves were assembled at Chaumont, and the corps of General Wrede at Andelot. General Count Wittgenstein* was advanced from Nancy upon Neuf Chateau. Prince Schwarzenberg established his head-quarters at Chaumont.

The whole of the Allied forces now collecting in the centre of France, it was no longer possible for

* Count Wittgenstein had moved on after the passage of the Rhine, upon Soriene; he had attempted a *coup de main* on the fortress of Phlasbourg, which not succeeding, he directed his corps on Nancy.

Buonaparte to remain absent from his own armies. He quitted Paris on the 25th, and arrived at Chalons on the following day. The effective army in the field, of which he took the immediate command, was composed of the corps of Marshal Mortier at Troyes, forming with the reserve, under General Dufour, which had been added to it from Paris, a force of 20,000 men; the corps of Marshals Victor and Marmont near Vitry, together about 28,000 men; the corps of Marshal Macdonald at Mezieres 10,000; and the reserve under Marshal Ney at Chalons 16,000: the whole amounting to 74,000 men. Buonaparte immediately brought together the corps of Marshals Victor, Marmont, and Ney, and the division of General Dufour detached by Marshal Mortier, and commenced his offensive operations. The first attack he directed, was upon St. Dizier, on the 27th, which was taken, and General Lanskoy driven from it upon Marshal Blucher's army, which was assembling at Brienne. Buonaparte having thus placed himself upon the flank of this army, and hoping to find it unsupported by Prince Schwarzenberg, moved on the 28th to Montierender and Vassy, and on the 29th, advanced to attack it.

Marshal Blucher aware since the 26th, that Buonaparte was moving against him, collected his forces, consisting of the corps of General Sacken and the division of General Alsusieff, and a part of the cavalry of General Wittgenstein under Count Pahlen; and with this force he had still determined to continue the offensive movement decided upon at Nancy, by which he purposed, by taking possession of Arcis sur Aube, to place himself upon the enemy's communications; with this view, the corps of General Sacken, on the morning of the 29th, had received orders to move in the direction of the bridge of Lesmont. It had, however, hardly commenced its movement in that direction, when the reports of Buonaparte's approach obliged Marshal Blucher to recall it, and prepare himself for the attack he was menaced with; he accordingly took up a position along the Chaussee, leading from Brienne to Paris, occupying the town with the division of General Alsusieff. The cavalry of Count Pahlen, was employed in covering the formation of the troops, and was seriously engaged with the advance of Buonaparte, which was unable, however, to prevent the accomplishment of its object. As soon as the French army was arrived, Buonaparte formed it into three columns. The right under General Chateau was to attack the castle of Brienne, the centre under General Decouz, the town, and the left under General Duhesme, to turn the right of the allied position. This latter attempt completely failed. The Russian cavalry having been sent back towards Brienne-la-Vielle, was ordered to make a circuit to its right, and when it should arrive on the left and rear of this column (which it was calculated it would do just at the fall of day), to charge and overpower it. This movement was crowned with entire success; eight guns were captured, and the French force in that part of the field was thrown into total confusion. The centre column, under General Decouz, was equally unsuccessful; it was repulsed by the infantry of General Alsusieff, at the same time that it was charged by the cavalry which had routed the division on its left. The attack on the castle was more fortunate; the troops which moved against it were concealed by the inequality of the ground, and Marshal Blucher, not suspecting their advance, had placed but a small force in occupation of that position. He was in the castle at the moment it was stormed and carried, and was nearly taken. This advantage procured to the enemy the means of descending into Brienne; where he was, however, unable to establish himself, although the efforts of the Allies to retake the strong post he had got possession of, were unavailing. Buonaparte, perceiving the advantage he had obtained in this part of the field, ordered the cavalry under General Lefebre des Nouettes, and the infantry of Generals Decouz and Meunier, to endeavour again to force the centre of the town: their efforts were fruitless, their troops were repulsed, and a considerable number of houses being set fire to, the action terminated in the night, the Allies remaining masters of the town, the French of the castle.

Marshal Blucher during the night drew back his infantry to Trannes, leaving his cavalry on the ground it occupied, with orders to fall back, if necessary, to the plain in front of the new position he had taken up. Buonaparte having advanced against this cavalry, through Brienne, on the 30th, it retired to the positions assigned to it, while the French army was placed on the ground extending from La Rothière to Dienville; Marshal Marmont arrived on the same day from St. Dizier at Vassy. The object of the French in this battle had failed; the Silesian army had resisted the desperate attack which had been made upon it, and was now in a position where it could be reinforced by the army of Prince Schwarzenberg. Buonaparte, notwithstanding, remained at La Rothière, and bringing the corps from Vassy, extended his army from Dienville to La Gibrie, with the force under Marshal Marmont, at Chaumenil and Morvilliers, and its advance at La Chaise. In this position he remained till the 1st of February.

The news of the action fought at Brienne reached Prince Schwarzenberg at Chaumont on the 30th; he immediately directed his army to advance in support of Marshal Blucher.

The 3d and 4th corps at Bar Sur Aube and Maisons were placed under the orders of that commander, the 5th and 6th were destined to attack Marshal Marmont at Vassy; the Austrian reserves and the 1st corps, together with the division of General Bianchi, the whole under Prince Colloredo, were ordered to move upon Vandœuvres, with the ulterior view of operating upon Troyes, and the Russian reserves were advanced to Colombé.

On the 1st, the troops being assembled on the points assigned to them, Marshal Blucher attacked the enemy. The 4th corps, under the Prince Royal of Wurtemberg, began the action by moving into the wood in front of La Gibrie, which after considerable resistance it succeeded in occupying; the village, however, being attacked, was defended with obstinacy; it was at first taken by the Allied troops, and afterwards re-occupied by Marshal Victor, who made every effort to maintain himself in this very essential part of the French position, and who succeeded in obliging the Allies, with the view of turning his right, to detach a part of their force upon Petit Mesgnil. While the contest at these villages was maintained with various success, the 5th corps, under General Wrede, which had marched from Doulevent *, moved out of the wood of Sou-

* Vassy having been evacuated by Marshal Marmont, the co-operation of the 5th corps with the 6th, which had been destined

laines in two columns, the right under General Hardegg, being directed upon Morvilliers, the left upon Chaumenil; in front of the last of which places Marshal Marmont was endeavouring to collect his forces. The Uhlans of Prince Schwarzenberg, however, who preceded General Hardegg, charged that part of the enemy which was moving from Morvilliers to effect this formation, and defeating it, took a great number of prisoners and a battery of artillery. General Wrede being at once enabled, by this success, to deploy the rest of his troops, advanced with them in two columns against the remainder of Marshal Marmont's corps at Chaumenil, while General Fresnel moved upon the left and rear of this village by the road from Brienne, which from the side of Morvilliers he had got possession of. Marshal Marmont, attaked by numbers so superior to his own, was driven from Chaumenil and Morvilliers, and with the loss of three guns, and a considerable number of men, was forced

to attack that place, became unnecessary; General Wrede in consequence moved from Doulevent, to take part in the action he was aware would be fought near Brienne. General Count Wittgenstein remained between Jionville and Vassy to retire to a position near the wood of Ajou. Buonaparte, feeling the importance of these positions, brought the division of General Guyot and a battery of artillery, supported by a brigade of cavalry under General Meunier, to the assistance of Marshal Marmont; notwithstanding which, this officer was unable to make head against the Allied cavalry, under General Frimont, which charged him in the plain, between Morvilliers and the wood of Ajou, and captured seven pieces of artillery.

In front of Marshal Victor, the Prince Royal of Wurtemberg, who had been re-inforced by a division of Russian grenadiers and two divisions of cuirassiers, renewed the attack upon la Gibrie and Petit Mesgnil, and, after a severe contest, succeeded in getting possession of these villages, by the capture of which he opened a communication with the 5th corps. The Prince Royal then pushed his cavalry between Petit Mesgnil and La Rothière, which, nearly at dark, fell upon the French cavalry under General Milhaud, which was formed in rear of Chaumenil, and drove it, with the loss of six guns, and a considerable number of prisoners, to the farm of

Beugné, to which place Marshal Victor had retired. The Wurtemberg regiment of the Prince Royal charged at the same time and carried a French battery, which had been placed by Marshal Marmont in front of the wood of Ajou, and which still was of considerable annoyance to the Bavarians in Chaumenil. Marshal Marmont then retired to the rear of this wood, establishing himself at the point where the roads from Brienne and Doulevent intersect each other, and from whence he connected himself with the corps of Marshal Victor, and with the rest of the French army.

The operations in this part of the battle having thus been detailed, it is necessary to return to the movements under the more immediate direction of Marshal Blucher; this officer, at the beginning of the action had formed the corps of General Sacken in two columns; the right, supported by General Alsusieff, he directed on La Rothière; the left, having the third corps in reserve, on Dienville; this column General Sacken afterwards brought to the main attack at La Rothière, leaving the third corps alone to pursue the movement which had been prescribed for it on Dienville*. The preservation of this post had been intrusted by Buonaparte, to the divisions of General Dufour and Ricard, under Count Gerard; who had placed an advanced guard at Unienville: General Guilay moved against this force, and having succeeded in defeating it, passed a brigade of infantry, supported by a regiment of cavalry and four guns, across the Aube, with the view of attacking Dienville from the left of the river; these troops he afterwards reinforced by the brigade under General Czollich, and a division of cavalry; while, with the division under the orders of General Spleny, he advanced against the front of the enemy's position: the action which ensued, and which was maintained throughout the day, led to no decisive results, and Dienville, at the close of the battle, was still occupied by the enemy. The same fortune did not attend the defence of La Rothière. General Sacken moved upon it, notwithstanding the contest which was still maintained at La Gibrie; and after an action, the

---

* An Austrian brigade also, under the orders of General Grimmer, was afterwards detached from this corps to co-operate in the assault of La Rothière.

more severe from the cover the French army was able to take advantage of in the enclosures which surrounded that village, carried it at the point of the bayonet, overwhelming the division of General Duhesme, which occupied it, and which was driven upon the corps of Marshal Victor, at that time retiring from La Gibrie. At the same moment the Russian cavalry under General Wassiltschicoff broke the enemy's centre, drove it upon the reserves, and took 24 guns belonging to Buonaparte's guard.

To repair these disasters, Marshal Oudinot moved up, at the head of the division commanded by General Rothembourg, and penetrated as far as the church of La Rothière, where he maintained himself till near ten o'clock at night; but he was afterwards defeated and driven back with very considerable loss, and obliged to retire upon Brienne.

In the attainment of these successes Marshal Blucher had distinguished himself, as much by the intrepidity with which he braved the dangers by which he was surrounded, as by the skill with which he directed the various and complicated attacks of so protracted an

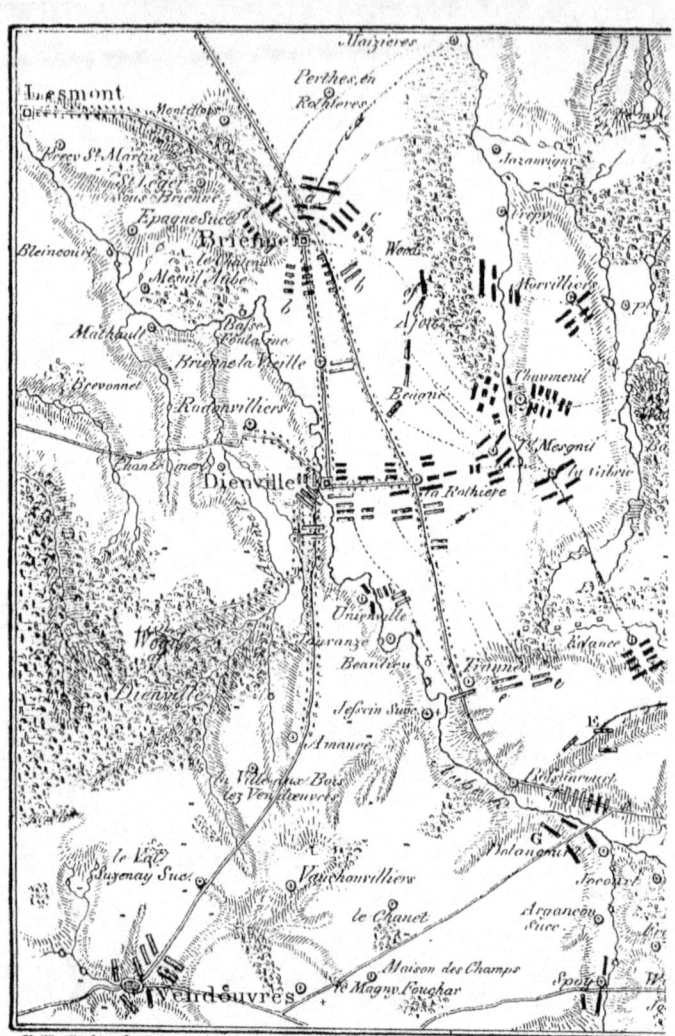

PLAN to serve for the ACTION BATTLE OF BRIENNE & LA BATTLE OF BAR S

Ba

a a. The French Army. b.b. The Allied Army. C. The attack of the C
 e. e. Position of Marshal Blucher on the 30th

Battle of the 1st of Feby.

Coloured
Green ---- Corps of Genl Sacken & Alsusief.
Yellow ---- Do. Genl Guilay.
Purple ---- Do. the P.R. of Wurtemberg.
Blue ---- Do. Genl Wrede.
Orange ---- Do. Cl Colleredo
Green ---- Russian & Prussian reserve having taken the position from w
              Marshal Blucher advanced.
Red ---- French Army.

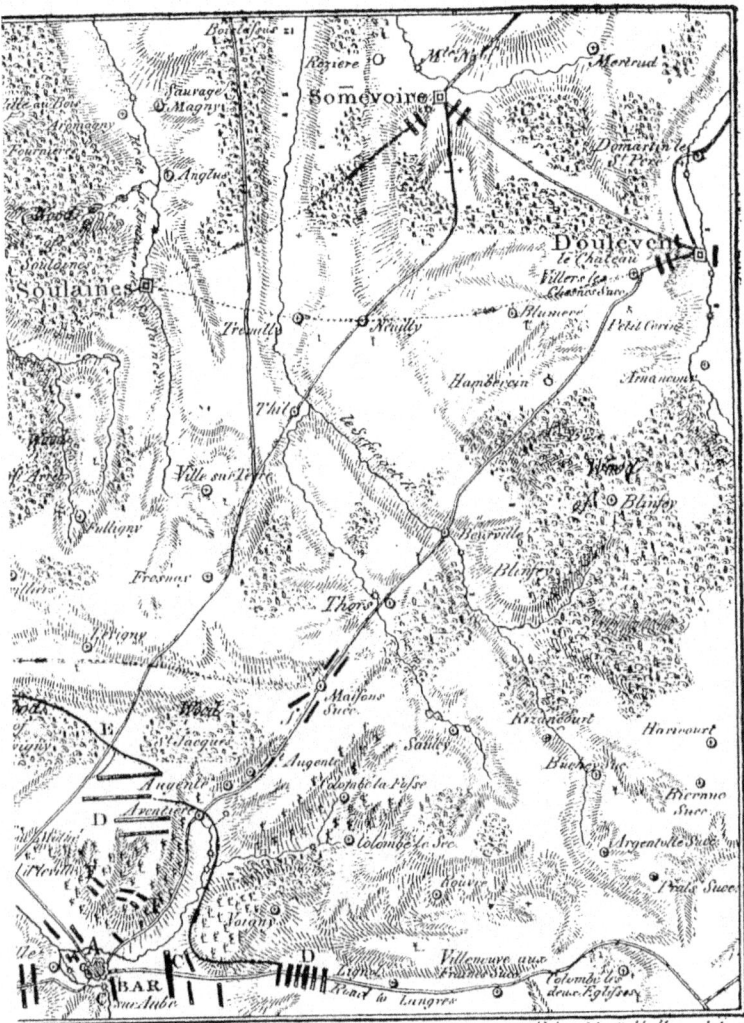

BRIENNE on the 29th of Jany., for the THIERE on the 1st of Feby., and for the AUBE, on the 27th of Feby. 1814.

29th

...shal Blucher. d. The attack made by the French on the Castle of Brienne.
J. J. Position of the 3d. and 4th corps on the 31st.

Battle of the 27th of Feby.

— A. French position.
— B. Cavalry of Genl. Kellerman.
— C. Position of Genl. Wrede, with his advance in a part of the town of Bar sur Aube.
— D. The 6th corps arriving from Colombé which formed on the heights of Aventiere.
— E. March of Count Pahlen upon Levigny & the bridge of Doulencourt.
— F. Position of the 7th corps of French Infy. & of the Cavy. of Genl. St. Germain.
— G. Division of Genl. Pacthod as it remained at the bridge of Doulencourt.

engagement: by the defeat of Marshal Oudinot he triumphantly closed this memorable action, and obliged Buonaparte at once to abandon Dienville; and on the morning of the 2d, to retire from his whole position; the Allies immediately afterwards took possession of Brienne; 4,000 prisoners and seventy-three pieces of cannon fell into their hands: the loss in killed and wounded on both sides was considerable*.

Buonaparte having retreated through Piney, left Marshal Ney's corps as a rear-guard at Lesmont, with orders to destroy the bridge, he afterwards fell back upon the corps of Marshal Mortier, which had remained at Troyes; on the 3d, he assembled his army in front of this place, having an advanced guard at the bridge of La Guillotiere, and another at La Maison Blanche, on the road from Bar-sur-Seine. Marshal Marmont, who had retired from Brienne through Ronay and Arcis, was on the same day at Mery.

On the side of the Allies, notwithstanding the successes of the battle of Brienne, their troops, on the evening of the 1st, were not directed to points

* See Appendix No. XI.

from whence they might annoy the enemy in the event of his retreat, but in greater numbers were collected on the field of battle, lest another action should still be fought. The reserves under the Grand Duke Constantine, which had arrived from Colombé at Bossancourt, were advanced to Trannes; and the corps of Prince Colloredo was ordered to suspend its movement from Vandœuvres upon Troyes, and to assemble at Dienville in support of General Giulay. The consequence of these dispositions (however much to be commended for the prudence by which they were dictated) was the inability to operate against Buonaparte in his retrograde movement, and the failure of any great or immediate results from the sanguinary battle which had been fought *.

---

* Buonaparte having ordered Marshal Ney, on the morning of the 2d, to protect his retreat, this officer, after destroying the bridge of Lesmont, took up a position on the left of the Aube, which he maintained throughout the day, notwithstanding the attempts of General Giulay and the Prince Royal of Wurtemberg to drive him from it. Marshal Marmont, who retired upon Ronay, was followed by General Wrede, who pushed a small corps of infantry across the Voire to dislodge him from the high ground on the right of that river which he had occupied. This effort was unsuccessful; but a body of the Austrian Uhlans having

The Sovereigns, together with the head-quarters of the two allied Armies, having united at the Castle of Brienne on the morning of the 2d, the plan for the future movements of the campaign was decided upon. Marshal Blucher uniting himself to the corps of Generals Yorck and Kleist (the former of which had captured St. Dizier on the 30th, and had since entered Vitry) was to operate along the Marne on Paris, Prince Schwarzenberg along the Seine. The Silesian army immediately began its march upon St. Ouen and Sommesous.

The disposition for the great army was, that the 5th and 6th corps should march upon Arcis, the 3d and 4th upon Piney; the whole Austrian corps, under Prince Colloredo, supported by the great reserves, upon Vandœuvres, and the Austrian light division, under Prince Maurice Liechtenstein, upon Frénoy and the bridge of Clerey. These movements having been executed on the 2d and 3d of February, Prince Schwarzenberg reconnoitred the enemy's position on the Barce, near the bridge of La Guillotière on the 4th: while occupied in so doing he re-

afterwards passed the river near Rance, thus threatening the enemy's left, Marshal Marmont retired to Rameru.

ceived a report, that a strong column of the enemy was moving by the road upon his left from Troyes to Bar-sur-Seine, that Prince Maurice Liechtenstein was attacked by it, and that he had been obliged to fall back from St. Thibault and Clercy*. The dread of an offensive movement in that direction, connected as it might be with the reported movement of Marshal Suchet, with a considerable force towards Lyons, induced Prince Schwarzenberg immediately to suspend the advance upon Troyes, which he had projected, and to carry the force within his reach, consisting of the great reserves and the corps of Prince Colloredo, to the left of Bar-sur-Seine, upon the road to Chatillon. The 3d, 4th, and 5th corps were ordered into the positions of Vandœuvres and Lusigny, and the 6th from Arcis upon Piney. The troops were assembled in these situations on the evening of the 5th, and morning of the 6th; the head-quarters were at Bar-sur-Seine.

It is impossible to pass by the mention of this

* The French corps engaged on this occasion was only the division of General Michel, supported by the cavalry of General Briche.

movement without remarking, that it was singularly unfortunate. After the decisive successes which had crowned the Allied arms at Brienne, it was natural they should be followed up with unremitted exertions; yet, upon the mere menace of an offensive operation by the enemy, in a direction which, if persevered in, must have separated the French army from its resources, and uncovered Paris, was the pursuit of that army given up, the connexion with Marshal Blucher abandoned, and the Allied troops harassed by an extended movement to counteract an operation which it would appear they most should have desired to see put in execution. Buonaparte immediately profited by the opportunity afforded him, and marched to Nogent, from whence, being no longer menaced by the proximity of the army of Prince Schwarzenberg, he was at liberty to act against Marshal Blucher. Troyes being thus abandoned, the Allies entered it on the 7th, the French rear-guard having quitted it the night preceding. The fatigue the troops had undergone during the last few days, induced Prince Schwarzenberg to allow them to remain in inactivity till the 10th, during which time, Buonaparte was supposed to have taken up a position at Nogent, with a view of defending the Seine; the idea, that profiting by the distance which separated the two Allied armies, he would operate upon the weaker, did not seem to be entertained; and a plan of operations was decided upon for the Allies; according to which the Austrian corps, lately under the orders of Prince Colloredo, now commanded by General Bianchi, (in consequence of Prince Colloredo having been wounded in a trifling affair on the 6th), together with the 3d corps, were to march on the 10th by the road to Auxon upon Sens; the 4th corps supported by the Russian reserves, by Villeneuve, upon the same place; the 5th corps by Trainel, as circumstances might require, either on Nogent or Sens; and the 6th corps from Mery, where it it had already arrived, upon Nogent. The object of these movements was to turn the right of the position the enemy was supposed to occupy, while Marshal Blucher was invited to act upon its rear through Sezanne.

In execution of these determinations, the 4th corps took Sens, after a severe contest on the 11th, and afterwards advanced upon Bray. General Hardegg.

commanding the advance of General Wrede, attacked the rear of the enemy between Romilly and St. Hilaire on the 10th, and on the 11th, assisted by the advance of the 6th corps, drove him into Nogent, which, after destroying the bridge, he evacuated on the following day.

Prince Schwarzenberg having ascertained on the 11th, that the corps of Marshals Victor and Oudinot were alone opposed to him, and that Buonaparte since the 9th had been moving against Marshal Blucher, immediately passed the 5th and 6th corps across the Seine at Bray and Pont-sur-Seine, directing them upon Donnemarie and Provins. General Bianchi, together with the 3d and 4th corps, was directed upon Montereau; the great reserves were assembled between Nogent and Bray. By this movement, Prince Schwarzenberg hoped to alarm Buonaparte for the safety of his rear, and recall him from the operation he was engaged in; while, at the same time, the Prince conceived that the position in which he had placed his army, extending from Montereau to Mery, in rear of the Seine, and protected by the 5th and 6th corps in advance of it, was such as would secure him from any movement the enemy might attempt, and would enable him, for a considerable length of time, (whatever should be the results of the operations against the army of Silesia,) to maintain possession of the vast extent of country he now occupied in his rear. We will, however, quit the detail of these transactions, to follow the movements of Marshal Blucher.

PART IV.

After the battle of Brienne, Marshal Blucher, marching by St. Ouen, reached Somepuis on the 4th. The day preceding, General Yorck had taken possession of Vitry, and had moved against the corps of Marshal Macdonald, which having lately been assembled at Chalons, had advanced to oppose his progress at Chaussée and Aulnay l'Estrée. General Yorck attacked this force in these positions, and drove it with the loss of some artillery upon Chalons, which by capitulation he occupied on the 5th. Marshal Blucher established his head-quarters on the 6th at Soudron. The corps of Generals Kleist and Kapsewitsch, which had reached Metz and Nancy on the 2d, were directed to assemble at Chalons on the 8th; Marshal Blucher was therefore on the point of concentrating a considerable army; this pleasing prospect was, however, considerably delayed by the events which it is now become our duty to detail. He ordered the corps of General Yorck to pursue Marshal Macdonald along the Marne towards Chateau-Thierry and la Ferté sous Jouarre, while General Sacken from Vertus should march upon the same points, by Mont-Mirail, supported by the division of General Alsusieff. In the execution of these directions, General Yorck arrived on the morning of the 10th at Chateau-Thierry, from whence the enemy had been driven the preceding evening by his advanced guard, combined with a detachment from the corps of General Sacken. This latter officer the same day entered la Ferté sous Jouarre, on the heels of the enemy retiring to Meaux after the affair of Chateau-Thierry, and placed his advance at Trilport, while General Alsusieff remained in reserve at Champ-Aubert. Generals Kleist and Kapsewitsch were assembled on the same day at Vertus, having reached that point from Chalons.

Buonaparte having made the necessary dispositions for the defence of the Seine and Yonne, which he intrusted to Marshals Victor and Oudinot and General Pajol, marched from Nogent with the guards and the corps of Marshals Ney and Mortier on the 9th, to unite himself with the force under Marshal Marmont, which, since the day preceding, was assembled at Sezanne. On the evening of the 9th, Marshal Marmont had pushed forward his advanced troops upon Baye, where, a trifling affair having taken place with a detached corps from the army of Silesia, Marshal Blucher, who had moved his head-quarters to Etoges, was induced to return to Vertus. On the 10th, Marshal Marmont advanced his whole corps upon Champ Aubert, where he surprised the isolated corps of General Alsusieff, and attacking it by its left, cut off its retreat on Marshal Blucher. Buonaparte, who was following with the rest of his troops, directed them upon the right of this unfortunate corps, which, thus overwhelmed, was broken and destroyed, 1,200 men alone escaping from it, the rest being either killed or taken.

As soon as the news of Buonaparte's movement upon Sezanne had been communicated to Marshal Blucher, he directed the corps of Generals Yorck, Sacken, and Alsusieff, to unite at Montmirail, while with the corps of Generals Kleist and Kapsewitsch he

K

marched upon Fère Champenoise, in the hope of calling Buonaparte's attention, and of preventing his advance upon the other division of his army as yet unconnected. Learning, however, on the 10th in the evening, the misfortune of Champ-Aubert, he moved back these last mentioned corps on the 11th, and assembled them at Bergères.

On the morning of the 11th, Buonaparte detaching the corps of Marshal Marmont to observe Marshal Blucher from Etoges, carried the rest of his army upon Montmirail, to which place the corps of Generals Yorck and Sacken from their respective positions were marching to concentrate. The French, however, forestalled them in the occupation of the town, and General Sacken found their army assembling under cover of the cavalry of General Nansouty in front of that place, and moving into a position near Bailly, its centre at Marchais, and its left at Pomesson, upon the Pt. Morin. From Vieux Maisons General Sacken made a corresponding disposition towards the right and attacked; not waiting for the junction of General Yorck, whose advance upon the road from Chateau-Thierry was already within his reach. The action which ensued was maintained with much valour throughout the day. Buonaparte watching the effects of the movements he had directed on the flanks of the Russians, by which they were induced to weaken their centre, carried by storm with the guards the key of their position at the farm of Lépine-aux-Bois, and Marshal Mortier, later in the day, possessed himself of the village of Fontenelles, by which he hoped to have cut off all communication between the corps opposed to him and General Yorck. In this, however, he was disappointed; General Sacken moved to his left, and after a contest which cost him many valuable lives, succeeded in forming his junction with the Prussians; the two corps immediately retired to Viffort, and on the following morning to Chateau-Thierry, leaving a rear-guard under General Katzler at the defile of Caquerets. On the 12th, Buonaparte followed up his successes by the road of Rosoy and Essises, and attacked this rear-guard; at the moment it was driven from its position, the French cavalry, led on by Marshal Ney, charged between the farms of Petit Baloy and La Motte, and defeated the Prussian cavalry, driving it from the support of the infantry, which consequently suffered severely in its retreat, harassed and pursued with all the means Buonaparte could accumulate against it. The brigade of the Prince William of Prussia, which was in garrison at Chateau-Thierry, moved out in front of that town, to protect the troops which were retiring, and by so doing, rendered essential service; and when at last, yielding to the superior numbers by which it was attacked, it retired across the Marne, the complete destruction of the bridge over that river was effected by it, and the immediate pursuit of the enemy thus put an end to. The allied officers continued their retreat in the direction of Soissons; on the 13th they pursued their march, General Yorck to Fismes, and General Sacken to Rheims. Buonaparte, delayed by the difficulties of re-establishing the bridge, was unable to follow them with any effect: he detached, however, Marshal Mortier to observe their movements, while he returned to oppose the operations of Marshal Blucher.

This officer had remained throughout the 11th and 12th in perfect tranquillity at Bergères; on the 13th, conceiving that Buonaparte had retired from his front, and that Marshal Marmont alone was keeping him in check, he advanced upon Etoges. The French corps, yielding to the superiority of numbers, retired disputing the ground to Fromentieres, Marshal Blucher establishing his head-quarters at Champ-Aubert. The following morning, the 14th, Marshal Marmont continued to fall back towards Montmirail, pursued by the Allies, till Buonaparte with the corps of Marshal Ney, and the guards, together with a force he had left at Vieux Maisons while in pursuit of Generals Yorck and Sacken arrived to his support.

Buonaparte immediately ordered the village of Janvilliers to be attacked, while the cavalry under Generals Grouchy on the left, and Lefebvre-Desnouettes on the right, co-operated, and the guards supported. The village was taken, the troops defending it were cut to pieces, and the Prussian cavalry charged and driven back. This sudden change from retreat to a vigorous offensive movement persuaded Marshal Blucher that Buonaparte was opposed to him; he therefore retired, forming his infantry in columns of mass, and protecting it with artillery and cavalry in the intervals. The French pushed forward with the greatest exertions, harassing and pursuing a body of men, which from its great inferiority, and the absence of all support, seemed menaced with total destruction. At one moment they succeeded in making some impression upon it, but Marshal Blucher, gaining courage from the dangers which surrounded him, animated the troops by his example, restored order where it had been broken, and, assailed on all sides, yet every where repelled the enemy, and continued his operation. A most trying situation awaited him, however, between Champ-Aubert and Etoges. General Grouchy, (after having made a rapid movement through the woods on the side of St. Martin d'Ablois,) had reached the high road near these places in rear of the Allies. Marshal Blucher hesitated not an instant in ordering his troops to advance, and force their passage through this new and formidable obstruction. The French had fortunately not succeeded in bringing up their artillery. General Grouchy charged, and at the same time Buonaparte, from his side, directed the cavalry of his guard, and the cuirassiers to do the same. Marshal Blucher, assailed in front and rear, still undaunted, repulsed the attacks which were made upon him, and clearing his passage through the opposing multitude, arrived at Etoges, where he found a corps of the enemy's infantry ; this unexpected obstacle did not check the gallantry of the Allied troops; they charged, and at the point of the bayonet carried the village, and retired to Bergères. At dark, Buonaparte gave up the pursuit. The Allies lost in the actions of this day 3,500 men and seven guns ; they continued during the night to fall back upon Chalons, where Marshal Blucher arrived on the 15th, and where he collected the corps of Generals Yorck and Sacken, which had retired from Chateau-Thierry to Rheims; he received also the intelligence of the arrival of General Winzingerode at Laon on the 12th, and of his having captured Soissons by storm on the 15th, taking there three general officers, 3,000 prisoners, and 13 guns.

Buonaparte, on the night of the 13th, returned with the guards and Marshal Ney's corps, from Champ-Aubert, to Montmirial ; leaving Marshal Marmont at Etoges, supported by the cavalry under General Grouchy: the Silesian army was consequently in a situation at Chalons where, collected, and free from the presence of an enemy, it might re-establish itself from the dreadful loss and disaster it had suffered.

The events, which have been described, naturally lead to some reflection on the causes which produced them. The talent shewn by Buonaparte, in seizing the opportunity of falling upon the divided force of his enemies, and the activity with which he pursued his advantages, must ensure to him the tribute due to military skill, which, perhaps, in criticisms on the battles of Leipzig and Brienne many persons had endeavoured to withdraw from him. It must at the same time, however, be admitted, that the Allies themselves seemed almost to have pointed out the movements by which their projects were to be defeated. The mode in which the communication between the army of Prince Schwarzenberg and the Silesian army was abandoned, leaving the enemy to establish himself in a secure position between them; as well as the delays which followed the occupation of Troyes, have already been detailed. That at the same moment Marshal Blucher's army should have been advancing in five unconnected columns, was a misfortune, which might have led even to greater disasters than it was the occasion of. The decision of the Prussian general, when he was aware of the storm that was breaking over him, was thought little calculated for the situation in which he was placed. To unite his advanced divisions at Montmirail, with the enemy already arrived at Sezanne, was a dangerous operation to undertake, and, as it proved, impossible to execute. The movement of Generals Kleist and Kapsewitsch to Fère Champenoise was unlikely to recall Buonaparte from an operation, the object of which he was at the very moment of attaining, while it rendered more difficult the assembling the Allied army, an advantage to which it would seem every other consideration should have been sacrificed. The Marshal's advance upon Champ-Aubert, by which he entangled himself with the whole of Buonaparte's force on the 13th, although a bold decision, and supported throughout with infinite firmness and valour, as well by the troops as by their commander, yet, as it was unfortunate in its results, so was it severely criticised *.

* Sir Hudson Lowe, and Lieut. Harris were present in these actions, and bore testimony to the gallantry displayed by Marshal Blucher and the troops under his orders.

It is necessary now to return to the operations of the great army. Prince Schwarzenberg received at Nogent, on the 15th, a report from Marshal Blucher, dated the 13th, detailing to him the events which were taking place, and calling for assistance. With a view of corresponding with this desire, the 5th and 6th corps were ordered to march, the following morning, from Donnemarie and Provins, to Sezanne, and the reserves from Pont sur Seine to Mery. The next day Generals Wrede and Wittgenstein were to continue their movement to a position between Sommesous and Arcis, General Giulay was to follow them. The Prince Royal of Wurtemberg was to take up the position from Bray to Nogent, supporting the advanced guards of the 5th and 6th corps at Provins and Nangis, which were not to be removed. General Bianchi with the Austrian troops under his orders was to remain between Montereau and Sens: General Platow in the vicinity of Fontainebleau. During the night, however, advice was received from the Russian quarter-master General Diebitsch, that the enemy was no longer pushing the Silesian army, and that Buonaparte had returned to Montmirail. The movement proposed was therefore counter-ordered, and Prince Schwarzenberg advanced on the 16th to Bray.

Meantime General Wrede, on passing the Seine on the 13th, at that place, had found Marshal Oudinot occupying a position at Cuterelles, with his advance at St. Sauveur. General Wrede attacked these troops, and entering this latter place, directed his right upon Luistraines, where, after a sharp action, he succeeded in forcing the enemy to retire, and in thus turning the left of his position. The remainder of his troops having come up, General Wrede commenced a general attack upon the centre of the French position; but a report from General Hardegg at Paroy, that he was engaged with a division of the corps of Marshal Victor, which was retiring from Nogent, on the road to Paris, put a stop to this operation. The Bavarians bivouaqued upon the ground they occupied; and in the morning the French having disappeared, they advanced to Nangis.

Buonaparte, being informed of the passage of the Seine by the Allies, directed Marshal Macdonald to advance by a forced march on the 14th, with the troops he had collected at Meaux, amounting to about 12,000 men, to Guigne, where he was to connect himself with Marshals Victor, Oudinot, and General Pajol. The whole of these corps, in consequence of orders from Paris, had retired on the 15th behind the Yeres, Marshal Victor to Chaulmes, Marshal Oudinot to Guigne, Marshal Macdonald to Solers, General Pajol to Cramayel, and Count Charpentier to Essonne and Corbeil. The Allies had, in the mean time, taken Moret and Fontainebleau, where the advance of General Bianchi was established; a separate corps of Austrians under Count Thurn, co-operating with Count Platow and General Seslavin, had occupied Nemours, and menaced Orleans. General Giulay was at Villeneuve la Guyard and Pont sur Yonne; the Austrian reserves and Prince Morice Liechtenstein between Sens and Joigny; the Russian reserves between Nogent and Bray; General Wrede at Donnemarie, with his advance at Nangis; to which place Count Wittgenstein had marched, by the misinterpretation of an order, on the 16th, but was directed on the 17th, to return to Provins, his advance, under Count Pahlen, remaining at Mormant.

Such was the situation in which Buonaparte found the great army, after he returned from his operations against Marshal Blucher. On the morning of the 14th from Montmirail, after issuing his orders to Marshal Marmont, whom he left in observation of the Silesian army, and to Marshal Mortier, who was to keep in check the corps of Generals Winzingerode and Bulow, he marched with the guards, and Marshal Ney's corps, by La Ferté sous Jouarre and Meaux, and on the 16th arrived at Guigne.

Buonaparte had lately received reinforcements from the armies opposed to Lord Wellington; he had in consequence formed four corps of cavalry under Generals Bordesoulle, St. Germain, Milhaud, and Kellerman, the whole amounting to nearly 20,000 men. The infantry which had joined him was incorporated with the corps as they already stood. The whole of the army he now took the command of in front of the Allies was estimated at about 55,000 men.

He commenced offensive movements against the

great army, on the morning of the 17th; Marshal Victor, flanked by the corps of cavalry under Generals Kellerman and Milhaud, overwhelmed the small force commanded by Count Pahlen at Mormant, and taking or cutting to pieces almost all its infantry, drove the cavalry upon the advance of General Wrede. General Hardegg, who commanded this corps, was also charged and driven back with some loss, the French possessing themselves of Nangis. From this point Buonaparte directed the pursuit of the Allies in three directions: Marshals Victor upon Montereau, Marshal Macdonald upon Donnemarie, and Marshal Oudinot upon Provins. Marshal Victor overtook a division of Bavarians under General Lamotte at Valjouan, which, with some loss, was forced to retire upon Bray, where the rest of General Wrede's corps effected its passage across the Seine without having been engaged. Count Wittgenstein retired from Provins to Nogent, the Prince Royal of Wurtemberg fell back to a strong position in front of Montereau; at the close of the day, therefore, the advantages obtained by the French were confined to the destruction of the infantry of Count Pahlen, and the loss occasioned to the corps of Generals Hardegg and Lamotte, the whole amounting to about 3,000 men. At the headquarters of the Allies, however, it was decided at a council of war held in the evening at Prince Schwarzenberg's, and at which were present the Emperor Alexander and the King of Prussia, that the Prince's aid-de-camp, Count Parr, should be sent to the French advanced posts, with a letter to Marshal Berthier, expressing surprise at the offensive movement which had been made by the French army, and stating, that the Allied Sovereigns having given orders to their plenipotentiaries at Chatillon to sign the preliminaries of peace, on the conditions which had been proposed by Mons. de Caulincourt*, they had directed

* A few days after the opening of the negotiations of Chatillon, the Russian plenipotentiary received an order to suspend all proceedings, until further directions were transmitted to him. On the same day, the 9th of February, Mons. de Caulincourt offered to negotiate an armistice, the basis of which should agree with the demands of the Allies, and for the attainment of which he proposed to surrender some of the fortresses which France was to sacrifice. The Allies desired that these stipulations might be agreed to in the form of preliminaries; and on the 13th, from Nogent, the Emperor of Russia ordered his plenipotentiary to accept these conditions. When Buonaparte found that the terms his negotiator had tendered were likely to meet the views of the Allies, he declined to adhere to them. See Appendix No. XII.

their army to abstain from any farther advance; that as it must be supposed Buonaparte would decide upon the same conduct as soon as he was aware of the circumstance; it was proposed immediately to agree to a suspension of hostilities *.

This letter, as might be expected, from the relative situation of the armies, remained for several days without an answer. Buonaparte, on the morning of the 18th, pushed the corps of Marshal Victor, supported by the reserve under Count Gerard from Montigny-Lancoup and Salins, upon Montereau. The division of General Pajol, which had moved the day preceding to Le Chatelet, was also directed to advance upon the same point. This town, situated to the south of the Seine, has a range of hills opposite to it on the other side of the river, which, as a strong military post, was occupied by the Prince Royal. The bridge was immediately in rear of this position, which was consequently extremely dangerous to a corps acting on the defensive,

* See Appendix, No. XIII.

a retreat being only to be effected over it, across the river, and at a time, most probably, when, the heights having been carried by the enemy, he would bring his fire to bear upon it.

Notwithstanding these disadvantages, the Prince Royal, relying on his own resources and the valour of his troops, hesitated not in fulfilling the letter of his instructions, and in fighting to defend the post intrusted to him. Marshal Victor and General Pajol were the first who attacked it; they were repulsed with loss, and their renewed attacks, till near two o'clock, terminated to their disadvantage. At that hour Buonaparte arrived with the troops under Count Gerard, supported by a part of the guards, when the contest became so unequal, that the Allies were obliged to fall back. This critical movement was executed with less loss than could have been expected. The Prince Royal distinguished himself both by his talent and his bravery; he was at one time in the midst of the French cavalry near the bridge, fighting and resisting its advance, and animating his troops by his example; he succeeded in gaining time for the passage of nearly the whole of his force across the river; it was re-organized on the other side, and retired unmolested to La Tombe and Bazoches. General Bianchi, from the left of the Yonne, and near the confluence of that river with the Seine, co-operated with his artillery in protecting the retreat of the Wurtemberg troops, and prevented the passage of any considerable body of the enemy in pursuit of them. The destruction of the bridge over the Yonne impeded the advance of the French upon him, and in the evening he fell back, according to his orders, towards Sens, from whence, in conjunction with the rest of the Austrian troops, he had been directed to retire upon Troyes. Buonaparte then pushed his army across the Seine, his advance establishing itself at Marolles.

Marshal Macdonald had moved in the morning upon Bray, but finding the village in front of it, and on the right bank of the Seine, occupied by the Bavarians, thus forming a *tête-de-pont* which it would be difficult to force, he limited himself to a partial engagement with their light troops throughout the day, and at night moved upon Montereau, where he passed the river. Marshal Oudinot, dreading the difficulties of forcing the position of General Wittgenstein at Nogent, moved at the same period from Provins upon Bray.

The whole French army was therefore assembled, on the morning of the 19th, between Montereau and that place; no very great advantage had been obtained by it, considering the extensive and unconnected position occupied by the Allies, at the moment it assumed offensive movements against them. This was attributed by the French officers to the separation of the three corps of their army after the successes at Mormant, an operation by which their force was frittered away, and rendered unable to make any serious impression. General Kellerman also complained that Buonaparte had not supported him, when he had so entirely overthrown the force under Count Pahlen, that he might have fallen upon Count Wittgenstein while moving upon Provins, and perhaps have prevented his retreat to Nogent.

At the moment the military council of the Allies had sanctioned the letter from Prince Schwarzenberg to Marshal Berthier, it was decided that the great army should retire to a concentrated position in front of Troyes, where, having effected its junction with the Silesian army which was already advancing from Chalons to Mery, a general battle was to be accepted.

The Emperor of Russia and King of Prussia left Bray on the morning of the 18th; they retired to Trainel, where a part of the Russian reserves were collected. Prince Schwarzenberg remained at Bray till the evening, when he moved his head-quarters to the same place. The left of his army, entirely composed of Austrian troops, retired from the Yonne towards Troyes, by Villeneuve l'Archevêque, where General Bianchi arrived on the 19th. The Prince Royal and General Wrede retired on the same day to Pont sur Seine and Mâcon, the Russian reserves to a position in front of Troyes. On the 20th, the left of the great army was between St. Liebault and Villemaure; the 5th corps was at Echemine, with its advance at St. Martin le Bosnay, the 4th retiring to Troyes, and the 6th at Mery, with its advance at Châtres.

By a reconnoissance made on the 21st, by detachments from the 5th and 6th corps, Buonaparte was known to have reached Nogent on the 20th, where he was collecting the greater part of his army; the 2d corps, from the command of which Marshal Victor had been removed, and which was placed under Count Gerard, being the only one detached to follow General Bianchi by Pont sur Yonne and Villeneuve l'Archevêque. In the course of this day, Marshal Blucher arrived upon the Seine. He had quitted Chalons on the 18th, moving his army, which had been collected there, and reinforced by the corps of Count Langeron and a considerable body of cavalry, in three columns; the right on Bergères and Etoges, the centre on Pierre-Morain, the left on Fère-Champenoise. On the 19th, in consequence of the intelligence received from the great army, he concentrated his troops at Sommesous; on the 20th he moved to Arcis; and on the 21st he relieved the sixth corps at Mery, which retired to Villacerf.

In consequence of the uncertainty with regard to the movements of the French army, Prince Schwarzenberg had directed a general reconnoissance to be made on the morning of the 22d, in which the whole of Marshal Blucher's cavalry was to be employed, as well as the cavalry under the orders of General Wrede. On the afternoon of the 21st, however, and immediately after the Silesian army had occupied the posts which had been given up to it by the 6th corps, it was attacked by the French divisions of Generals Boyer and Gruyère, who endeavoured to force the passage of the Seine, The bridge over the river, which was of wood, was set fire to; but not being entirely consumed, a part of the enemy's forces succeeded in passing to the right bank. During the contest at this point, the town of Mery, which was in the possession of the Allies, was on a sudden discovered to be in flames in several places, which extending with great rapidity, rendered it impossible for the support destined for the Allied troops engaged near the bridge to arrive to their assistance. Marshal Blucher, in consequence, drew up his army in two lines in the rear of Mery, and there waited to receive whatever portion of the French army should choose to pass the river and attack him. This disposition put an end to the enemy's advance; the troops they had already brought into action were recalled, who in their retreat, being attacked by the Allies, were defeated with considerable loss. In consequence of this affair, the reconnoissance, which had been ordered for the morning of the 22d, was countermanded; and the Prince Marshal having received intelligence that Marshal Augereau had collected a force at Lyons, with which he was advancing against the Austrian troops in that quarter, detached immediately General Bianchi upon Dijon to reinforce them; and at the same time, giving up the idea of accepting a battle, if Buonaparté were inclined to offer it, he withdrew all the infantry of his army, with the exception of the fifth and sixth corps, which remained as a rear-guard, through Troyes, and across the Seine.

On the 22d, the French army leaving a corps to observe Marshal Blucher, moved forward towards Troyes, preceded by its cavalry, which arrived about two o'clock at Pavillon, Les Grez, and Villemaure; the whole of the Allied cavalry, assembled in the plain in front of these places, was ordered to advance upon it. This movement was, however, so slowly executed, and there was so much apprehension of engaging in an action where the strength of the opposing forces was not exactly known, that the enemy was not molested. The French army was concentrated in the evening between Villeneuve l'Archeveque Avon la Peze, Echemine, and Les Grez, with the guards in reserve at Chatres.

PART V.

PRINCE Schwarzenberg, on receiving the news of the offensive movements commenced by Marshal Augereau, recommended the retreat of the army under his orders behind the Aube as far as Chaumont and Langres, and of the Silesian army to Nancy. This plan was agreed to by the sovereigns, and the necessary orders despatched. On the evening of the 23d, the corps of General Giulay retired on the road to Bar sur Seine: Prince Morice Liechtenstein being left to cover its movement, with orders to follow in the morning to Bar, from whence it was to form part of the corps of General Bianchi, joining that officer at Dijon. General Wrede was placed with the 5th corps in the town of Troyes, which he was to defend till the morning of the 24th; the rest of the great army retired by the roads of Piney and

Vandœuvres; the road by Arcis and Lesmont being pointed out for the army of Silesia.

By these combinations the two most effective corps of Austrians attached to that part of the great army which was operating immediately against Buonaparte were separated from it, and, together with the Austrian reserves which had arrived at Basle, were placed under the orders of the Prince Philip of Hesse-Hombourg; so that there remained only with Prince Schwarzenberg, of troops of his own nation, the 3d corps, the force under General Frimont attached to the 5th corps, a brigade incorporated with the 4th corps, and a division of grenadiers and one of cuirassiers under General Count Nostitz.

The army of the south, which henceforth composed almost the entire Austrian force in France, being thus rendered infinitely superior to the corps opposed to it, drove back Marshal Augereau from Lons le Saulnier, and on the 21st of March was established in Lyons.

It is of interest here to remark, that the army of Prince Schwarzenberg had retired from Bray for the purpose of being concentrated near Troyes, where, in connexion with Marshal Blucher, who was invited to move on Mery, it would be in a situation, with a vast superiority of numbers, to meet the enemy in a decisive action. This object was obtained on the 22d, the two Allied armies united within the space of a few miles, and, opposed only to the force Buonaparte had collected against one of them, appeared to be in possession of every advantage the most successful military combinations could produce. Elated with the prospect before him, Marshal Blucher proposed to pass the Seine, and in conjunction with the great army to fall upon the enemy. Other counsels, however, prevailed: the troops under Generals Bianchi and Prince Morice Liechtenstein being at this crisis removed, the Allied armies were thought to be unequal to such an enterprise, and a general retreat was proposed, which, had it been effected to its entire extent, would have abandoned half the French territory which had been conquered, and might have considerably delayed the eventual successes of the Allies.

In the afternoon of the 22d of February, Prince Schwarzenberg received an answer to the letter he had addressed to Marshal Berthier from Bray, enclosing a letter from Buonaparte to the Emperor of Austria, in which he stated, " that fortune having smiled upon him, he had destroyed the Russians and Prussian army, commanded by Marshal Blucher, and the Prussians under General Kleist. Under these circumstances, notwithstanding the prejudice which existed in the Austrian head-quarters, his army was stronger in infantry, cavalry, and artillery, than that of the Allies ; and if the knowledge of this fact was necessary to the determinations of the Emperor, he should have no difficulty in shewing his troops to a person of sound judgment, such as Prince Schwarzenberg, Count Bubna, or Prince Metternich. He thought it right to write this letter, because a struggle between his forces and an army principally Austrian, appeared contrary to the interests of both empires. If the Austrian army were successful, the Emperor's situation would only be more embarrassing. If the Allies were beaten, how would they retire from France, the population of which was exasperated to the last degree by the crimes of the Cossacks and the Russians. In this state of things he proposed to the Emperor to sign a treaty of peace without delay, upon the basis which was offered from Frankfort, and which the French nation and himself had adopted as their ultimatum; indeed, it was the only ground-work upon which could be re-established the equilibrium of Europe; if conditions differing from it were imposed upon France, peace could not last. The Allied plenipotentiaries had proposed terms at Chatillon, the knowledge of which in France would excite universal indignation. It was the realization of the dream of Burke, who wished to make France disappear from the map of Europe. There was no Frenchman who would not rather prefer death than accept conditions which would make him the slave of England. Such could neither be the intentions nor the interest of the Emperor of Austria. What view could that Sovereign have in forcing the restitution of Antwerp from France, and thereby destroying its marine. By the propositions of Frankfort Austria would become a maritime power; what object could she have, therefore, in exposing her flag to be outraged and violated as it formerly had been by England? What object could she have in placing the Low Countries under a Protestant Prince, who was one day destined to ascend the throne of England? At all events these hopes, these projects, were beyond the reach of the coalition. If the battle which would soon be fought against the Allies should be unsuccessful, he had still the means of fighting two more before Paris should be captured; were even this to happen, the rest of France would never bear the yoke to be imposed upon her, The convulsions of the nation would quadruple its energies and its force. He never would yield Antwerp or the Low Countries. A peace upon the basis of Frankfort could alone enable France to look to the re-establishment of its marine and of its commerce. If the Emperor of Austria persisted in making his interest subordinate to the views of England and the resentments of Russia, the Genius of France and Providence would be against him. The Emperor Alexander should not entertain sentiments of vengeance; before the capture of Moscow he offered him peace, he did all in his power to stop the conflagration, which had been lighted in that capital by the Emperor's orders. After all 200,000 men were in arms at Paris; they knew what the Russians had been guilty of; they knew the fallacy of their promises, they knew the fate which would await them. He pressed the Emperor of Austria, therefore, to avoid the chances of a battle, to conclude an immediate peace, grounded on the proclamation published by Prince Schwarzenberg, upon the declaration of the Allies of the 1st of December 1813, and upon the propositions of Frankfort. These he had accepted, and he would still accept; not but that the position of the Allies was now far different from what it was at that time, and that in the judgment of every impartial man, the chances now were in his favour. He should take leave to tell the Emperor of Austria, that notwithstanding all that Sovereign had done against him since the invasion of France, notwithstanding his forgetfulness of the ties by which they were united, and of the interests which connected their people, he retained towards him the same sentiments, and he could not see with indifference, that if the peace now offered was refused, it would be the misery of the Emperor's life, and of his people; while by a single word all might be conciliated and lasting tranquillity secured to Europe. If he had been base enough to accept the conditions offered to him, the Emperor of Austria ought to have dissuaded him from doing so, since he knew that what degraded thirty millions of people could not last. The Emperor of Austria might at once finish the war, secure the happiness of his people and of Europe, and end the miseries of a nation, which was a prey to the crimes of the Tartars of the Desert, hardly deserving the appellation of men. He could hardly be asked why he addressed himself to the Emperor of Austria; he could neither do so to the English, who thought only of the destruction of his marine, nor to the Emperor Alexander, whose only feeling was vengeance against him. He could only address that Sovereign who had lately been his ally; and who, from the strength of his army and the greatness of his empire, was considered as the principal power in the coalition; the Emperor of Austria, who, whatever were now the sentiments he entertained, yet had French blood in his veins."

The letter from Marshal Berthier expressed nearly the same sentiments to Prince Schwarzenberg, calling upon him to use his influence to bring the war to a termination, upon the terms of the Frankfort basis, and assuring him, that those which had been proposed at Chatillon, far from leading to the signature of preliminaries, as had been stated in his letter from Bray, had been refused by Buonaparte, who would die rather than agree to them *.

The first determination upon the receipt of these letters was to return no immediate answer to them, since the principle upon which the original proposition had been made from Bray had not been very generally approved. With a view, however, of gaining time for the arrival of the reinforcements which were moving to join the Allied army, Prince Wenceslas Liechtenstein, in the afternoon of the 23d, was sent to Buonaparte's head-quarters, to notify the wish of the Allies to negotiate for a suspension of hostilities. Buonaparte held most exulting language to this officer; he stated his army to amount to 100,000 men, the most effective he had ever commanded, and he called upon the Austrians not to sacrifice themselves to the wretched policy of England, and to the artifices of Russia, but to retire from

* It is singular that the terms inveighed against in both these letters were precisely those proposed in Monsieur de Caulaincourt's letter, which has already been referred to.

the coalition against him. He, notwithstanding, consented to the propositions which were made to him, and appointed Count Flahaut the French commissioner to treat for an armistice; he was to meet the officers named on the side of the Allies, at Lusigny, on the following day.

The French army advanced in three columns on the 23d upon Troyes; a part of the corps of Count Gerard made a successful charge on the cavalry of Prince Morice Liechtenstein, near Fontvannes, and captured six pieces of cannon. Troyes was summoned; General Wrede in reply stated, that the place would be evacua'ed the following morning; this not being considered by the French as sufficiently advantageous to them, they made preparations to assault it, which was twice unsuccessfully attempted during the night. On the 24th, the town being evacuated, Buonaparte entered it, and was received with acclamations; the wounded and sick left by the Allies were dragged into the streets to grace his triumph. He immediately ordered a ci-devant emigrant, who had waited upon the Emperor of Russia, and had worn the order of St. Louis, to be tried by a military commission; the sentence of death which was pronounced against him, was executed within a few hours. The French troops followed the Allies upon the roads to Vandœuvres and Bar sur Seine; not however with much vigour. Prince Schwarzenberg removed his head-quarters on the 25th to Bar sur Aube, and on the following day to Colombé les deux Eglises. The Russian reserves retired to Chaumont and Langres; the 5th corps was placed at Bar sur Aube; the 6th, in support at Colombé; the 4th corps was removed to Montfan les Froneles, Blessonville, and Chateau Vilain, to connect itself with the 3d, which had retired from Bar sur Seine upon Arc en Barois.

From the manner in which the great army had been followed in its retreat from Troyes, it became evident that Buonaparte was occupied in some other operation besides the pursuit of it; yet no suspension of the preconcerted movements took place with the Allies till the 26th, when the small force, by which General Wrede was attacked at the bridge of Dolancourt and at Bar sur Aube, induced him to assault that town after it had been occupied by the enemy.

He succeeded in retaking a part of it, and in proving that he was able alone to cope with the troops which were opposed to him. The 6th corps was however, ordered up from Colombé on the morning of the 27th, to support General Wrede, and to attack the enemy.

The French force, under the orders of Marshal Oudinot, and composed of the 2d and 7th corps of infantry, and of the cavalry under Generals St. Germain and Kellerman, was occupying the greater part of the town of Bar, the villages of Ailleville, and Arsonval, and the bridge of Dolancourt. The cavalry under General Kellerman was on the left of the Aube, upon a height above Bar, on the road to Spoy. General Wrede had placed his troops in position opposite to Bar and across the road leading to Chaumont; his advance in the Faubourgs of the town, with a detachment of light troops marching through Bayel and Bajol upon the heights of Ste. Germaine. Prince Schwarzenberg joined him at the moment the 6th corps arrived from Colombé; which he directed to move in rear of General Wrede, and ascend the heights of Arentière, from whence the ground falling towards the

Aube, and intersected by ravines, was commanded. Count Pahlen marched upon Levigny, from whence he was to move towards Bossancourt, and menace the bridge of Dolancourt. As soon as these dispositions were discovered by the enemy, Marshal Oudinot formed the 7th corps of infantry, supported by General St. Germain, across the ravines above mentioned, his right supported by the 2d corps under General Gerard, which was in occupation of Bar. The action commenced about twelve o'clock, by an attack made by the French Brigades of Generals Montfort and Belair, which moved from the ground in front of Ailleville. The right of these columns stormed a height, which was the connecting point between the 6th corps and the force under General Wrede. The Russians, who occupied it, were driven back. Count Wittgenstein directed a heavy column of infantry, supported by a division of cuirassiers, to retake the position; the cavalry arriving first, charged, but was repulsed; the infantry, however, executed the duty imposed upon it. The other French column was equally driven back, and the whole of the 6th corps, being assembled on the heights, commenced a general advance upon the enemy; this operation was, however, arrested by a forward movement of the French cavalry, which had already been in action, reinforced by the corps under General Kellerman, which having descended from the heights on the left of the Aube, had been formed upon the right of Arsonval. Count Pahlen was recalled from Levigny to assist in repelling this attack, a charge of which had already been successful against the Russian cavalry; its further progress was resisted near Arentière, where Count Wittgenstein concentrated his troops, and where his artillery was served with considerable effect. Prince Schwarzenberg directed Count Pahlen in consequence of this success, to return to Levigny, and continue the operation he was originally charged with; he ordered also the right of the 5th corps to advance along the foot of the heights of Arentière, towards Ailleville, thus menacing the right and rear of the enemy's force engaged with the 6th corps. Count Wittgenstein at the same time pushed forward. The French thus overwhelmed by numbers, and forced to retire, defended themselves in the different positions afforded by the ravines, which intersect the road as far as the bridge of Dolancourt, and succeeded in crossing the Aube without any considerable loss. The artillery of Count Pahlen, which had advanced from Levigny, did some execution upon their rear guard while passing the river. Count Gerard, attacked by the Bavarians, evacuated Bar, which, being occupied by General Wrede, terminated the action. Count Wittgenstein, who, as well as Prince Schwarzenberg, had been wounded in this affair, retained, notwithstanding, the command of his troops, and placed them along the right of the Aube; the French formed upon the left of it, one of their brigades being posted upon the road to Spoy, the rest of their army between the bridge of Dolancourt and Vandœuvres. The result of this action was favourable to the Allies; though with their great superiority of numbers, and a position commanding the ground on which the enemy was formed, and from whence he was in danger of being driven into the river immediately in his rear, it is to be lamented that the contest was so prolonged, and that its success was not more decisive*. The

* The French had about 17,000 men engaged in this action, the division of General Pacthod, which remained at Dolancourt, not included. The Allies had the 5th and 6th corps, which, although reduced from their original numbers, could not be less than 35,000 men.

enemy on the following day retired to a position in front of Vandœuvres, he was not pursued; Prince Schwarzenberg was unwilling to risk his troops in any advanced movement till he had ascertained the strength of the corps of Marshal Macdonald, which had moved from St. Usage, upon Clairvaux, and La Ferté sur Aube. Neither did he wish to depart at once from the new system of operations he had decided upon, and which a few days before had been announced to the army in a General Order, of which the following is a translation :—

" I have already directed all the officers commanding the various corps and detachments belonging to this army, to seek to diminish the ill effects by which a retrograde movement is so frequently accompanied, by requiring them to maintain on one side the strictest discipline among their troops, while on the other they shall take care that every measure conducive to that object, shall punctually be carried into effect.

" At the present moment when the operations of the great army and of the army of Marshal Blucher, are taking a decided character, I think it my duty to point out to the commanders of corps, the object to which our movements are directed, in order to place them in a situation clearly to understand the point of view according to which they are to consider the operations of the army.

" On approaching its reserves, (which have already crossed the Rhine,) the great army will assume the offensive with a considerable part of its forces in the south of France: it will keep the defensive on the line on which it is now operating, till Marshal Blucher by forming his junction with Generals Winzingerode and Bulow, and by resuming the offensive upon the rear and flanks of the enemy, shall compel him to divide his forces, and thus procure to the great army (reinforced by its reserves,) the opportunity of striking a decisive blow. With these views the commanders of corps will be pleased to rectify, as far as may be necessary, the opinion in general, and give to the spirit of the troops under their orders, the most favourable direction.

" I cannot at the same time too strongly urge that the strictest measures be taken to remove from the sphere of the operations of the army, the endless train of baggage which encumbers it *."

(*Signed*) Schwarzenberg.

The plan which is here explained was formed at Bar Sur Aube on the 25th, in a council, at which the Emperor of Russia and the King of Prussia were present. It was brought about by a report received from Arcis, that the Silesian army had not retired through that place, as had been concerted, but, having thrown three bridges across the Aube at Anglure, had taken a direction different to the one recommended to it.

The Prince Royal of Wurtemberg received instructions from Prince Schwarzenberg on the 27th to advance with the troops under his orders, taking also the command of the 3d corps, against Marshal Macdonald. On the evening of this day the Prince Royal passed a body of cavalry across the Aube at La Ferté; but the division of General Milhaud, supported by the infantry under Generals Broyer and

* The order of the day, of which the above is a translation, is published in the " *Aperçu de la Campagne de l'Armée des Alliés et de l'Armée Française in* 1814."—Weimar, 1815.

Amey, obliged it to retire. On the 28th the Prince Royal, with the 4th corps, marched upon Clairvaux, with the view of turning the left of the French position, while he directed the 3d corps to pass the river at the bridge of Silvarouvre, and endeavour to turn its right. Marshal Macdonald, who had received orders from Buonaparte to take the command of the whole force left to observe the great army, had assembled the divisions of Generals l'Héritier and Albert at Fontette, with a view of forcing his way to Bar sur Aube or Vandœuvres; but the Wurtemberg cavalry, which had passed through Clairvaux, having intercepted the roads leading to these places, he was forced to abandon his intentions.

General Giulay attacked the divisions of Generals Broyer and Milhaud at La Ferté and Silvarouvre, and after a sharp contest, passed the river, and drove them from their positions; he was aided in this operation by the corps of Cossacks under General Seslavin, which operated upon his left. These divisions retired upon the troops under Marshal Macdonald near Fontette, from whence the whole fell back on Bar sur Seine, to the environs of which place it was pursued by the Allies. In consequence of these successes, and of a despatch received from Marshal Blucher, dated La Ferté sous Jouarre the 28th, by which his offensive movement towards Paris was explained, Prince Schwarzenberg, on the 1st of March, ordered a reconnoissance to be made towards Vandœuvres by the cavalry of the 5th and 6th corps. General Frimont advanced by the road from Spoy, Count Pahlen by Amance upon Val Suzenay and Vauchonvilliers; these movements succeeded beyond the objects for which they were undertaken.

Marshal Oudinot, alarmed by the advance of Count Pahlen on his left, abandoned Vandœuvres, which was occupied by General Frimont. It became now no longer necessary to persevere in the plan which had been announced to the army. Prince Schwarzenberg received a report from General Tettenborn, dated Vertus the 27th, informing him that Buonaparte was on that day at Arcis, that his guards were marching by Sezanne and Fère Champenoise, and that it was evident he was directing his forces against Marshal Blucher. Notwithstanding this intelligence, considerable objection was felt by many distinguished officers to advance towards Troyes; a plan even was proposed by which the Russian troops attached to the great army should be moved towards Châlons, where, embodied with the Silesian army, as well as with the army of the Prince Royal of Sweden, the whole should be placed under the Emperor Alexander, while Prince Schwarzenberg, retaining the Bavarian and Wurtemberg troops, should join the army already to the south, and operate on Lyons. According to another view, Prince Schwarzenberg was to move the greater part of his army to the right, connecting it with the corps arriving from the north, and undertaking, under the protection of the force so assembled, the siege of Mayence. These plans were grounded upon a supposition, that the line of country upon which the great army was operating, was exhausted; that no further supplies could be derived from it, and that the hostility of the peasants, which had lately begun to shew itself, would render it impossible to remain upon it. The weakness of the enemy in front, and the facility with which his positions were abandoned, made it impossible, however, to listen to any of these suggestions.

Prince Schwarzenberg advanced his head-quarters

to Bar sur Aube on the 2d of March, and having received a report from the Prince Royal of Wurtemberg, stating, that he had driven Marshal Macdonald from Bar sur Seine to La Maison Blanche, he resolved to attack the enemy, now occupying with his advanced troops the same position along the Barce, which had been taken up by Buonaparte after the battle of Brienne, and if possible to take possession of Troyes. On the 3d Count Wittgenstein moved against the French position, turning its left, while General Wrede advanced upon the bridge of La Guillotière; the troops under these officers arrived at their destination at one o'clock. Count Pahlen, who had reached Dosches the day preceding, had moved upon Laubressel and Bourenton in the morning; the latter village not being occupied by the enemy, he passed through it, and fell upon the French train of artillery which was retiring to Troyes, and, dispersing the troops which escorted it, took the greater part, and occasioned considerable confusion in the rear of the enemy's position. The cavalry of General St. Germain, however, obliged Count Pahlen to fall back, and wait the arrival of the troops in his support. At two o'clock, the 6th corps, advancing from Roully and Mesgnil Selliers, began its attack on the villages where Count Pahlen had already been engaged, while General Wrede, having passed five battalions across the Barce near Courteranges, co-operated with the Russians, and forced Marshal Oudinot to retire. When Prince Schwarzenberg perceived the enemy giving way, he directed the Bavarians to storm the bridge of La Guillotière, which being successfully executed, General Gerard was obliged to abandon the direct road to Troyes, and to retire along the marshy ground to his right; by this movement he joined the rest of the French army in its position at Saint Parre aux Tertres where it had been driven, with the loss of several pieces of cannon and 2,000 prisoners. The Russian divisions of the Prince Eugene of Wurtemberg and Prince Gortschakow had distinguished themselves in the attack of Laubressel, from whence the enemy had been repulsed, after a contest of some duration; the Russian cavalry, which was in support of the infantry, having made several very successful charges. On the morning of the 4th, the Russians again attacked the corps of General Gerard, which had been left as a rear-guard at St. Parre, the main body of the enemy having retired through Troyes in the night, and drove it from its position. General Gerard proposed to capitulate for the town, but was answered that an hour would be allowed him to evacuate it. As soon as the time had elapsed, the Allied cavalry passed through Troyes, and pursued the enemy on the road to Nogent. Prince Schwarzenberg, with great valour and distinction, directed the movements of these troops, who drove the French cavalry upon its infantry at Les Grez, occasioning it very considerable loss*.

Marshal Macdonald, who had been directed by Buonaparte to take the command of the whole of the French army in observation of Prince Schwarzenberg, had retired the troops he, till then, had separately commanded, from la Maison Blanche on the night of the 3d, connecting their retreat by Pavillon with the corps from Troyes; so that the Prince Royal of Wurtemberg, with the 3d and 4th corps, was enabled, without opposition, to reach that town at the same time with the rest of the

* On the day on which Troyes was re-captured, the negotiations for an armistice, which had been carried on at Lusigny since the 24th of February, were put an end to, Count Flahaut refusing the conditions to which the Allies were willing to subscribe.

Allied army. Marshal Macdonald fell back to Nogent, where he placed the whole of the troops now collected under his orders in a position along the left of the Seine, occupying Bray and Montereau, with his head-quarters at Provins.

Prince Schwarzenberg ordered his army to advance on the 5th; on the 7th the corps of Count Wittgenstein was cantoned between Romilly and Nogent, that of General Wrede between Trainel and Grisy, with its advance opposite to Bray; the 3d and 4th corps at Villeneuve l'Archeveque, with their advance in occupation of Sens and Pont sur Yonne. In these positions this army remained till the 13th, when, in consequence of the news from Marshal Blucher of the assembly of his army at Laon, Prince Schwarzenberg concentrated the 6th corps between Pont sur Seine and Mery, the 5th at Arcis sur Aube, the 3d at Prunay, and the 4th at Avon le Peze. The Russian reserves were at the same time ordered up from Chaumont to a position between Brienne and Montierender. The corps of Prince Morice Liechtenstein, which, instead of continuing to form a part of the army of the south, had been recalled by Prince Schwarzenberg, was directed upon Tonnerre and Auxerre, where it arrived on the 11th, and at Joigny on the 13th. General Seslavin was at St. Valerien on the same day, General Alix being opposed to him, and in occupation of Montargis and Nemours. The intelligence of the victory obtained by Marshal Blucher induced Prince Schwarzenberg, on the 15th, to move his headquarters to Pont sur Seine, with a view of attacking Marshal Macdonald at Provins with the 4th, 5th, and 6th corps, while he directed the 3d to establish itself at Sens. Marshal Wrede, on the morning of the 16th, advanced from the neighbourhood of Arcis sur Aube and Plancy through Traconne upon Villenoxe and Villigrue, while General Rayefski, who had succeeded Count Wittgenstein * in the command of the 6th corps, was directed to penetrate by St. Fereol Fouchères and St. Martin de Chennetron upon Provins. The Prince Royal of Wurtemberg was to pass the Seine at Nogent, and establish himself at Meriot.

The 6th corps was alone engaged in the action of this day; the division of the Prince Eugene of Wurtemberg drove the enemy from l' Echelle upon Corme-

* Count Wittgenstein had retired in consequence of ill health.

ron and Richebourg, while Prince Schafskoy established himself at Sordun and in the forest which surrounds it. General Gerard was in consequence recalled from his position near Nogent, and the 4th corps pushed its advance without opposition to Meriot. Marshal Macdonald, menaced by superior forces, abandoned his position during the night, and retired to La Maison Rouge, with his right at Donnemarie, and his left at Cucharmoy; his cavalry in front at Rouilly.

During this action, Prince Schwarzenberg received a report of the defeat of the corps of General St. Priest near Rheims; he immediately directed the troops who were engaged, to suspend their movements, and the 5th corps to march upon Arcis, to which place he immediately transported his headquarters; the 3d corps he at the same time directed to fall back from Sens to Villeneuve L'Archévêque.

On the 17th the 5th corps was moved into a position between Rameru and Arcis, the 6th was ordered to advance upon Charny, the 4th was brought to Mery, and the 3d to a position between

Nogent and Pont sur Seine. The Russian reserves were assembled at Donnement and Donmartin.

We have thus traced the movements of the great army through a period during which its operations have frequently been criticised. Whatever reasons might be assigned for delaying to assume decided offensive measures previous to the capture of Troyes on the 4th, yet, from that period to the 17th, during which time Buonaparte was known to have concentrated his forces against Marshal Blucher upon the Aisne, the comparative inactivity of this army has constantly been remarked upon. The grounds upon which the movements it pursued were adopted, were set forth at head-quarters, in a memoir dated the 7th of March, and which stated, "* that the superiority of numbers on the side of the Allies enabled them to operate so as to force the enemy to divide his army, thus taking from the part of it where Buonaparte was not present the advantage which as sovereign he possessed, and which was entirely wanting to the Allies, where troops of so many nations were combating together. According to this principle the battle offered by Buonaparte at Troyes was not accepted: Marshal

* Extract from the Memoir drawn up at the head-quarters of Prince Schwarzenberg.

Blucher could not have debouched from Mery, and the enemy with a small force could have kept him in check at the moment of the greatest exertion. The two armies therefore separated; so that while one army retired, the other could operate on the enemy's rear and upon his communications.

" Success had justified this principle; Marshal Blucher, by having gained a few marches, would not be drawn into an engagement with the principal force of the enemy, till he was in sufficient strength to accept a battle; while the great army, having beaten the inferior numbers opposed to it, had re-occupied its former positions, and the debouchés of the Seine.

" At the same time this army, by leaving the guards and reserves at Chaumont, had given them time to recruit from their fatigues, and had kept them as a point on which it might fall back, or operate as the occasion might require; while the troops employed in the advanced movements necessarily requiring rest, they ought not immediately, at least, to be forced anew into active operations.

" News of the Silesian army, whether it had fought with success, or had still continued to avoid an engagement, would in the mean time be received.

" If it had gained a victory, the great army would push on with vigour upon the left of the Seine, followed by the guards and reserves, while the army of the south, after destroying Marshal Augereau, might move by Orleans, and form its junction near Paris. If the Silesian army was beaten, the great army would then so far impose upon Buonaparte, as to prevent his following up his victory; he would be forced to weary his troops by marches and countermarches, and Marshal Blucher would thus be enabled to resume offensive movements against the forces of the enemy, which would be left to act against him.

" If Buonaparte was successful, he would move upon Troyes or on the Marne to menace the right of the great army. It would then be of interest to know if his victory had been purchased at the expense of many lives, which would decide whether the great army should accept a battle on the Aube or in any other position.

" The enemy could only venture to move towards the sources of the Marne, if his loss had been but trifling; in that case the great army would only risk an action, when it should be in a situation to cover the roads by Langres and Bourbonne-les-Bains. Such a position would allow it to receive reinforcements from the army of the south, with which, in all cases, it must remain in communication. If the army of Silesia should, in the mean time, be in a situation to act with vigour against the force left by the enemy to oppose it, the great army would then have the time to see consolidated the successes of the army of the south, and by reinforcing itself by detachments from it, to continue its operations along the Seine, while its detached corps would annoy the enemy's rear, and would menace Paris.

" Such were the only principles on which the Allies ought to act; it would be easy to shew the fallacy of any others. One only operation differing from them might seem plausible; which was, to march at once to a position between the Aube and the Marne; thus placing the great army upon the enemy's flank. This movement could only be effected, from the actual dislocation of the troops, in four marches, which would bring it to the 11th of the month before this operation could be completed: by that time the fate of the Silesian army would be decided, and, supposing it to have been defeated, the great army would be placed in such a position as to have no option, but that of risking the fate of the campaign by a general battle: the disadvantages attendant on its being obliged to do so would be, that having left a corps upon the Seine, as it must necessarily have done, it would have lost its numerical superiority over the enemy, and it would have been separated from the army of the south, which, in case of disaster, was its only support. Isolated and divided, therefore, the great army would have abandoned the commanding situation it at present occupied, and if defeated, would end by being obliged to fight its way through a line of fortresses but imperfectly blockaded. But even if it should gain a victory, it would always be obliged to re-cross the Seine, to operate upon Paris, the only true object of all its movements."

In addition to these arguments it was stated, that

the hostility of the people of the country, at this time driven to desperation by the conduct of the contending armies, were forming themselves into armed bands, and thus rendered the further advance of the Allies into the heart of France a measure of doubtful policy, particularly since the success which had already attended Buonaparte's movements against both the Allied armies, while separated, was a just cause for acting with circumspection so as to prevent the possibility of a similar result on the present occasion. The fate of the war in France being therefore, for the present, left to rest on the Silesian army, we will return to the detail of its movements from the 23d of February, when it crossed the Aube at Anglure.

PART VI.

Marshal Blucher took upon himself the responsibility of declining to conform to the plan decided upon at Troyes, and, boldly adventuring again to bring the whole of Buonaparte's force against him, detached himself from Prince Schwarzenberg, and marched upon Marshal Marmont, who had arrived at Sezanne. This officer, perceiving the Silesian army in advance upon him, retired to La Ferté Gaucher, and the following day to La Ferté sous Jouarre, whither Marshal Mortier, having learnt the movement of Marshal Blucher, had also retired from Chateau Thierry. These forces, thus concentrated, moved upon Meaux on the 27th. The Silesian army, having reached La Ferté Gaucher, was, on the same day, advancing in two columns, the right by Rebais upon La Ferté sous Jouarre, the left by Coulommiers on Trilport and Meaux. The advance of General Sacken had already entered a part of this last mentioned town when the French Marshals arrived there; he had also sent detachments on the road to Paris as far as Lagny. Marshal Blucher, seeing an opportunity of establishing a passage across the Marne at La Ferté sous Jouarre, recalled the troops under General Sacken from his left, and crossed the river. He left General Yorck to protect the bridge, over which he had passed his army, with orders to remove it on the first appearance of the enemy; with the rest of his troops he proposed to form his junction with the corps of Generals Winzingerode, Langeron, and Bulow; the two former, who had moved to Rheims, were ordered along the Aisne upon Soissons, while the latter, which had reached Laon on the 24th, and had taken La Fère on the 26th, was ordered to move upon the same point, and assist in its attack*.

Marshal Blucher in the mean time directed General

* Soissons had been abandoned by General Winzingerode, when he was directed by Marshal Blucher to move upon the Marne, and Marshal Mortier had placed a garrison in it.

Kleist to take up a position at Neufchelles, with his advance at Gué à Treme, while General Sacken should support him from Lisy. In the evening of the 28th, however, Marshals Marmont and Mortier, having been reinforced by 5,000 men from Paris, advanced against Gué à Treme, and after a sharp action obliged the troops in occupation of it, to fall back on Neufchelles. Marshal Blucher determined, in consequence of this affair, to pass the remainder of his army (consisting of the corps of Generals Yorck and Kapsewitsch,) across the Ourcq at Crouy, and attack the French army; but the bridge at this place having been destroyed, General Yorck was unable to cross the river, and was consequently obliged to move to Fulaines; where General Kleist, who had retired on the Chaussée to Soissons, had arrived. It was nearly dark when the junction of these two corps was effected, so that the attack which originally had been intended, could no longer take place. General Kapsewitsch in the evening passed a part of his advanced guard across the Ourcq at Gesvres, which brought on an affair with Marshal Marmont, who was defending the river, and who obliged the Russians to fall back: the French Marshals established their positions along the Ourcq,

Marshal Mortier in front of Lisy, opposite to General Sacken, and Marshal Marmont at May-en-Multien.

As soon as Buonaparte was aware of the offensive movements undertaken by Marshal Blucher, he prepared to follow him. On the 27th he left Troyes, and conveying with him the guards and the corps of Marshals Ney and Victor*, together with a considerable force of cavalry, arrived on the evening of the 1st of March at La Ferté sous Jouarre. He was only enabled to pass the Marne on the 3d, the guards at La Ferté, the corps of Marshals Ney and Victor, and Generals Grouchy and Arrighi, at Chateau Thierry. He directed Marshals Marmont and Mortier to cross the Ourcq, and the whole army to follow up Marshal Blucher, and, by moving to the right upon Fismes and Braine, to endeavour to bring him to action on the left of the Aisne.

* Marshal Victor, after the affair at Montereau, and in consequence of the anger Buonaparte had expressed at his want of energy on the preceding day, had desired to retire. His request was answered by an order to make over the command of the 2d corps to General Gerard, and to assume the direction of two divisions of the young guard, under Generals Charpentier and Boyer de Rebeval, which were at that time forming at Charenton.

On the 2d of March, the Silesian army commenced its movement upon Soissons; the corps of General Yorck, by Oulchy le Chateau; the corps of Generals Sacken and Kapsewitsch by Ancienville and La Ferté Milon. General Kleist made a reconnoissance in the direction of May-en-Multien; his advance under General Zieten had an affair near Neufchelles with the division of General Merlin, which being driven upon Generals Ricard and Lagrange, was enabled, thus reinforced, to re-assume the offensive, obliging the Prussians to retire towards Mareuil la Ferté. Marshal Marmont at this place came up with the corps of General Kleist, but was unable to prevent its passage of the Ourcq. In conjunction with Marshal Mortier he afterwards passed through La Ferté Milon, and marching upon Neuilly St. Front, again overtook General Kleist, who repulsed the attacks made upon him, and continued his march upon Soissons. This place having been attacked by General Bulow and Count Woronzow on the 1st, surrendered on the 2d, at night. General Moreau, who commanded there, having capitulated on condition to retire with his troops, which he effected on Villers Coterets. The whole Silesian army passed through Soissons on the 3d, and the morning of the 4th, and leaving there a strong garrison, took up a position between the villages of Laffaux, Cerny, and Ailles, with the Aisne in front, and the Lette in rear. Buonaparte had established his head-quarters at Montreuil aux Lyons, and hoping to have enclosed Marshal Blucher, is reported to have felt the greatest disappointment on the morning of the 4th, when it was discovered he had crossed the Aisne, and escaped him, as he represented it, by the capture of Soissons. He ordered Marshals Marmont and Mortier to retake that place, but after an action which lasted till night on the 5th, they were obliged to abandon the attempt. Buonaparte moved upon Braine, from whence he drove the advance of General Winzingerode, and detached a corps upon Rheims, which took possession of it, obliging the greater part of the garrison to surrender.

Buonaparte had now opposed to him the whole of Marshal Blucher's army; the corps of Generals Winzingerode, Bulow, and Langeron, having formed their junction. It amounted to near 80,000 men, concentrated, and in a position in every respect advantageous. Notwithstanding its superiority to the French force,

Buonaparte continued to operate against it, and on the 5th pushed forward General Nansouty, who being successful in a charge upon the Russian cavalry near Bery au Bacq, took that place, while the divisions of Generals Friant and Meusnier established themselves on the heights in front of it. On the 6th, Buonaparte having collected the corps of Marshals Ney and Victor, and having ordered Marshals Marmont and Mortier to move upon Braine and Fismes, advanced upon Corbeny. Marshal Blucher had put his army in motion upon Craone, to counteract the attempt of the enemy to turn his left; but perceiving that object was already in part effected, he detached General Winzingerode with a corps of 10,000 cavalry by Chevregny and Bruyères upon Veftud, while he directed the corps of General Bulow to occupy Laon. On the morning of the 7th he moved the corps of Generals Yorck, Kleist, and Langeron, through Pancy upon Fetieux, with the intention of uniting them with General Bulow from Laon; and, in conjunction with the cavalry of General Winzingerode, of attacking the right of Buonaparte whilst engaged against Count Woronzow, who, supported by General Sacken, was placed in a position on the heights opposite to

Craone, between Vassogne and Ailles, having in his front the farms of Heurtibize and Les Roches, and the village of St. Martin.

Buonaparte ordered a reconnoissance of this force, in the evening of the 6th, from the mill of Pontoise, which was supported by Marshal Ney, who moved upon the village of St. Martin; an engagement ensued, in which the farm of Heurtibize was taken by the French, and afterwards retaken by the Russians. On the morning of the 7th, Buonaparte directed Marshal Ney to advance through St. Martin upon the village of Ailles; this attack was intrusted to the division of General Boyer de Rebeval, while Generals Meunier and Curial supported it by moving upon its left. The action upon this point being severe, Marshal Victor advanced from the Abbey of Vaucler upon the farm of Heurtibize, endeavouring thus to co-operate with the troops engaged. He was however wounded, and the command of his corps was afterwards given to General Charpentier. The whole of the force thus employed being unable to dislodge the Russians, Buonaparte sent forward General Grouchy with his cavalry, with orders to débouché upon the left of Marshal Ney; this officer was wounded while endeavouring to execute this object, and the troops he commanded driven back. Count Woronzow seized this opportunity to charge the divisions of Generals Meusnier, Curial, and Boyer de Rebeval, which he drove into the wood in their rear, completely defeating them: General la Ferriere, who attacked the flank of the Russians, while executing this movement, was severely wounded, and his cavalry repulsed. The same good fortune had attended the Russians in the valley of Vassogne, where General Nansouty was driven back by the cavalry under General Benkendorf.

In this state of the battle the Allied troops received orders from Marshal Blucher to retire from the ground they were defending, and concentrate with the rest of his army at Laon; this decision was produced by the failure of the operation projected upon the right of the French. From the badness of the cross roads, the troops destined for this movemant were unable to arrive in sufficient time; the cavalry of General Winzingerode, and the corps of General Kleist, reaching Fetieux only at four in the afternoon, and the remainder still being at that hour considerably in the rear. It was in consequence determined to bring the Silesian army to Laon, and there accept a general battle. General Sacken immediately obeyed the orders he had received, leaving, however, his cavalry under the orders of Count Woronzow; who, perceiving the critical situation into which he might be thrown by retiring in face of the enemy, determined to wait a more favourable opportunity, and therefore continued the defence of his position. Buonaparte ordered General Charpentier, supported by General Colbert, to advance upon the farm of les Roches, and Marshal Mortier, who was just arriving on the field of battle, to press forward and assist their attack. These officers, together with the division of General Friant, at length succeeded in taking the village of Ailles, in the assault of which the corps of Marshal Ney co-operated. Count Woronzow, in consequence of the advantages thus gained by the enemy, began his retreat, which was conducted with the greatest order, without the loss of a single gun or prisoner. Buonaparte directed General Belliard with the cavalry of the guard, to connect itself with the corps of General Nansouty, and turn the Russian right; this movement was prevented by the cavalry of Generals Wassiltschikow and Benkendorf, assisted by a battalion of light infantry, which, taking advantage of the cover afforded by some enclosures, mainly contributed to check the enemy's advance. Count Woronzow retired by Chevregny, Chavignon, and l'Ange Gardien, whence being joined by the garrison of Soissons, which had been recalled by Marshal Blucher, he moved upon the position of Laon.

This was the best fought action during the campaign; the numbers engaged on both sides were nearly equal, the superiority, if any, being on the side of the enemy. The French suffered severely*; the corps originally engaged were defeated; the number of fresh troops they at last brought into action, at the moment the support of General Sacken was withdrawn from Count Woronzow, renders the retreat of this officer, then executed, as honourable as the victory he had previously gained.

Buonaparte moved, with the force which had been

* The numbers of killed and wounded on the side of the French were reckoned at 8,000; on that of the Russians, about 5,000.

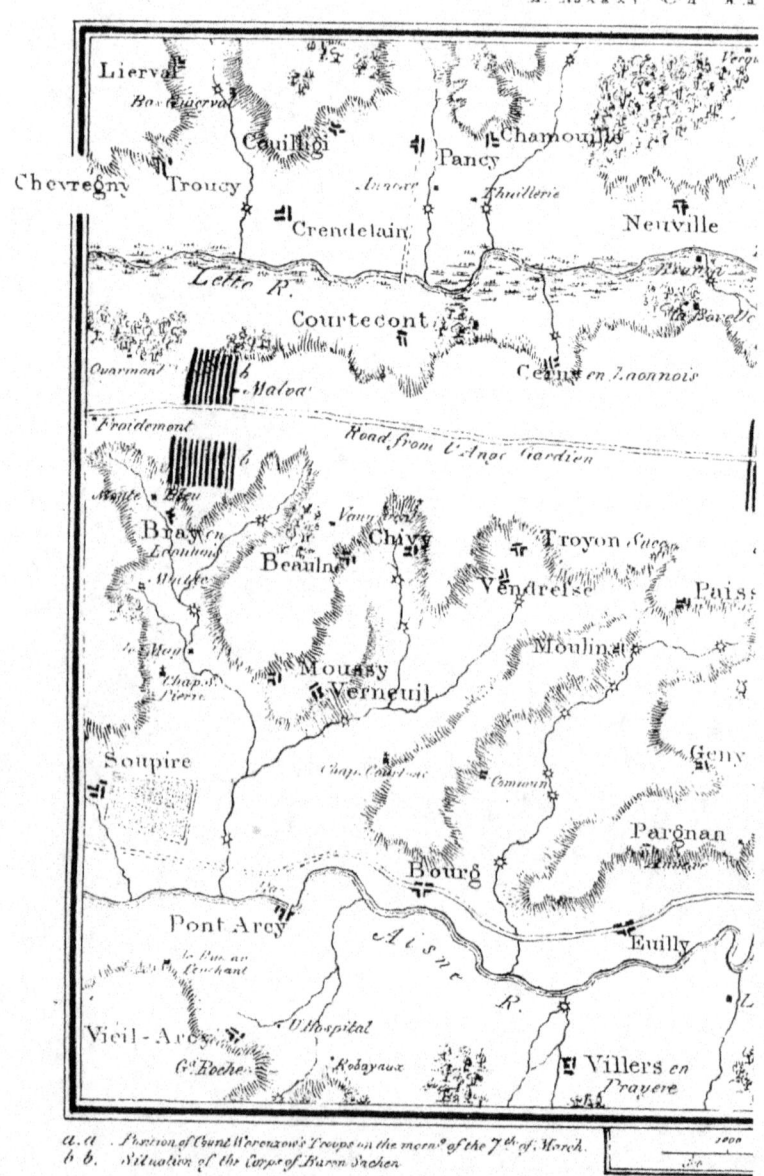

PLAN OF TI

a. a. Position of Count Woronzow's Troops on the morn.ᵍ of the 7.ᵗʰ of March.
b. b. Situation of the Corps of Baron Sachen.
c. c. The

BATTLE OF CRAONE

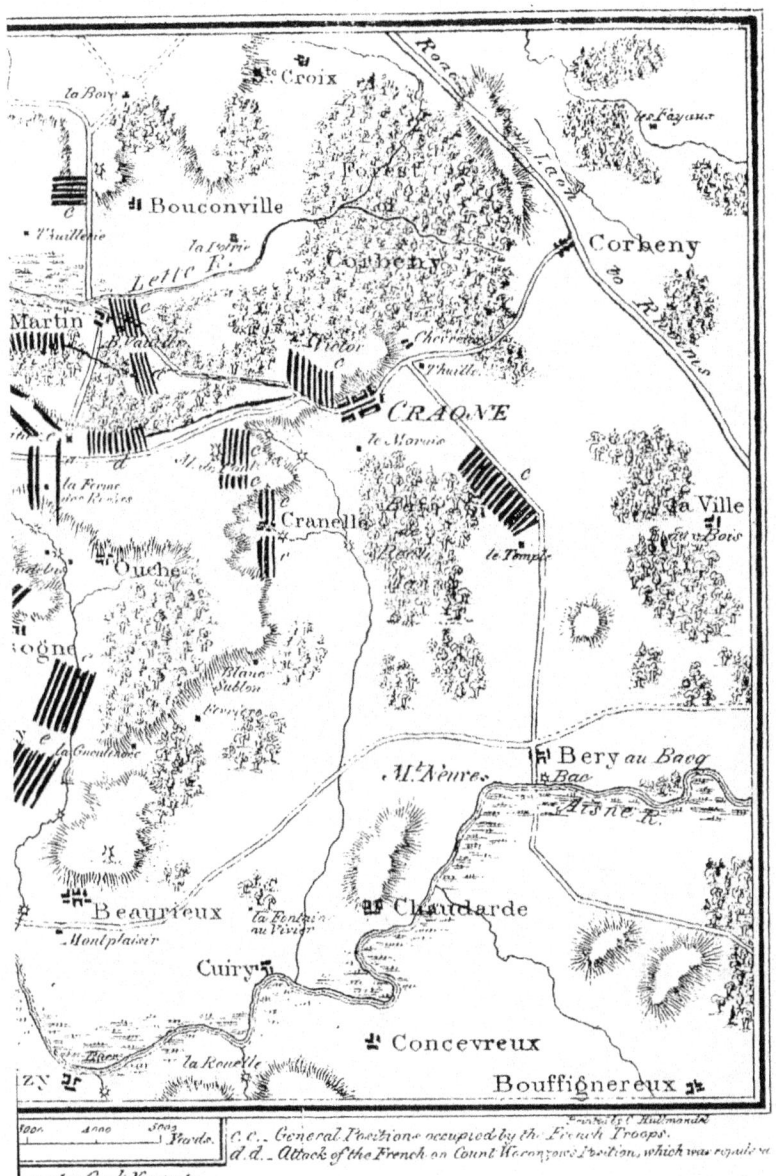

c.c. — General Positions occupied by the French Troops.
d.d. — Attack of the French on Count Woronzow's Position, which was made
under Genl. Nansouty.

engaged at Craone, by Chavignon upon Etouvelle, thus menacing the right of the Allies, while Marshal Marmont was directed to advance from Bery au Bacq, by Corbeny and Fetieux. He was to communicate with Buonaparte by Bruyères, and attack the left of the position of Laon. Marshal Blucher, occupying that town with the corps of General Bulow, had placed Generals Sacken, Langeron, and Winzingerode upon the right, in rear of the Chaussée, leading to Crepy, and Generals Kleist and Yorck between Vaux, and Athies on the left; his advanced guard was in rear of the marshy ground near Etouvelle. Marshal Ney arrived opposite to this place on the 8th at night, he immediately attacked and drove back the corps which defended it, and opened a passage for the cavalry of General Belliard, which was ordered to move upon Laon, and by a coup de main so unexpected, to endeavour to get possession of it. Buonaparte was disappointed. General Belliard was received at the foot of the position in front of the town, by a destructive fire of artillery, which put an end to his operation. On the morning of the 9th, Marshals Ney and Mortier advanced and occupied the villages of Semilly and Ardon, while the rest of the French army was formed in rear and across the great road to Laon.

Marshal Blucher at eleven o'clock (when by the dispersion of a thick fog which covered the country, he was enabled to discover the positions of the enemy,) moved the corps of Generals Bulow and Woronzow upon these villages, and carried them after a short resistance, defeating the troops opposed to him, and driving them with great loss upon the cavalry of General Belliard. This officer, by the judicious distribution of the force under his orders, assisted also by Marshal Ney, stopped the pursuit of the Allies, and at a later period enabled the division of General Pont de Morvon to re-enter Ardon.

The Allied Cavalry was at this time directed to operate upon the left of the French, supported by the division of General Schowouski, which moving on the road to Anizy, took Clacy, the point on which the left of Buonaparte's position rested; the corps under General Charpentier was consequently ordered, in concert with the divisions of Generals Friant and Curial, to attack it. This village became the scene of a violent contest; Count Woronzow ordered up the greater portion of his troops to assist in repelling the assaults of the enemy ; and at dark, it remained occupied in part by each of the contending armies. At the same time, Ardon was again carried by General Bulow, and the French division occupying it, nearly destroyed; General Pont de Morvon and Colonel Leclerc were killed. This terminated the action on the right of Marshal Blucher; on his left he had already been triumphantly successful : Marshal Marmont, having débouchéd at one o'clock from Fetieux, advanced by Aippes upon Athies, in rear of which the corps of Generals Yorck and Kleist were placed, supported by Generals Sacken and Langeron, who had been detached from the right to their assistance. Marshal Marmont, anxious to receive orders from Buonaparte, ordered a corps of cavalry to his left, with directions to communicate with him; in the meanwhile he engaged in an affair in front of Chaufour, and succeeded in establishing himself in a part of the village of Athies. He maintained himself, however, in this position but for a short time, General Yorck assumed the offensive by attacking the troops under General Lucotte, with the brigade of the Prince William of Prussia, supported by Generals Horn and Klux; while the cavalry of General Zieten, passing near Salmoucy, fell upon the force under General Bourdesoulle, and defeating it, pushed forward upon the enemy's right. General Kleist at the same time advanced upon the great road from Laon, and menaced his left. The brigade of General Lucotte, being completely overthrown near Athies, fell in confusion upon the remainder of the French infantry, which, menaced by the advance of General Kleist, was driven with the loss of forty-one pieces of artillery to Fetieux, whence it was pursued by the cossacks and light cavalry to Bery au Bacq; the Allies took near 3,000 prisoners, 41 pieces of cannon, 131 caissons, and a great quantity of baggage. The successes of this day having been decisive, Marshal Blucher ordered Generals Yorck, Kleist, and Sacken, to advance upon Bery au Bacq, and General Langeron upon Bruyères, thus menacing the right and rear of the French troops now remaining in his front. Buonaparte, notwithstanding, did not retire; and, after having repulsed several attacks made by Count Woronzow against the village of Clacy on the morning of the 10th, he directed the divisions of Generals Meunier and Curial to assault the town of Laon. This movement, attempted with bravery, but against forces it was impossible to combat with, was immediately checked, and the troops employed in it defeated. Buonaparte, still unwilling to fall back, conceived the possibility of turning the right of Marshal Blucher's position, and for that purpose detached Generals Drouot and Belliard to reconnoitre beyond Clacy, upon the road from Laon to la Fère. These officers, having convinced themselves of the impossibility of the projected operation, persuaded Buonaparte no longer to expose his army in the dangerous situation it was placed in, but to fall back upon Soissons. About four o'clock this movement was undertaken, and on the following day the French army took up a position in front of that town. Marshal Marmont had retired to Fismes, from whence he again connected himself with Buonaparte. Marshal Blucher advanced upon the Létte, with his left pushed forward to Bery au Bacq.

The results of the operations which here terminated were disastrous to the French; their losses were calculated at from 10 to 12,000 men, and they were obliged to retire before an army, in the destruction of which alone they could have hoped for a successful issue to the contest they were engaged in. Buonaparte seems, however, not to have been discouraged by these reverses; he adhered to the rejection of the propositions made to him at Chatillon, a conduct by which the Congress, assembled at that place, was dissolved; its last sitting was held on the 19th of March.

On the morning of the 12th General St. Priest, who was in march to join Marshal Blucher's army from Vitry, seizing an opportunity which appeared to be offered him, of taking possession of Rheims, stormed and carried it, capturing 12 guns and 2,000 prisoners. As soon as the intelligence of this event reached Buonaparte, he ordered Marshal Marmont, on the 13th, from Fismes, to advance upon Rheims, with the view of retaking it before the garrison could receive assistance from Marshal Blucher, following, himself, with the rest of his army, the corps of Marshal Mortier alone being left to occupy the positions about Soissons. The advanced guard of Marshal Marmont

PLAN OF THE BATTLE OF LAON.
On the 9th & 10th of March 1814.

Prussians { 1. Corps under General York.
           { 2. .... Kleist.
           { 3. .... Bulow.

Russians { 1. Corps under General Sacken.
         { 2. .... Langeron.
         { 3. .... Wintzingerode.

French { 1. Imperial Guard.
       { 2. Corps under M. Marmont.

appeared opposite the outposts of General St. Priest, about eleven o'clock; the Allies immediately took up a position across the road leading to Soissons, from whence a heavy fire of artillery was maintained till about four, when the troops brought by Buonaparte having arrived in support of Marshal Marmont, a general advance of the French line, flanked by its cavalry in masses, commenced. At this moment, while his advanced troops were falling back upon the main position, General St. Priest was severely wounded and taken from the field; the Russian cavalry, under General Emmanuel, was driven in from the left by General Sebastiani, while the right and centre gave way before the superior numbers which were pressing against them. The Allies retired into the town of Rheims, which was defended till ten o'clock at night, when, with the loss of above 3,000 men and 11 guns, they fell back upon Neufchatel, the road to Bery au Bacq, on the right of the Vesle, being intercepted by the cavalry of General Excelmans, which Buonaparte had pushed across that river at the bridge of St. Brice. On the 14th Marshal Marmont pursued the Allied troops to Courcy, where, meeting with the Prussian cavalry under General Katzler, his advance was driven back with considerable loss; he then took up a position near Cormicy, his cavalry at Sapigneules.

Marshal Blucher had placed his army during this time in a position extending from Chauny to Craone and Corbeny, where it remained to collect provisions and to recover from the incessant fatigues it had lately undergone.

Buonaparte moved Marshal Ney to Chalons, while the corps of Generals Vincent and Colbert took possession of Epernay. He remained with the guards at Rheims, re-forming his army, and uniting with it a corps of 4,000 men under General Jansens, till the 17th, when he marched to Epernay, and with a force not exceeding from 25 to 30,000 men, began his offensive movement against the great army now assembled upon the Aube and Seine. Marshal Marmont was left in conjunction with Marshal Mortier to observe the Silesian army; the troops under their orders were estimated at 18,000 men.

Buonaparte had sent orders to General Durette,

who commanded the 3d military division, to assemble a body of 12,000 men from the different fortresses in rear of the allies, and to join the effective army at Chalons; he had also given directions to the officers commanding these places to encourage the insurrection of the inhabitants, and to fall upon the baggage and communications of the Allied armies which were operating in advance of them. Marshal Ney is said to have offered to undertake the charge of assembling and directing the forces which might thus be brought into action, but Buonaparte refused his proposal.

PART VII.

The French army, now assembled at Chalons and Epernay, advanced on the 18th; the right upon Fère Champenoise, whence the cossacks, under General Kaisarow, were driven by General Sebastiani, and the left upon Sommesous. Prince Schwarzenberg had been impressed with the conviction, that after the capture of Rheims on the 13th, the operations of the French army would again be directed against Marshal Blucher. The orders he had issued on the 17th, for the concentration of his army between Arcis and Pont-sur-Seine, with the reserves at Donnement and Dommartin, were given out with the intention of moving from those positions upon Somepuis and Vitry; and thence upon Chalons, and upon the rear of the French army while engaged in this supposed operation. The attack before Fère Champenoise, in which a part of the cavalry of the French guard had been engaged, proved, however, that Buonaparte was marching upon the Aube. This unexpected intelligence having reached Arcis in the afternoon, the Emperor of Russia having arrived there at the moment from Troyes, a council was held, where it was stated that the 6th corps, when the last intelligence was received from it, not having established itself, as directed, in the positions of Charny and Plancy; the passage over the Aube at those places, towards which the enemy appeared to be moving, was unoccupied; that this corps, together with the 3d and 4th, now concentrated near Mery, if directed to march upon Arcis, might find the French already across the river, and in a situation to oppose their movement; they might, in consequence, be obliged to fall back thus leaving the 5th corps, and the Russian and Prussian reserves, the only troops now about to be assembled at Arcis, exposed to the attack of the whole of Buonaparte's army; if it was thought advisable to run the hazard of such a contest, the idea of concentrating the army at Arcis might still be adhered to; but if this project should be abandoned, it was recommended that the three corps above-mentioned should at once retire from Mery to Troyes, and on the following day to Vandœuvres; that the 5th corps, leaving an advanced guard in Arcis, should fall back towards Pougy, where the head-quarters would be placed on the 19th, and that the great army should be assembled on the 20th, with the reserves, in a position between Brienne and Bar sur Aube, at which latter place the head-quarters were to be established. Such was the plan proposed and adopted, and for the execution of which the following Order of the Day was issued:

Disposition for the 19*th and* 20*th of March.*

Arcis sur Aube, 18th March, 1814.

"The 5th corps will to-night retire to the left bank of the Aube at this place, and will dispute the passage of that river. To-morrow it will place itself in echellons as far as Pougy.

"The 3d, 4th, and 6th corps will retire to-morrow to Troyes; General Seslavin will remain with a detachment strong enough, if possible, to defend the défilés of Bray and Nogent.

" The guards and reserves will take up their position behind the Voire to defend it till the 5th corps shall arrive at Lesmont, after having defended the left bank of the Aube from Arcis to that place during the 19th.

" On the 20th, the 3d, 4th, and 6th corps will march to Vandœuvres; the guards and reserves to Trannes and Maisons.

" The 5th corps will on that day take up the position of Brienne, leaving a rear-guard at Ronay and Lesmont.

" The head-quarters will be the 19th at Pougy, the 20th at Bar sur Aube.

" The 5th corps will leave a corps of observation upon the Aube, which, in case of necessity, will rejoin it by Dienville. The Prince Royal of Wurtemberg will conduct the pontoons to Bar sur Aube, and will leave a detachment sufficient to observe the Seine. If this force should be obliged to abandon this river, it will retire towards Prince Maurice Lichtenstein, and will fall back upon Dijon."

In order to understand the measure thus adopted, it is of consequence to observe that it was decided upon, at about four in the afternoon, when the report of the attack made upon the cossacks at Fère Champenoise was received. The distance from this place to Arcis, or to Plancy, was greater than from Mery to either of them, so that the concentration of the Allied army could hardly have been impeded, even if the whole force of Buonaparte (instead of its advance only under General Sebastiani) had been assembled there. From the lateness of the hour it was also improbable that the French army, after a long march to Fère Champenoise, could continue to advance to the Aube, or be in a situation to force a passage across that river, supposing the 6th corps alone to be in position to oppose it. Notwithstanding these circumstances, together with the certainty that the troops, which Buonaparte was bringing with him, must be infinitely inferior to the great army, this retreat was undertaken; and but for the total inability of the enemy to profit by the first advantages it afforded him, might have been attended with the most serious consequences to the Allied armies.

On the evening of the 18th General Sebastiani arrived at Gourganson, Semoine, and Herbisse, while the column on his left advanced to Sommesous. On the 19th he pushed forward about midday towards Plancy, which place, after a trifling affair with the cossacks near Coursemain, he took possession of. Buonaparte soon after arrived there, and directing the divisions of Generals Excelmans and Colbert, under General Sebastiani, upon the road to Arcis, he marched with the division of General Letort upon Mery, where he fell in with the rear of the 4th corps, which was covering the march of the troops retiring to Troyes. General Letort passed the Seine at a ford below Mery, and followed this rear guard to Les Grez, without reaping, however, any other advantage than the capture of thirteen pontoons, which had been left at Chatres. Buonaparte returned in the night to Plancy.

The little progress which had been made by the

enemy on this day decided Prince Schwarzenberg to alter the march of the three corps directed from Troyes upon Vandœuvres, and to concentrate them with the 5th corps and the reserves, in front of Arcis. With this view the Prince Royal of Wurtemberg, to whom the command of the 3d, 4th, and 6th corps was intrusted, was ordered to march from Troyes on the morning of the 20th upon the roads to Plancy and Arcis, with his cavalry on St. Etienne and Nozai. General Wrede was to assemble the infantry of his corps at Chaudray; while General Frimont, with the cavalry, was to observe the enemy, and retire, upon his advance, upon Mesnil la Comtesse.

The Russian reserves were to occupy Longsols and Onjon; their cavalry, from the heights of Mesnilettre, was to support the corps of General Frimont, and to establish the communication between General Wrede and the Prince Royal of Wurtemberg.

On the same day, Buonaparte directed General Sebastiani, who had moved the preceding evening to Bessy, to advance upon Arcis, from whence he conceived the Allies were retiring, as they were from

Mery; the guards from Plancy, and the division of General Letort, which was recalled from Les Grez, were destined to support him; while Marshal Ney, who on the other side of the river had reached Riverelle and Viapre, was to concentrate upon the same place. He directed also, the force under Marshal Macdonald, from Provins, to arrive by forced marches at Arcis; notwithstanding, however, the greatest exertions on the part of the troops under this officer's command, the corps of Marshal Oudinot and the cavalry of General St. Germain, only reached it on the 21st, in the morning; the second and eleventh corps, with the fifth and sixth of cavalry, on the 22d.

General Sebastiani having approached Arcis, discovered the cavalry of General Frimont extended in the plain in front of it, he was in consequence induced to delay his movement against the town, to allow the troops in his rear to arrive to his support, which having taken place about two o'clock he pushed forward, and with little opposition took possession of it. Marshal Ney arrived there nearly at the same time. These officers having reconnoitred in their front, discovered a considerable force of the Allies assembled on the side of Mesnil, la Comtesse, with the apparent intention of attacking them; they immediately established themselves in a position to defend Arcis, while they pressed the arrival of the troops from Plancy, and reported to Buonaparte the change they had observed in the dispositions of the Allies. They were soon after attacked by the fifth corps, which advanced in two columns; the right, chiefly composed of Austrians, upon Grand Torcy; the left, in which were the Bavarians, upon the high ground on the road from Troyes; and by the cossacks under General Kaiserow, supported by General Frimont, who charged General Sebastiani, and drove him back in confusion, with the loss of four cannon and 300 prisoners, upon Arcis. Buonaparte arrived at this moment, and the division of General Friant, assembling in front of the town, re-established order, which, by the defeat of the cavalry, had been considerably broken. The defence of Grand Torcy immediately occupied his serious attention; he sent there the whole of Marshal Ney's corps, supported by detachments from the corps of General Friant. This village was taken and re-taken several times, and the contest for its possession lasted till after dark; it was set fire to in the night, and the troops on both sides were forced to evacuate it.

Meanwhile, the left column of the Allies had arrived on the ground marked out for it, from whence, supported by the sixth corps (advancing from Troyes) it was to have attacked the town of Arcis and the right of the French position. General Raefsky being, however, unable to pass the Barbuise in time, this operation was given up, and after a cannonade maintained till the close of day, the Bavarians returned to near Chaudrey, where, in conjunction with a division of Russian grenadiers, they were placed in support of the troops engaged in Grand Torcy. Upon their left was placed another division of Russian grenadiers together with a part of the Russian cavalry of reserve, the whole of which, under General Miloradowitsch, had arrived on the field of battle during the action. These troops communicated by their left with General Raefsky, and were in support of the cavalry of General Kaiserow. General Sebastiani, reinforced by 2,000 cavalry under General Lefebre Desnouettes, who joined him at the close of day, made a charge upon these forces in the night, which (although the occasion of considerable alarm) was successfully resisted.

On the side of the Prince Royal, the cavalry which was in his advance, and upon his left, fell upon a detachment of mounted grenadiers and Mamelouks of Buonaparte's guard near Premierfait, took 200, and drove the rest into Mery.

The action of this day appeared to be only the prelude of the great battle which was to be fought on the following morning. Prince Schwarzenberg, under this impression, ordered the Prince Royal to concentrate his troops on the right of the Barbuise, near St. Remy; the Russian reserves were placed on the heights of Mesnil la Comtesse, and the corps of General Wrede, supported by a division of Russian grenadiers, at Chaudrey. A detachment of the cavalry of the Russian guard, under General Oscherousky, was placed beyond the Aube near Rameru, and General Kaiserow on the left of the Barbuise, between Nozai and the mill of Becheret. In this position the army remained till near ten o'clock, when a forward movement of the enemy's cavalry under General Sebastiani, along the Chaussée leading to Troyes, seemed to indicate a general advance. The 3d corps, which was in march to take the position assigned to it, immediately formed, and in alignement with the rest of the troops under the Prince Royal, shewed a force so considerable as to put an immediate stop to this operation.

Prince Schwarzenberg, observing the hesitation of the enemy, decided to assume the offensive, but delayed his advance till the necessary preparations were completed. About twelve o'clock, however, a column was perceived marching from Arcis on the right of the Aube, and in the direction of Vitry; as it continued filing from the town, its force was discovered, and it became evident that the French army was retiring. The Allies were immediately ordered to fall upon its rear; Arcis was attacked, and after a short contest was taken. The rear-guard which remained in occupation of it was inconsiderable, and retired to a position in the fauxbourgs, on the right of the Aube, from whence it defended the passage of the river. General Raefsky, who commanded the attack upon the town, displayed considerable spirit and ability in the mode of conducting it.

The following disposition for the movements of the army was immediately issued.

Heights above Mesnil la Comtesse,

March 21st, 6 o'clock, p.m.

" In consequence of the direction of the enemy's march towards Vitry, the army now assembled will pass the Aube, and place itself on the Puis, in the following order :

" The fifth corps behind the Meldenson, between Donnement and Jasseinnes. The fourth and sixth corps will be directed, by his Royal Highness the Prince Royal of Wurtemberg, by the shortest line behind the Puis, in the neighbourhood between Corbeil and Dampierre, and he will ensure the appui of their left flank on the Aube. As it is essential this flank march should be concealed from the enemy, it is necessary the commanders of corps should so conduct it, as to attain their object without its being

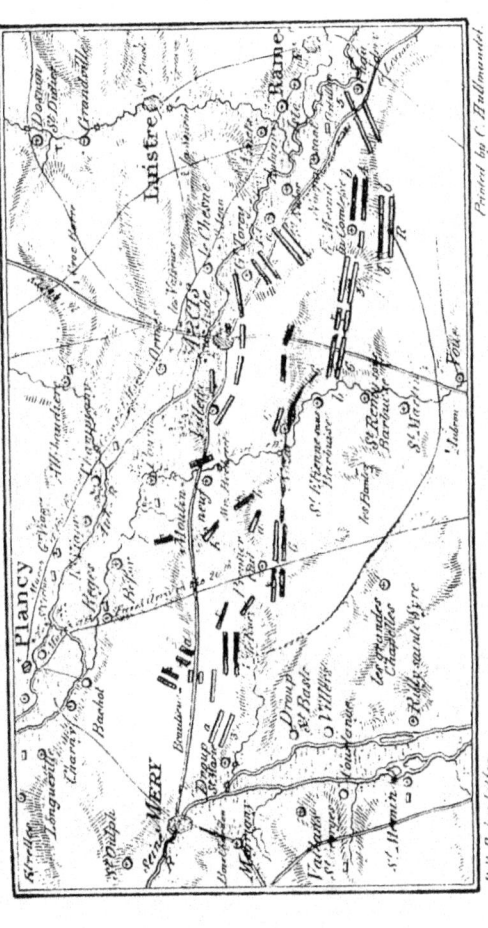

perceived. The guards and reserves will march by Lesmont on Precy, and place themselves on the left bank of the Voire, to ensure the possession of the defiles of that river. The head-quarters will go to Ronay.

"The third corps remains in possession of Arcis, and will defend this point. General Kaisarow will particularly observe the country between the Aube and the Seine; while General Seslavin will remain on the other side of that river for the same purpose. The prisoners to be sent to Pougy."

These movements were undertaken to counteract the supposed intention of the enemy to turn the right of the great army by St. Ouen, and to operate upon Brienne, on its rear. A very different object was in his contemplation. Buonaparte moved to Somepuis, leaving directions for the troops under Marshal Macdonald, who were arriving from Sezanne at Orme and Viapre, to be placed in support of Marshal Victor, who had remained in command of the rear-guard at Arcis

In concluding the account of the two days thus

passed by the contending armies in presence of each other, it is equally worthy of remark, that Buonaparte, with a force not exceeding 25 or 30,000 men, should have risked himself in such a position in front of 80,000 of the Allies, as that the latter should have allowed him to escape them with impunity.

On the morning of the 22d, the apprehension lest the enemy should be moving round the right of the Allied army having been dissipated by the reports of his further progress towards Vitry, Prince Schwarzenberg retained his head-quarters at Pougy. In the course of the day, the 3d corps attempted to carry the bridge of Arcis, but was repulsed by Marshal Victor, who defended the right of the Aube at that point, till night. Marshal Macdonald moved with the whole of his force, which in the course of the 21st and the morning of the 22d was assembled in the environs of Arcis, to Dosnon. Buonaparte transferred his head-quarters to Olcomte, and directed Marshal Ney to summons the Prussian Commandant of Vitry to surrender, and in case of his refusal to endeavour to intimidate the garrison, and get possession of the place; this object, although pressed with considerable ability and courage, was not obtained, and the French troops were obliged to bivouaque at Blacy and Vitry le Brulé, from whence they passed the Marne near Frignicourt, while their cavalry with the head-quarters proceeded on the 23d to St. Dizier.

Prince Schwarzenberg, on the morning of this day, directed a general advance of the Allies upon Vitry, with the view of attacking Buonaparte, who was supposed to be assembling his army there, and of connecting himself with Marshal Blucher, who having been at Bery au Bacq on the 19th, and having retaken Rheims with the corps of General Winzingerode, was expected at Chalons. General Oscherousky moved upon Somepuis, and fell upon the train of artillery belonging to Marshal Macdonald, which was passing from Pleurs (where it had remained during the march of that officer's corps upon Arcis) towards Vitry. He took twenty pieces of cannon and a considerable number of prisoners; amongst them a courier despatched from St. Dizier, from whom the first information of Buonaparte's movement in that direction was obtained*. On its being received by Prince Schwar-

* See Appendix, No. 14, the letter from Buonaparte which was found upon the courier.

zenberg, he returned from near St. Ouen to Pougy to hold a council with the Emperor of Russia and King of Prussia, who had joined the army since the 20th, and had been present in the actions in front of Arcis. He there explained, that unexpected as was the intelligence he had just received, and unwilling as he should have been to allow the enemy to establish himself in a situation to menace his communication with the rear, yet, as that object was now actually effected, he would not waste his time in seeking to counteract its immediate consequences, but by placing himself on the rear of Buonaparte, and following him with rapidity, he proposed to visit upon him the evils he had prepared for the Allies.

He stated himself to be aware of the many difficulties he should have to encounter; his magazines at Chaumont would most probably, fall a prey to the enemy*, and before he could re-establish others, or secure a new basis for his operations, the French army would be increased by the garrisons of the fortresses in the rear, which it was evidently Buonaparte's

---

* By the able dispositions of the adjutant-general of the Austrian army, General Köller, the capture of these magazines was averted.

intention to call to his assistance; he had, however, but one line to pursue, which he was determined to follow up with vigour.

With these views the march of the different corps of his army was continued. The Prince Royal of Wurtemberg followed Marshals Macdonald and Victor, who were retiring from Arcis and Dosnon to join Marshal Ney, who on the right of the Marne near Vitry, was waiting to protect their passage across that river. The Prince Royal was, however, only able to open a cannonade upon them, which at different times was renewed till the close of the day. Marshal Wrede moved upon Courdemange, from whence it was conceived he might have attacked Frignicourt, and have intercepted the corps pursued by the Prince Royal, which, not arriving at that point till night, would have had to contend in front, with the corps of Marshal Wrede, supported by the Russian grenadiers, and in its rear with that of the Prince Royal.

From some apparently overstrained feeling of precaution this operation was not attempted, and the French, in presence of two superior corps of the Allies, and between them and the fortress of Vitry, which was in their possession, passed the Marne unmolested, and pursued their march to join Buonaparte. Prince Schwarzenberg established his head-quarters on the same evening at Somepuis; the advance of General Winzingerode, under Generals Czernischew and Tettenborn, communicated with the cavalry of Count Pahlen, and thus formed the junction of the Silesian army.

On the morning of the 24th the Allies were ordered to continue their movement in pursuit of Buonaparte. Prince Schwarzenberg was, however, overtaken, soon after he had quitted Somepuis, by an aid-de-camp of the Emperor of Russia, requesting he would wait his arrival, which took place immediately afterwards. A conference was then held, in which the Emperor strongly enforced the propriety of marching upon Paris; he was supported in this opinion by the King of Prussia, and by the officers of his own staff, Prince Wolkonski and Generals Debitsch and Toll. Prince Schwarzenberg, notwithstanding the arguments which were used against it by several officers holding high situations in his head-quarters, agreed to the wishes of the Emperor, and at once took measures for the execution of the plan proposed. Orders for the different corps to halt upon the ground they occupied were immediately despatched, and the cavalry under General Winzingerode, which joined at Vitry, was directed upon St. Dizier, to engage the attention of the French army, and cover the operation of the Allies upon Paris.

PART VIII.

The corps of Marshals Mortier and Marmont, which had been left by Buonaparte upon the Aisne, and amounting to about 18,000 men, were on the 18th at Soissons and Berry au Bacq. The first of these was, however, on that day moved to Rheims, leaving the division of General Charpentier between Soissons and Compiegne; the other remained in its position. Marshal Blucher directed Generals Yorck and Kleist to advance upon Berry au Bacq and Pontavaire; General Winzingerode, with the cavalry under his orders, upon Asseld la Ville. Constrained by these movements, and after a trifling engagement at Pontavaire, Marshal Marmont retired upon Fismes, to which place he was followed by the corps of Generals Yorck and Kleist, General Winzingerode advancing upon Rheims.

Marshal Mortier, fearing that his communication with the 6th corps would be intercepted, abandoned Rheims on the morning of the 19th; meeting, however, Marshal Marmont at Junchery in march to join him, the two Marshals decided upon re-occupying Rheims, and General Belliard, with the cavalry, proceeded immediately with the view of executing that object: he arrived there almost at the same moment with the advance guard of General Winzingerode, but time enough to drive it back, and take possession of the place. During the period, of the execution of this service, the Marshals upon further consultation had given up the plan they had agreed upon, and had sent orders to General Belliard to retire upon Fismes, who consequently after defending himself through the day, evacuated Rheims at dark, and without loss executed their directions. On the 20th, the two French corps moved into a position at Mont Saint Martin, with their advance at Fismes; the division of General Charpentier was recalled from Soissons, and placed upon their left; while General Winzingerode, who during the night had occupied Rheims, advanced with his cavalry upon the Marne at Chalons. In this state of things Marshal Blucher directed Generals Yorck, Kleist, and Sacken, to assemble their corps in front of Fismes, while General Bulow should undertake the siege of Soissons; and Count Langeron, with the infantry of General Winzingerode's corps under Count Woronzow, should concentrate upon Rheims. On the 21st, Marshals Mortier and Marmont received orders to join Buonaparte at Vitry; they immediately moved to Chateau Thierry, the following day to Montmirail, the 23d to Bergères and Etoges, and the 24th to Vatry and Soudé St. Croix. General Winzingerode had, in the mean time, captured Chalons and Epernay, and, with 8,000 horse, was moving towards Vitry. Generals Yorck and Kleist, who had moved upon the Ourcq at Oulchy, Billy, and Cugny, their cavalry at La Ferté Milon, advanced on the 24th upon Chateau Thierry. General Sacken had joined the corps in occupation of Rheims on the 23d, and on the following day had advanced in conjunction with it to Chalons, where Marshal Blucher established his head-quarters.

Generals Pacthod and Amey, who had assembled a French force at Sezanne, having received orders to join Buonaparte, moved on the 24th to Etoges, in the hopes of connecting themselves with Marshal Mortier; but learning at that place the march of this officer upon Vatry, they reported to him their situation, and requested orders as to their future movements. Such were the general positions occupied by the opposing armies on the morning of the 25th, when the Allies commenced their operation upon Paris.

The Prince Royal of Wurtemberg, with the cavalry of the 4th and 6th corps in front, advanced upon the road to Fère Champenoise, the Russian reserves followed in the direction of Montrepeux; the 3d corps, which had remained near Arcis, moved upon the same point by the great road from Troyes, and the 5th corps formed the rear-guard of the whole army. Marshals Marmont and Mortier, not suspecting the vicinity of the Allies, broke up from their positions on the left of the Somme-Soude, and were commencing their movement upon Vitry, when Count Belliard, who commanded their cavalry, was attacked by Count Pahlen at Dommartin l'Estrée and Soudé Notre Dame: in the mean while Prince Adam of Wurtemberg turned the left of Marshal Marmont, who, leaving a detachment of infantry to stop the progress of the Allies at Soudé Sainte Croix, retired upon Sommesous, where he was joined by Marshal Mortier from Vatry. The Allies continually charged the French during these operations, the detachment left at Soudé Sainte Croix was taken, and the cavalry under General Bordesoulle overthrown; the rear of Marshal Mortier was broken near Estrée, and the position of Sommesous, (turned on its left at Montepreux, by the cuirassiers under General Nostitz,) was carried, and the enemy defeated and driven upon Conantray and Lenhare. Near the former of these places the cavalry of the Russian guard, charging through the French cuirassiers, fell upon the infantry, which, although formed in squares, was broken; the brigade of General Jansen was cut to pieces, that of General le Capitaine suffered considerably, two Generals, twenty-four pieces of cannon, and a great number of prisoners were taken. The Prince Royal advanced his cavalry towards Fère Champenoise, and by thus threatening to intercept the retreat of the French, threw them into complete disorder; the arrival of a regiment of cavalry, which formed in front of that village protected their escape and saved them from the total destruction with which they were menaced. The Marshals retired to the heights of Linthe, where they re-formed their troops and from whence a cannonade being heard which was supposed to be the return of Buonaparte, on the rear of the Allies, their cavalry charged the Austrian cuirassiers, and obtained over them a momentary success; this advantage was, however, immediately checked by the Wurtemberg troops and the Cossacks of General Seslavin, who drove the enemy back upon their position. The Marshals continued their retreat to Allement, where for a short time they established themselves.

For a considerable time during the day a cannonading had been heard on the right and in front of the allied columns. When the Sovereigns and Prince Schwarzenberg passed through Fère Champenoise, they perceived a body of infantry in the direction of Ecury le Repos engaged with cavalry, which latter was ascertained to be the advance of General Blucher under General Korf; who, moving from Chalons upon the road to Montmirail, had fallen in with the troops under Generals Pacthod and Amey, at Villeseneux, on their march towards Vitry. As these officers had a convoy attached to them, they immediately formed and for a considerable time defended themselves; perceiving however that the numbers of the Allies were increasing, they commenced their retreat upon Clamanges, where, being more closely pressed, they abandoned their convoy, and proceeded towards Fère Champenoise. The moment they were perceived by the Emperor of Russia, he stopped a train of light artillery which was passing forward at that moment towards Linthe, and placed it under the orders of Lord Cathcart, while Prince Schwarzenberg recalled a part of the cavalry in advance, and with these forces, connected with the troops already engaged, fell upon the French columns, which, after a gallant resistance, while attempting to get to the marshes of Saint Gond, were broken, and all who composed them either killed or taken.

The losses of this day to the enemy were very considerable, amounting altogether to between 8 and 9,000 men, either killed, wounded or taken prisoners, amongst the latter were eight Generals; above 60 pieces of cannon, together with a great number of caissons and waggons, fell also into the possession of the Allies.

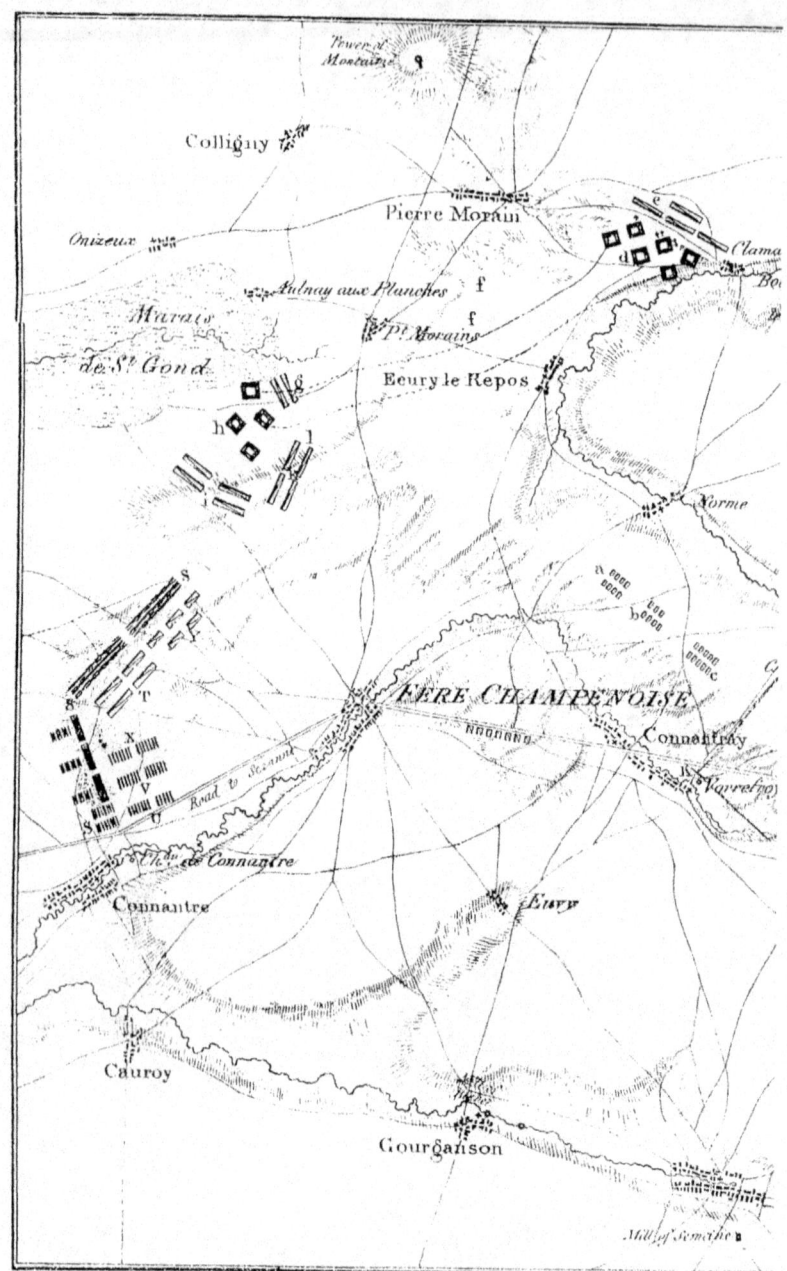

BATTLE OF

On th

A. & B. *The corps of Marshal Marmont's division.* C. & D. *2nd position of these co* of the French corps. J. M. *2nd deployment of the Allies.* N. O. P. *Arrival of the corps* S. S. *Position taken up by the French corps near Linthes* T. U. V. X. Y. *The last pos from the army of*

a. b. & c. *Advance of the Allies.* d. & e. *The action at Clamanges.* f. *Retreat of the*

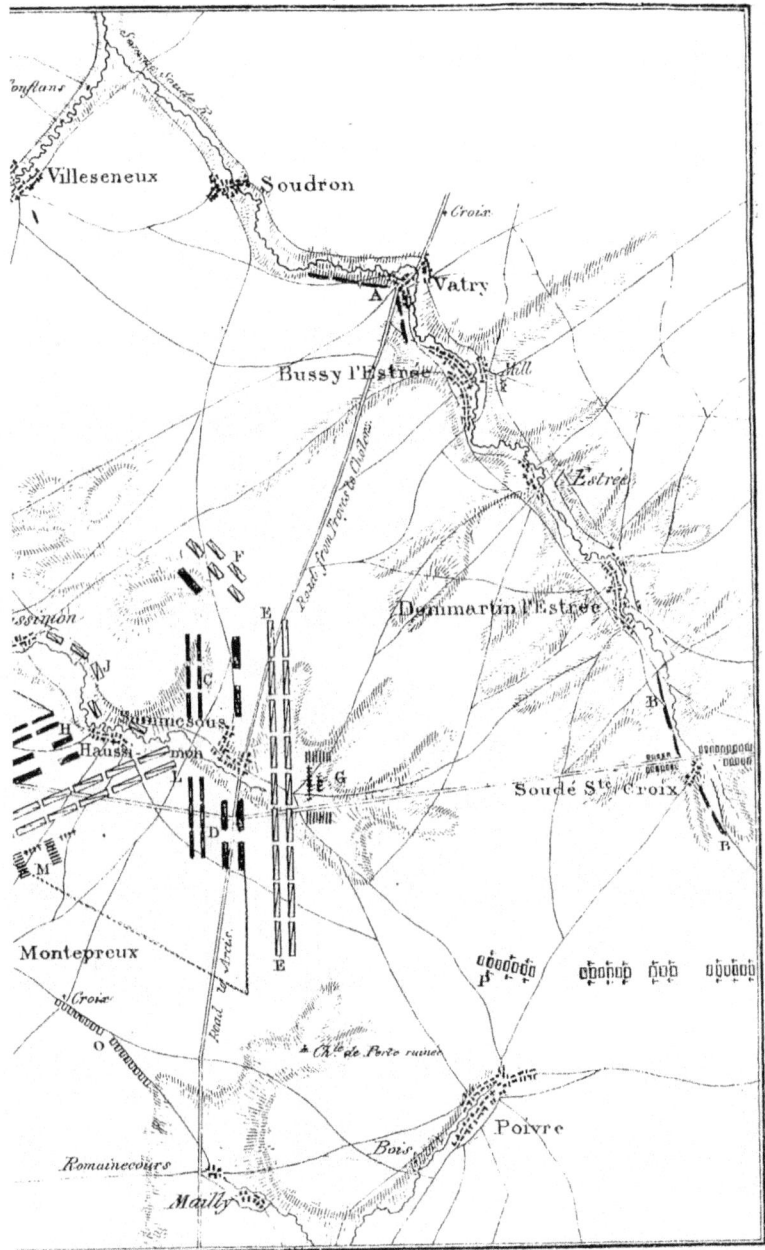

CHAMPENOISE.

March 1814.

1.st deployment of the force of the Allies under the P. R. of Wurtemberg. H. 3.rd position Grand Duke Constantine. I. K. Movement of the French corps to the rear.
Q. The corps of Gen.ls Pacthod & Amey with the convoy in rear. R. The cav. detached r. under General Korf.
last position. g. i. k. l. the Allies having surrounded them

Colonel Campbell, the British officer who was attached to the corps of General Rayefsky, and who was particularly distinguished on this occasion, was severely wounded by a cossack, who, taking him for a French officer, forced his pike through his back. Colonel Rapatel, the aide-de-camp of the late General Moreau, was killed nearly at the same moment when, urged by his distress at seeing his countrymen and former fellow-soldiers so bravely, yet so uselessly, sacrificing their lives, he had approached them to entreat they would surrender.

The corps of Generals Yorck and Kleist marched on this day, the 25th, from Chateau Thierry to Montmirail, from whence they detached their advanced guard of cavalry, under General Ziethen, to Sezanne: General Compans, who occupied that place with a French division, abandoned it in the night, taking his direction upon La Ferté Gaucher, near which place, he had an engagement on the following morning with the brigade of the Prince William of Prussia, which had previously occupied it. The French troops were forced to retire upon Chailly, where they were, attacked by the cavalry under General Horn, and driven, with the loss of 400 men, to the heights of Montanglaust beyond Coulommiers.

Marshals Marmont and Mortier retired during the night from Allement, and arriving at Sezanne, found it occupied by a part of General Ziethen's cavalry; as it was still dark, the officers on both sides, ignorant of the force respectively opposed to them, were unwilling to engage in an affair which might compromise the existence of their corps. At the break of day, however, the French, ascertaining the small number of the Allies, forced their passage through the town, and continued their retreat upon Esternay and Reveillon, halting for four hours at Mœurs. The cavalry of the Prince Royal of Wurtemberg, in consequence, came up with them, and operating by Courgivaux and St. Martin du Bauchet, thus menacing the road from Reveillon to Moutis, forced Marshal Marmont to retire upon La Ferté Gaucher, in the endeavoured to pass through which place, Marshal Mortier had already been defeated by the corps of Generals Yorck and Kleist which were now established there; the two Marshals in consequence took up a position for the night at Chartronges, near the farm of Larniere. Their direct road upon Paris was intercepted; they determined in consequence to march through Courtacon and Champcenetz upon Provins, the only point from whence they still could hope to reach the capital before the Allies. This movement was effected without loss. On the 28th they continued their operation by Nangis, from whence Marshal Mortier moved through Guignes upon Brie Comte Robert, and Marshal Marmont through Melun. On the 29th they reached Charenton, and took up a position between that place and Vincennes. General Compans retired on the 27th upon Meaux and Trilport, where he was joined by General Vincent with a small corps of cavalry. These officers attempted to defend the Marne, but being menaced by the advance of the two Allied armies, after blowing up a powder magazine at Meaux, and destroying the bridge, they retired on the 28th to Claye and Villeparisis, where an engagement took place with the advance of the Prussians, who having pursued them from Meaux, were repulsed by a charge of the French cavalry with the loss of 200 men. The two Allied armies, during these days, were pushing forward *en masse;* the head-quarters of Prince Schwarzenberg were moved from Fère Champenoise on the 26th to Treffaux, on the 27th to Coulommiers, and on the 28th to Quincy, a village to the south of Meaux.

The army of Marshal Blucher was on this day collected near Trilport. The disposition for the 29th was, that the corps of Generals Sacken and Wrede should remain near Meaux as a rear-guard to the army: the corps of Marshal Blucher should assemble on the road from Soissons to Paris, and advance by Charny, Mory, and Aunay: the 6th corps, supported by the Russian guards and reserves, by Claye and Bondi; and the 3d and 4th corps, under the Prince Royal of Wurtemberg (who, not being able to pass the Marne at Lagny, was forced to move by Meaux), by Charmentré and Chelles.

Considerable delay attended the execution of these movements; on the night of the 29th the centre column having driven the French out of Bondi, advanced to Pantin and Noisy le Sec. The Silesian army only reached Aunay, Le Bourget, Ville-pinte, and Blanc Mesnil, and the 3d and 4th corps Annet.

The Sovereigns and Prince Schwarzenberg established their head-quarters at Bondy; the plan of attack for the following morning was determined there. The Silesian army was to advance by Aubervilliers upon Montmartre, La Chapelle and la Villette, and through the plain of Clichy upon the barriers of Paris; a force was also to be detached from it to observe St. Denis. The centre column, consisting of the 6th corps, and the guards and reserves under the orders of Marshal Barclay de Tolly, was to advance upon Les Maisonnettes, Prés St. Gervais, Romainville, Bagnolet and Belleville. The 3d and 4th corps, under the Prince Royal of Wurtemberg, were to follow the right of the Marne, and possessing themselves of the wood of Vincennes and the bridges of St. Maur and Charenton, were to assist the centre column by operating on its left at Charonne. The Allied troops were to be assembled on the ground, from whence they were to commence their attack at nine o'clock. Unfortunately, by a delay in the transmission of the orders, the army of Marshal Blucher did not break up from its cantonments till so late as to be unable to commence its fire till two in the afternoon. The column under the Prince

Royal had so great a distance to march, that its arrival on the ground assigned to it was at a still later period. The 6th corps, notwithstanding, began the engagement at the hour appointed.

The French force opposed to the Allies was composed of the corps under Marshals Mortier and Marmont, the garrison of Paris under General Hulin, comprising the divisions of Generals Compans and Ornano, and the National Guard, amounting to about 12,000 men, in a state of activity, 6,000 of whom took some part in aid of the regular army. The troops of the line amounted to about 20,000 infantry and 6,000 cavalry; Joseph Buonaparte commanded in chief, the Duke of Conegliano was at the head of the National Guard.

In consequence of a reconnoissance made by the French officers on the 29th, it is understood to have been determined that Marshal Marmont should occupy the positions extending from the canal of L'Ourq near Pantin, to Charonne and Montreuil, covering the heights of Belleville, and connecting his left at Les Maisonnettes with Marshal Mortier, who, extending from thence, was to occupy La Villette, La Chapelle, Clignancourt, and Montmartre, with his advance in occupation of Aubervilliers, and his cavalry in the plain of Clichy. Joseph fixed his station on the heights of Montmartre, near the five wind-mills.

On the morning of the 30th Prince Eugene of Wurtemberg, supported by the cavalry of General Kretow, advanced through Pantin upon Les Maisonnettes; while General Mezenzow attacked the plain in front of Romainville, covered on his left by Count Pahlen, who advanced upon Montreuil. Marshal Marmont, who at this moment had arrived upon the ground assigned to him, had placed the division of General Arrighi, in this last mentioned place, and at Malassise; the brigades of Generals Fournier and Joubert in line, in front of Bagnolet, with their left connected with the division of General Ledru des Essarts, which occupied the wood of Romainville; from whence the division of General Compans at Prés St. Gervais, connected the whole of his position with the troops in Les Maisonnettes. In rear of this line was the division of General Ricard in the park of Bruyères, and the division of General La Grange behind Bagnolet; the whole supported by the artillery at the But des Tourelles. The cavalry of Generals Vincent and Bordesoulle were in two lines between Montreuil and Charone.

From these positions Marshal Marmont assumed the offensive, and for a moment succeeded in driving back the Allies upon the villages of Pantin and Romainville, repelling the cuirassiers of General Kretow, who, on the right of the Prince Eugene of Wurtemberg, endeavoured to support the troops which he had thrown forward towards Les Maisonnettes, and which having been resisted by the divisions of General Boyer de Rebeval and Michel, were forced to retire, and obliging General Mezenzow to suspend the movement he was engaged in. Marshal Mortier was enabled to support the operation of his colleague, by placing the divisions of Generals Charpentier and Curial between the But of Chaumont and La Villette, while that of General Christiani occupied this latter place and La Chapelle, with the brigade of General Robert at Aubervilliers, and the cavalry of General Belliard in the plain upon its left.

As soon as these dispositions had been observed by Marshal Barclay de Tolly, he directed three divisions of Russian grenadiers, to move forward in support of General Mezenzow; these troops immediately advanced upon Montreuil, and the wood of Romainville, and at the first of these places, being conducted by General Mezenzow, supported by Count Pahlen, succeeded in defeating the enemy, while at the other they were resisted till the arrival of the cavalry of the Prince Royal of Wurtemberg near Fontenay and Vincennes; Marshal Barclay de Tolly was then enabled to advance the troops from Montreuil upon Malassise, Bagnolet, and Charonne, which after some contest they took possession of, while the Russian grenadiers, under the direction of General Miloradovitsch, notwithstanding the efforts of the division of General Ricard, headed by Marshal Marmont, carried the park of Bruyères and the wood of Romainville, thus establishing themselves on the centre of the enemy's position; who still retaining, however, the village of Prés St. Gervais, formed himself on a new line extending from this place in front of Belleville to Menilmontant and the But of Fontarabie.

During the period of these operations the troops under the Prince Eugene of Wurtemberg in Pantin had been reinforced by the Prussian and Baden guards, and by two brigades of Prussians under Generals Katzler and the Prince William of Prussia, which had been detached from the corps of General Yorck, and had passed the Ourcq on a bridge between the farm of Rouvroy and Pantin. Prince Eugene thus reinforced, moved upon Prés St. Gervais, while the division of General Zermolow and the troops under General Katzler, attacked Les Maisonnettes and the bridge across the Ourcq, over which passes the road leading from this place to La Villette; on the extreme left, about the same time, Generals Mezenzow and Count Pahlen advanced upon Menilmontant and Fontarabie; all these operations succeeded, the enemy was forced back upon Belleville, and in rear of Les Maisonnettes and La Villette, where he was enabled only for a short time to maintain himself. The Prussian guards, supported by the Prince William of Prussia, made a most brilliant charge upon the heights of Beauregard between Prés St. Gervais and the But of Chaumont, from whence they drove the division of General Boyer de Rebeval, with the loss of all its cannon; by which the whole of Marshal Marmont's position being turned, he was obliged to evacuate Belleville, and, at the head of his staff, to cut his way through the Allied troops, which, already in advance of Les Maisonnettes, intercepted his retreat to the barrier of Paris. The heights which covered the town in the neighbourhood of Belleville were thus in the possession of the Allies, and from an elevated spot near the telegraph a fire was immediately commenced upon it. It is a singular circumstance that the first shot directed upon this capital was from the Russian battery of light artillery, which last retired from Moscow when it was abandoned to the French, and that in both instances this battery was under the immediate direction of General Miloradovitsch, who commanded the Russian infantry of reserve.

The relation of these events has been continued without interruption, because the decisive struggle for the possession of Paris was maintained by the troops engaged in them. As collateral operations, we must now return to the movements of the armies of Marshal Blucher and the Prince Royal of Wurtemberg.

About two o'clock the corps of Generals Yorck and Kleist, supported by Count Woronzow, arriving by the chaussée of Senlis, passed the canal of St. Denis, opposite to La Villette and La Chapelle, while General Langeron, driving General Robert from Aubervilliers, and leaving a small corps to observe St. Denis, moved the forces under his orders to the chaussée leading from St. Ouen to Paris; thus avoiding the obstacles which, along the canal which traverses the plain, the enemy had prepared to oppose to him: he extended his cavalry to the neighbourhood of Clichy.

Marshal Mortier observing these dispositions, brought Generals Charpentier and Curial to support the division of General Christiani, and directed a charge of cavalry against the brigade of General Horn, at that time advancing upon La Chapelle, but which was totally repulsed by the hussars of Brandenburg, who captured twenty pieces of cannon. La Chapelle and la Villette were then attacked by the Allies, and although the defence of these posts was conducted with skill and bravery; yet, by the combined exertions of Generals Yorck and Kleist, together with the successes of General Katzler which have already been described, and a vigorous effort made by the troops under General Count Woronzow, (two battalions of the chasseurs of which took 12 guns, and drove the enemy from the entrance of La Villette to the barriers of Paris) the whole of these positions were captured. General Count Langeron advanced at the same time towards Montmartre, and his cavalry, under General Rudzewitsch, was approaching the barrier of Clichy.

It was at this moment that Marshal Mortier received an order from Buonaparte, despatched on the 29th from the bridge of Dolencourt, to negotiate directly with Prince Schwarzenberg for a suspension of hostilities, upon the ground that Monsieur de Caulincourt had been sent to the Emperor of Austria with proposals of peace, such as the Allies had stated themselves to be ready to assent to.

An answer, such as might have been expected at such a period, was returned, declaratory of the perfect union amongst the Allies, and of their determination to regulate their conduct according to the declaration which had been issued after the rupture of the negotiations at Chatillon. A short time after this communication had taken place, an aid-de-camp of Marshal Marmont reached the ground where the sovereigns and Prince Schwarzenberg were assembled, and proposed an armistice, stipulating the surrender of all the positions without the walls of Paris, and the evacuation of the town by the French troops in the course of the night.

These conditions having been agreed to, a cessation of hostilities was immediately directed; the successes, however, of Count Langeron were not arrested till he had driven General Belliard from Clignancourt, and with the divisions of Generals Kapzewitsch and Rudzewitsch had carried the heights of Montmartre and the faubourg of Batignoles, and had pushed his right, under General Emmanuel, to the barrier of Neuilly.

On the extreme left of the Allies we have already mentioned the arrival of the cavalry of the Prince Royal of Wurtemberg at Fontenay. This officer, leaving the Austrian corps of General Giulay at Neuilly-sur-Marne, directed the infantry of the 4th corps to advance in two divisions, the left upon St. Maur, the right by the wood of Vincennes, leaving a force to blockade the Castle, and afterwards to cooperate with the column on its left. St. Maur was immediately carried by these troops: the Prince Royal then advanced upon Charenton, which he also succeeded, without much resistance, in occupying; a part of his cavalry advanced towards the Barrière du Trône, Count Pahlen moved from the neighbourhood of Montreuil to communicate with it; observing, at the same time, a French battery of twenty pieces of cannon on the road to Vincennes, he charged and carried it, cutting to pieces and capturing the greatest part of the national guards and military cadets who defended it.

Count Pahlen afterwards moved upon the cavalry under Generals Bordesoulle and Chastel, driving it from Fontarabie and Menilmontant, within the walls of the capital.

In these positions the armistice having been proclaimed, the Allies bivouaqued for the night, anxiously awaiting the triumphant recompense of their efforts, in the occupation of Paris, which, without defence, now lay prostrate before them. This seat of empire, from whence destruction had been hurled on the various countries from which the soldiers who composed the army before her walls had been collected, was now doomed to feel the weight of an hostile occupation.

The capitulation of the town, which was signed during the night, stipulated that the French troops of the line should evacuate Paris by seven o'clock on the morning of the 31st, with the artillery which belonged to them; hostilities were only to re-commence two hours afterwards; the arsenals and all military magazines and establishments were to be given up to the Allies in the state in which they existed; all the French wounded, marauders, &c., found in Paris after nine o'clock, were to be considered prisoners of war. It was also agreed, that the National Guard and the Gendarmerie, being distinct from the army of the line, might be preserved, disarmed, or dissolved, at the will of the Allied Powers. The town of Paris was recommended to the generosity of the Allies.

Towards day-break on the 31st, the municipality of Paris arrived at the head-quarters of the Allies at Bondy, with the view of obtaining whatsoever alleviation they were able, in the future occupation of their capital. Amongst the persons who composed it, it was singular to observe Monsieur de Caulincourt, who the day before had been stated to be on a distant mission. This negotiator, when Buonaparte became acquainted with the capitulation of Paris, was directed by him to seize whatever opportunity his acquaintance with the Emperor of Russia might afford, to obtain a peace upon the conditions France had refused at Chatillon, or to receive from him any other proposals he could be induced to · offer; he was, however, obliged to return with an understanding, that the Allies would no longer treat with the Sovereign he came to represent.

The Emperor of Russia declared to the Municipality, "that he did not make war on France, but against
" one man whom he had once admired, but whose
" ambition and want of faith had obliged him to pur-
" sue even to the heart of France; that his inten-
" tions and those of his Allies would soon be known:

" —he meant not to conquer or rule in France, but to
" learn in Paris (the focus of French feeling) what
" was the wish of the French nation, and then to give
" it his support."

He agreed to the request of the Municipality, that
the National Guard should remain to perform the
service of the capital, and assured them, that in General Sacken, whom he had named Governor, they
would find a wise and benevolent protector.

Soon after the return of the deputation to Paris, the
Emperor of Russia and King of Prussia, accompanied
by Prince Schwarzenberg at the head of detachments
from all the corps of the army, entered Paris, and
proceeding along the boulevards from the Porte St.
Martin to the Champs Elysées, passed their troops
in review there, while the cavalry under Count Pahlen,
and General Emmanuel, pursued the French on the
road to Fontainebleau, as far as Juvisy and Antony.

To conceive the singularity of the scene which presented itself on this occasion, it must be recollected,
that since the Allies had entered France they had never

met with any very marked demonstration of national feeling, except from the peasantry, who at a distance from the general operations of the war, and exasperated by the conduct of the troops detached from the main army, had at times shewn considerable hostility. They had seldom witnessed the expression of any satisfaction on their entry into any of the considerable towns they had taken possession of; nor had any sentiments of a contrary nature been manifested. In entering the capital of the country little variation from this line of conduct was expected. As Paris had, however, been the focus of the Revolution; as it was supposed to contain every class of persons, who, through the changes of the previous twenty years, had rendered themselves conspicuous, and had either directed or profited by the convulsions of their country, a feeling of more hostility was rather expected from it than from the places which had already been occupied. A few moments indeed before the entry of the sovereigns, a subaltern officer, escaping from the town in considerable alarm, approached the Grand Duke Constantine, and assured him he had been fired upon, and that the interior of the town was in open insurrection. This statement was but little attended to, and was not communicated to the Emperor of Russia, but it served to heighten the contrast which was immediately afterwards exhibited. From the first moment of the entry of the troops, the populace assembled in crowds within the barriers of Pantin, commenced a general applause, which, seconded by the immense number of persons collected in the streets and houses, lasted during the whole passage of the Allies to the Champs Elysées, and continued there while the troops were defiling. It is impossible to describe the apparent enthusiasm of this expression of popular feeling; every rank of persons took their share in it, many officers were observed as being conspicuous, and the rich vied with the lower classes in proclaiming their joy at the political change about to be effected. The display of the white cockade, which first took place near the Porte St. Martin, was received with universal acclamations.

During the passage of the troops, an individual in the crowd called out " A bas la statue," a sentiment in which a considerable number of persons appearing to coincide, they moved in a body to the Place Vendome, where having placed a cord round the neck of Buonaparte's statue, they endeavoured to displace it. This attempt was the only one expressive of hostility to the late government which, in the course of the day was not generally approved; few persons were added to the original number employed in the proceeding, so that the weight of metal bid defiance to the assailants, and the statue, for some days at least, remained. It was covered with a white sheet, which being told to Buonaparte he is reported to have said of the Parisians,—" Ils font bien de me cacher leur honte."

For several days after the entry of the Allies, the same universal joy continued to be expressed. At the theatres, at all public places, a feeling of participation in the triumph which had been obtained seemed alone to occupy the French people; crowds of them were constantly surrounding the palace where the Emperor of Russia had fixed his head-quarters, giving expression to their apparent devotion and attachment to him, and to the cause of which he was considered the main spring and support: towards England, the most undisguised sentiments of respect and friendship were constantly manifested*; and with regard to the Royal Family of France, the white banners as pledges of attachment to it, were paraded through the streets, and every where appeared to be received as the happy symbols of a regenerated country.

When, at a later period, the French Marshals came to grace the triumph of the Allied Sovereigns ; when on the Place Louis XV., on the very spot where Louis the XVIth had been beheaded, they attended the *Te Deum* sung in presence of the Allied army to commemorate its victories, it was little to be supposed that within a year the individual, at whose fall there appeared such general satisfaction, would on the same ground be again triumphant, and without an

---

* The English officers who entered Paris with the Allied armies with which they had been engaged during the previous campaign, were, the Earl of Cathcart, Lord Stewart, Lord Burghersh, Colonel Sir Hudson Lowe, Lieutenant Colonel H. Cooke, Major the Honourable Frederick Cathcart, Captain Wood, Lieutenant Aubin, Lieutenant the Honourable George Cathcart, Lieutenant Harris, who carried the account of the capture of Paris to England.—Thomas Sydenham, Esq., John Bidwell, Esq., and Doctor Frank.

army have traversed France, and subdued her to his authority.

As soon as the Allies were masters of Paris, the Prince of Benevento received a message from the Emperor of Russia, calling upon him to step forward on the present occasion, and save his country from the ruin with which, by the continuation of hostilities, it was menaced; and announcing to him that it was his intention to take up his residence in his palace. When the Emperor arrived there, a council was held, at which the Prince of Benevento, the Duke D'Alberg, and Baron Louis assisted; together with Prince Schwarzenberg and the Allied ministers, the result of which was the following proclamation, signed by the Emperor of Russia:

" The armies of the Allied powers have occupied the capital of France. The Allied Sovereigns accede to the wishes of the French nation.

" They declare that the conditions of peace formerly insisted upon in order to bind the ambition of Buonaparte might now be moderated, since France, by returning to a wise government, will herself offer a pledge of peace.

"The Sovereigns consequently proclaim, that they will no longer treat with Napoleon Buonaparte, or with any of his family.

"That they respect the integrity of France, such as she anciently existed under her legitimate kings; and may, perhaps, grant her an extension, since they always profess the principle, that, for the happiness of Europe, France must be great and powerful.

"That they will recognise and guarantee the constitution which the French nation may choose for itself: they consequently invite the Senate to select immediately a provisional government, which may furnish the means necessary for the administration of the country, and prepare such a constitution as may suit the French people.

"The intentions which I have now expressed are in common between all the Allied powers and myself.

(Signed) " ALEXANDER.

"*Paris*, 31*st March*, 1814."

A note verbale was at the same time transmitted to Buonaparte, to the following purport:

"The Allied Powers have yielded to the wishes of France. They have taken upon themselves the engagement no longer to treat with the Emperor Napoleon, who has been the only obstacle to peace. They will not object to negotiate with him as to what regards his personal interests or those of his family; with these might be comprehended, all the persons present with him and under arms.

"In this transaction they will be guided by the most liberal sentiments.

"A place may be fixed upon, where the Emperor Napoleon might proceed to terminate these arrangements. From the moment of his doing so, an armistice might be established, and the effusion of blood put a stop to; if he should refuse, he alone would be responsible for the miseries which press upon France and upon Europe."

The first result of these measures was, that the Municipal Council of Paris unanimously declared itself in favour of the recall of the Bourbons to to the throne of France, and of the deposition of Buonaparte from a power he had so long abused. This was followed by a decree of the Senate, which had been convoked by the Prince of Benevento, by which a Provisional Government, consisting of five members, namely, the Prince of Benevento, Count Jaucourt, the Abbé Montesquieu, General Bournonville, and the Duke D'Alberg, was established, and to which was delegated the charge of presenting to the Senate the project of a Constitution which might be suitable to the French nation. In consequence of these dispositions, on the 3d of April it was declared by the Senate, that Napoleon Buonaparte had forfeited the throne of France; that the right of hereditary succession in his family was abolished; and that the French people and the army were released from their oaths of fidelity to him. The Corps Legislatif, in the course of the same day, adhered to this decision.

While these decisive steps towards the establishment of a new Government were rapidly succeeding each other, a discussion of considerable importance arose amongst the legions of the National Guard, whether, as a body, they should follow the example set by many of the individuals belonging to them, and adopt the white cockade. The Duke of Montmorency, who had succeeded to the Duke of Conegliano in the command of these troops, would anxiously have desired to see this proposal agreed to; but General Dessolles, who was appointed to the command of the whole French force in Paris, finding that six out of twelve legions only were unanimous upon the subject, declared that the measure would be adopted when the National Guard received an order for that purpose from the Government. This circumstance, as well as the delay of the Provisional Government in proclaiming the re-establishment of the family of the Bourbons in their ancient rights, gave rise to considerable discussions, in which the partisans of the different pretensions which were set forth for the chief rule in France, supported the claims they were anxious to see successful with warmth and violence. These animosities were, however, soon after appeased; but the leading features of the revolution having thus far been detailed, it is necessary to return to the military operations which succeeded the march of Buonaparte upon St. Dizier.

PART IX.

The plan which Buonaparte had adopted was, to force Prince Schwarzenberg to fall back, by marching upon Chaumont, thus menacing Bar sur Aube and Langres, consequently the whole line of the operations of the Allied army; leaving himself in a situation to profit by the disorder which must ensue, and possibly to obtain a decisive advantage.

Various opinions as to the propriety of this measure existed in the French army. It deviated totally from a plan which, but a short time before, had been proposed, and according to which Buonaparte should have moved from Rheims, so as to operate by Sezanne and Provins. The advantages of thus concentrating the French army with the corps under Marshal Macdonald at Provins, and of being able, from that position, either to support or call to aid the corps of Marshals Marmont and Mortier, left upon the Marne (while the garrisons in rear of the Allies should be directed to collect and harass their communications), were of such importance, that it was with reluctance the adoption of the present system of operations was seen by many of the most distinguished amongst the French officers. The die was, however, cast, from the moment the French troops passed the Marne at Frignicourt; and although, looking retrospectively at the subject, there might appear a preference in favour of the movement on Provins, and on the left of Prince Schwarzenberg's army, yet it should be remembered, that in the reduced state of the French forces since the defeat of Laon, the only chance of success which remained for them, was by keeping separate the two great armies of the Allies; an advantage which Buonaparte appeared to promise himself by directing his operations against the rear and upon the resources of Prince Schwarzenberg's army; and which, as the possibility of gaining a victory was almost precluded by the diminished number of his troops, seemed to be the only means left to him of effecting the great object he had in view. Nor was he very far from succeeding. The order of the day given out at Arcis on the 18th, already proved a disposition on the part of the Allies to fall back, while the movements directed from the heights of Mesnil la Comtesse, on the 21st, were calculated to meet Buonaparte's supposed intention of operating on the communications of the Allied army upon the Voire. That he should attempt the same thing by so wide a movement as through St. Dizier, was never contemplated, and consequently, the means of opposing it were not prepared; and when the first suspicion was excited, by the knowledge of Buonaparte's arrival at St. Dizier, from whence he was considerably nearer to Chaumont than the Allies, it was too late by falling back to prevent the accomplishment of his views. The concealment, therefore, with which the march from Arcis to St. Dizier was effected, was one of the causes which contributed the most to the failure of Buonaparte's combinations.

The French army continued its movement from St. Dizier to Joinville on the 24th. The advance of

General Winzingerode, who was ordered to pursue it, having followed its rear-guard, under Marshal Macdonald, as far as Thieblemont. On the 25th, the French advance-guard took possession of Bar sur Aube and Chaumont, where it created the greatest alarm and disorder*. The rest of the army was placed between Doulevent, Vassy, and Humbecourt. The advance of General Winzingerode, under General Tettenborn, (after an affair with the division of General Gerard, near Hoiricourt,) was established at Eclaron; while Count Czerniczeff moved from Vitry to Moutierender. On the morning of the 26th, Buonaparte, who till then had been convinced the whole of the Allied armies were pursuing him, determined (in consequence of the reports which had been circulated of the march of the Allies upon Paris,) to ascertain by a reconnoissance what force was actually in his rear. With this view,

---

* The Corps Diplomatique, which was returning from Chatillon, was obliged to abandon Chaumont with great precipitation; and many of them, amongst whom were Counts Rasoumoffsky and Stadion, and Lord Aberdeen, were forced to bivouaque upon the road half-way between that place and Langres, whence they joined the Emperor of Austria, at Dijon.

General Tettenborn was attacked and driven over the Marne, on the right of which General Winzingerode had formed his troops in two lines, extending from St. Dizier to near Perthe. Buonaparte brought his whole army to attack this position; under the cover of the cavalry of General Sebastiani, supported by Generals Kellerman, Milhaud, and St. Germain, he passed the guards and the corps of Marshal Macdonald and General Giraud across the river at the ford of Hallignicourt, while he directed Marshal Oudinot upon St. Dizier. General Winzingerode, at too late a period to remedy the mischief, perceived the very superior forces which were about to fall upon him; he directed General Tettenborn to cover the road to Vitry, while he endeavoured to save the infantry he had placed in St. Dizier, and from that point to take his direction upon Bar le Duc. In manœuvring to effect these objects, he was broken in upon, and defeated with great loss, by the French cavalry, and driven to Les Trois Fontaines and to Saudrupt, while General Tettenborn with difficulty maintained himself near Perthe. General Winzingerode lost in this action near 2,000 men, and nine guns.

However brilliant the result of this affair was to the French arms, yet the knowledge which Buonaparte derived from it of the movement of the Allies upon Paris must have counterbalanced, in his mind, the feelings of satisfaction he would otherwise have experienced. On the morning of the 27th he pushed forward upon Vitry, driving before him General Tettenborn and the troops under Count Czerniczeff, which had rejoined that officer from Montcirender, and endeavoured to get possession of that place; but finding, from the fidelity of the Prussian commandant, and the strength of the fortifications, that he had no chance of succeeding, he returned at night to St. Dizier, from whence he put his army in motion through Bar sur Aube and Troyes towards Fontainebleau. Two other plans are reported to have been projected by him; the first, to continue the pursuit of a part of the original object of his movement, by collecting the garrisons from the rear, and thus having reinforced his army, to operate against the Austrians in the south of France; the second, to march by Sezanne and Coulommiers upon Paris. After a discussion with Marshals Berthier and Ney, these ideas were abandoned. On the 28th Marshal Oudinot was recalled from Bar le Duc, where he had established himself, and the whole French army was concentrated between Bar sur Aube and Vassy, with the head-quarters at Montierender. Buonaparte on the 29th moved forward with a detachment of the cavalry of the guard towards Troyes. At the bridge of Dolencourt he was met by a courier from Joseph Buonaparte, announcing the approach of the Allies towards Paris, and their arrival at Meaux. He immediately despatched the order which has already been mentioned to Marshals Marmont and Mortier, desiring them to endeavour to open a negotiation for peace with Prince Schwarzenberg; he had previously, on the 25th from St. Dizier, directed Monsieur de Caulincourt to announce his readiness to treat with the Allies to the Emperor of Austria, who being at Bar sur Aube when the great army moved from Vitry upon Paris, had been obliged to separate himself from the other Sovereigns, and retire upon Dijon. Prince Metternich had replied to this communication on the 27th by stating, that he would notify it to the rest of the Allies *.

* It was at Bar sur Aube on the 22nd of March that the first communications from persons in Paris attached to the cause of the

At the same time that the order was despatched to the French Marshals in front of Paris, the following notification was issued to the French army by Marshal Berthier, and Buonaparte pushed forward with a small escort towards Fontainebleau.

"All the couriers from Paris are arrived. The spirit in that city is good. The Marshals Dukes of Treviso and Ragusa, *who have not suffered*, and all the troops that could be collected at Paris, are in action, with a numerous artillery on the heights of Claye. Blucher was to enter Meaux this day (the 29th). The Emperor will be to-night at Troyes, and to-morrow at Nogent. We must march day and night, taking only such intervals of repose as are indispensable."

Bourbons was received by the Allies; they were brought by two individuals, and purported that if the cause of the ancient royal family of France was espoused by the Allied Sovereigns, they might rest assured that aid and assistance would be afforded to them: it was consequently determined to place the Provinces of France which were occupied by the Foreign armies, the revenue of which was estimated at 142,232,800 francs, under the government of the Comte D'Artois, and a communication to that effect was made to him, at the same time that he was invited to repair from Vesoul, where he had till then remained, to Nancy.

The French army was on this day concentrated between Lusigny and Troyes; General Winzingerode, who followed it, reached Montierender. On the following day the guards, and a portion of the French army, reached Villeneuve l'Archevêque, from whence Buonaparte proceeded in the afternoon to Villeneuve la Guyard, and on horseback as far as Fontainebleau; where he got into a carriage, and hastened towards Paris, still in the expectation of reaching it before the Allies could enter, and of stopping their advance till the arrival of his army. Marshal Berthier and Monsieur de Caulincourt accompanied him. On reaching la Cour de France, an inn on the road to Paris, he was met by General Belliard, who, by virtue of the capitulation signed by Marshals Mortier and Marmont, was retiring to Fontainebleau. Buonaparte got out of his carriage, and walked along the road with General Belliard, when the following conversation is said to have taken place *.

Taking General Belliard's hand, Buonaparte ex-

* This conversation appears in the valuable work of the Chevalier Koch on the Campaign of 1814.

claimed, "Why, Belliard, what is all this? How come you here with your cavalry? Where is the enemy?"—" At the gates of Paris."—" And the army?"—" It is following me."—" And who guards the capital?"—" The Parisian guard."—" What is become of my wife and son? Where is Mortier, where is Marmont?"—" The Empress and the King of Rome set out the day before yesterday for Rambouillet; and from thence I believe for Orleans. The Marshals are, doubtless, still in Paris, to complete their arrangements." He then recounted to Buonaparte, with rapidity, the operations of the army, which was left on the 19th of March on the Aisne, and gave him a concise account of the battle of Paris. At that moment Marshal Berthier and Mons. de Caulincourt came up.—" Well, gentlemen," said Buonaparte, " you hear what Belliard says. I must go to Paris; —come—Caulincourt, call up my carriage."

During this conversation they had advanced about a mile and a half. General Belliard represented to Buonaparte that he could go no further, as there were no troops at Paris. "Never mind," he replied, " I shall find the National Guard; the army will join me to-morrow or next day, and I shall retrieve matters."—" But I repeat to your Majesty that you cannot go to Paris. The National Guard, according to the treaty, occupies the barriers; and though the Allies are not to enter till seven o'clock, it is possible they may have proceeded on, and that your Majesty might meet them on the Boulevards."— " Never mind, I will go there; my carriage! follow me with your cavalry."—" But, Sire, your Majesty exposes yourself to be taken, and Paris to be sacked; more than 120,000 men occupy the neighbouring heights: besides, I came out by virtue of a convention, and I cannot return."—" What convention? who made it?"—" I do not know, Sire; the Duke of Treviso informed me that it existed, and that I was to move to Fontainebleau."—" What is Joseph about? Where is the Minister of War?"—" I know not, we have received no orders from either during the day; each Marshal acted for himself. To-day they have not been seen with the army, at least at the corps of the Duke of Treviso." " Come, I must go to Paris, wherever I am not, they make nothing but blunders." Marshal Berthier and Monsieur de Caulincourt united with General Belliard to dissuade Buonaparte. He called incessantly for his carriage, Monsieur de Caulincourt announced it, but it was not come up. Buonaparte, in his impatience, walked in a hurried and uncertain manner, repeating questions upon points already explained. " They should have held out,'' he said repeatedly, " and tried to have awaited the army; Paris should have been stirred, which cannot like the Russians; the National Guard, which is good, should have been put in action, and the defence of the fortifications, which the minister ought to have erected, and planted with artillery, should have been intrusted to it. The National Guard would have defended them well, while the troops of the line would have fought on the heights and in the plain."—" Sire, I repeat to you, that more has been done this day than appears possible; the entire army, mustering from 15 to 18,000 men, resisted above 100,000 until four o'clock, hoping that you might arrive every moment. The report of your arrival having been circulated in Paris, and having reached the army, the troops redoubled their ardour, and forced the enemy to turn the town by the plain of Neuilly and the Bois de Boulogne. The National Guard also distinguished itself, both by its sharp shooters, and by defending the miserable redoubts which covered the barriers."—" That is wonderful! how much cavalry had you?"—" Eighteen hundred horses, Sire, including the brigade of Daulincourt." —" But Montmartre fortified, and provided with heavy artillery, should have made a vigorous resistance."—" Fortunately, Sire, the enemy had the same opinion, and therefore approached it with so much circumspection—but it was not so, and there were only seven six-pounders."—" What then has been done with my artillery? I ought to have had above 200 pieces at Paris, and ammunition to supply them for a month."—" The truth is, Sire, that we had only field artillery to oppose to the enemy; and, after two o'clock, we were even obliged to employ that sparingly for want of ammunition."—" Well, I see every one has lost his head. This comes of employing men who have neither common sense nor energy! And yet Joseph imagines himself capable of leading an army; and the *routinier* Clarke has all the vanity of a good minister; but the former is a fool, and the latter, perhaps, a traitor, for I begin to believe what Savary used to tell me of him." The conversation continued in this style, till at about a league and a quarter's distance from la Cour de France they met a column of infantry. Buonaparte asked what troops they were; and was answered by General Curial, that it was the corps of Marshal Mortier. He ordered him to be called, and was told he had remained at Paris. Then, upon the reiterated representations and entreaties of Marshal Berthier, Monsieur de Caulincourt, and General Belliard, Buonaparte consented to return to la Cour de France, where he supped, and immediately after set off for Fontainebleau, having ordered all the troops to take up a position in the neighbourhood of Essonne, which was executed by them as fast as they arrived from Paris."

In the course of this day the French army, which was following Buonaparte, had reached the environs of Villeneuve l'Archévêque. It arrived, on the 31st, at Pont sur Yonne; and on the 1st of April at Fontainebleau. Buonaparte during these days was occupied with the re-organization of his troops, and after the discussion of various plans for his future operations, he decided to advance upon Paris. With this intention, on the 3d of April, he assembled his guards in the court of the palace of Fontainebleau, and addressed them in the following words:

" Soldiers! the enemy has stolen three marches upon us, and has made himself master of Paris. He must be driven out of it. Unworthy Frenchmen, emigrants, whom we had pardoned, have adopted the white cockade, and have joined our enemies. Wretches! they shall receive the reward of this new crime. Let us swear to conquer or to die, and to cause to be respected that tri-coloured cockade, which, during twenty years, has found us in the paths of glory and of honour."

The troops, by their acclamations, testified their adherence to the sentiments which were thus expressed, and immediately afterwards commenced their march to the advanced positions marked out for them on the Essonne; along the line of which river the French army was assembled, having its right at Melun, and its left at La Ferté Aleps. The corps of Marshal Marmont was at Corbeil and Essonne, and that of Marshal Macdonald occupied Villiers,

Chailly en Biere, and Fontainebleau, thus forming the line of support, while the cavalry was cantoned between St. Germain and Boissise le Roi.

On the part of the Allies, immediately after the occupation of Paris, their troops had been pushed forward on the roads of Lonjumeau and Juvisy. The army of Marshal Blucher, which, in consequence of the indisposition of that chief, was now commanded by Count Barclay de Tolly, had its advance at Montlhery and Arpajon; the 3d, 4th, and 6th corps of the great army, under the Prince Royal of Wurtemberg, were at Villeneuve le Roi and Athis, on the right and left of the road to Fontainebleau; and the 5th corps and the Russian grenadiers of the reserve were at Paroy and Rungis. The Russian guards remained in occupation of Paris, reinforced by the greater part of the corps of General Bulow, which was called, from the blockade of Soissons, the brigade of General Thumen alone being left for that service.

The head-quarters of Prince Schwarzenberg were transferred on the 2d, to Chevilly; but before we give an account of the transactions which took place there, it will be of advantage to describe the general situation of the other contending armies throughout France.

It has been already stated, that Brussels was taken possession of by the Allies, on the 1st of February, General Maisons having evacuated it, and having retired with the troops under his orders, to Tournay. where he arrived on the 10th. General Borstell was detached to Ath, to observe this officer, and to protect the march of General Bulow from Brussels, which he quitted on the 13th, upon Laon, which he reached on the 24th, having marched by Soignes, Genappe, Mons, and Pont sur Sambre. General Maisons, on the 17th, retired behind the Marque, with his left at Armentieres; thus abandoning Tournay, which General Borstell took possession of. General Maisons afterwards collected the greater part of his troops at Courtray and Oudenarde, and made several movements, which induced the Duke of Saxe-Weimar (who had been reinforced by a division under the orders of the Prince Paul of Wurtemberg), to bring together a force amounting to about 8,000 men, and, having driven General Maisons from Oudenarde on the 5th, to attack him at Courtray on the 7th; when, notwithstanding a resistance continued throughout the day, that officer was defeated, and forced back upon Mont Halluin, in front of Lille. The Duke of Weimar, having been completely successful in this operation, remained in tranquillity till the arrival of General Thieleman, with a reinforcement of 8,000 Saxons, when (his army amounting to 27,000 men) he conceived the project of besieging Maubeuge. For this purpose, he placed General Thieleman at Tournay, to observe General Maisons; Generals Borstell and Ryssell at Bavay and St. Ghislain, to watch Landrecy, Condé, and Valenciennes; while General Lecocq was to undertake the siege.

The movements for the execution of this plan commenced on the 17th of March; on the 19th and 20th, Maubeuge was invested, but the resistance of the garrison, under Colonel Schouller, proving greater than had been anticipated, General Lecocq, on the 24th, converted the siege into a blockade, and fell back upon Requigniés. General Maisons being made aware of the result of these operations, took advantage of the concentration of the principal force of the

Allies upon his right, to attempt the enterprise on Ghent, which, with a view of communicating with Antwerp, he had for a long time meditated. He commenced his march from Lille on the morning of the 25th, with 8,000 men, and 20 pieces of cannon; and driving before him the Allied troops which were in garrison at Menin and Courtray, took possession of those places, and moved an advanced corps to Pelleghem. The following day, he pushed forward upon Ghent, which, with little opposition from the small garrison which occupied it, he made himself master of; and immediately detaching a party to communicate with Antwerp, directed General Roguet, with 4,500 men, to leave that place, and establish himself at Alost.

In this state of things, the Duke of Weimar (whose force had been diminished by the march of the corps of Generals Ryssell and Borstell to join Marshal Blucher) was considerably alarmed for the safety of Brussels; he was fortunately reinforced by the corps of General Walmoden, which he placed in advance of Louvain; while that of General Thieleman occupied Oudenarde. From these positions he decided to march against the enemy. General Maisons, however, on the morning of the 30th, retired with the whole of his corps, amounting now to above 12,000 men, and moved upon Pelleghem and Courtray. General Thieleman immediately proceeded to Awelghem; from whence, on the 31st, he attacked the enemy in front of Courtray; but being entirely unsuccessful, he was obliged to fall back beyond Awelghem, with the loss of six guns, and near 800 prisoners. General Maisons, elated with this success, attempted to get possession of Tournay; from whence, however, having failed in his object, he moved upon Lille. On the 4th of April he marched, with the view of relieving the garrison of Maubeuge, to Valenciennes, where the events in Paris being made known to him, he returned to Lille. The Duke of Weimar had, at the same time, concentrated his troops: placing General Thieleman at Tournay; General Lecocq at Mons; and the corps of Count Walmoden and General Gablentz (who had been relieved from before Antwerp by a division of the Swedish army) in reserve at Ath and Lessines.

As connected with the Duke of Weimar's army,

and as a proof of the facility with which France was invaded, it is of interest to trace the progress of a partisan corps, amounting to about 800 men, exclusive of a body of Cossacks under the orders of Colonel Giesmar, which rendered the most important services. This very intelligent officer quitted Leuze on the 14th of February, and marching by Renaix, Courtray, Cassel, Lilliers, St. Pol, Doulens, Albert, Braye, Roye, Noyon, and Chauny, all which places he took possession of, he put himself in communication from Sincenis, on the 27th with the corps of General Bulow, which had arrived on the Aisne. On the 1st of March, he moved upon Nayon and Roye, thence upon Compiegne, which not having succeeded in occupying, he retired on the night of the 8th by Chauny and Jassy to Ribemont, where he fixed his headquarters on tne 10th, from whence after alarming the country in all that neighbourhood, he moved upon St. Quintin, which he captured on the 13th with the great depôt of artillery which had been established there, he afterwards took possession of Montdidier, St. Juste, and on the 19th, of Clermont; from this place he returned by Montdidier to Roye, from whence he marched on the 27th upon Cuvilly, and co-operating in an unsuccessful attack on Compiegne on the 1st of April, he moved on to Pont St. Maxence, Beaumont, Pontoise, and on the 5th, to Meulan. In the course of the service here described, Colonel Giesmar took a very considerable number of prisoners, rescued a great many of the Allied troops, who were in the hands of the French, (amongst them some English), took several fortified places, and spread terror and alarm throughout the provinces in which he was operating.

During the period of these operations, Lieutenant General Sir Thomas Graham had conceived, and nearly executed, one of the most daring enterprises that have ever been undertaken. He had remained since the 6th of February, when the bombardment of Antwerp was given up, in observation of that place and of Bergen-op-Zoom. This last-mentioned fortress, the strongest perhaps in the world, and completely garrisoned, he determined to assault. The British troops under his orders being divided into four columns, the first consisting of 1,000 men was destined to enter the place by the bed of the river Zoom, where it passes out of the town on the side of the Scheldt, it was then to proceed along the ramparts to its right to facilitate the entry of the 2nd column of 1,000 men which was to turn the outworks on the left of the road to Antwerp by their right, and afterwards to assault the bastion immediately in rear of them. The 3d column was to attack the bastion on the left of the gate through which passes the road to Breda. The 4th column was destined for a false attack upon the works which cover the road from Steenberg.

Of these columns, the 1st entirely succeeded, having overcome every obstacle, and its advanced-guard consisting of 300 men was pushed along the ramparts to the bastion on the right of the road to Breda; but the main body having by some accident divided itself, a part, consisting of 200 men, moved to the left of the Zoom and was soon cut off from the rest of the detachment by the rising of the tide in the river, while the remainder halted upon the first bastion, which it took possession of, and which covered the water-port gate; the advanced-guard being thus left without support, was obliged to fall back to the 2nd column, which by this time had established itself on the bastion it was destined to attack; this column communicated with the troops remaining at the water-port gate and sent a detachment of 300 men along the ramparts to its right to get possession of, and to open the Antwerp gate, and to facilitate the attack of the 3d column, which not succeeding however, in carrying the bastion on the left of the road to Breda, was conducted to the point at which the 2d column had entered the town, where it was formed in support of it.

In consequence of this want of success on the part of the 3d column, the 300 men which had been sent to its assistance were exposed to the whole force with which the enemy was defending that part of the ramparts, and being surrounded near the Antwerp gate, which it was unable to force, after a desperate resistance, was obliged to surrender; a force, however, of 2,500 men, in complete communication with each other, was now assembled within the place, while the false attack on the Steenberg side of the town was completely successful in its object, as it occupied the enemy, and retained a considerable force in observation of it.

In this situation the troops remained, though constantly under the fire of the enemy, till the break of day, when the garrison being formed into three columns of attack, was enabled to move upon the 200 men who on the right of the Zoom were cut off from their comrades, and to force them to surrender, the troops at the water-port gate being then exposed to the attack of two of the enemy's columns, a part of which from the arsenal and the ramparts on the right of the Zoom commanded their position, they were obliged to retire to the marsh between the water-port gate and the fort on the Scheldt, where although reinforced by 600 men from the 2d column, they were in part reduced to a capitulation, while the rest escaped across the ramparts on the side of Antwerp.

This loss induced Major General Cooke who commanded the assault, to endeavour to withdraw the remainder of the British troops who were by this time attacked by the whole of the enemy's force, it was found impossible, however, from the positions the French had occupied upon the adjoining bastion, although they were twice driven from them at the point of the bayonet by the 69th and 55th regiments, to execute entirely this determination, a part only of

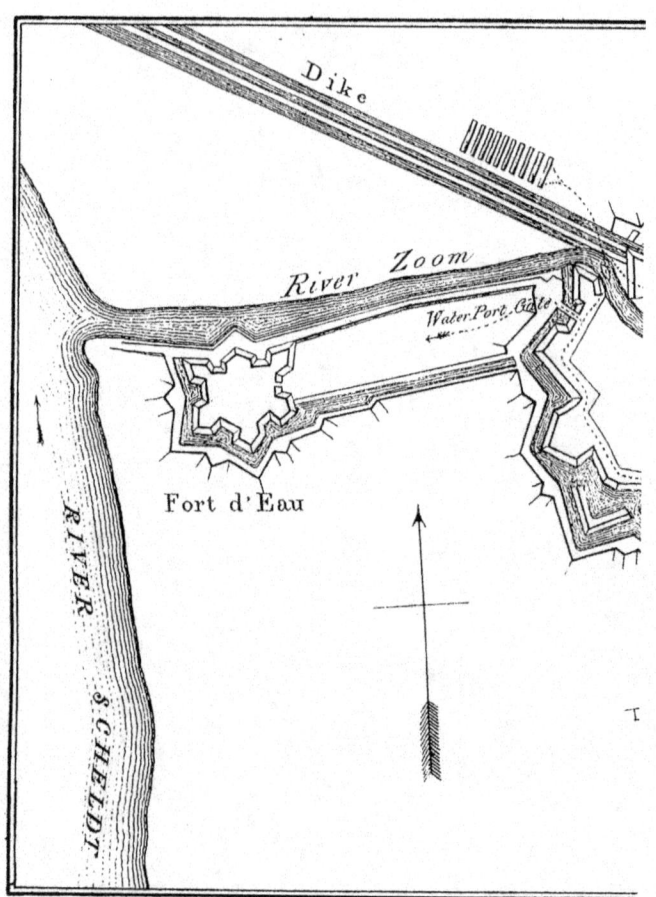

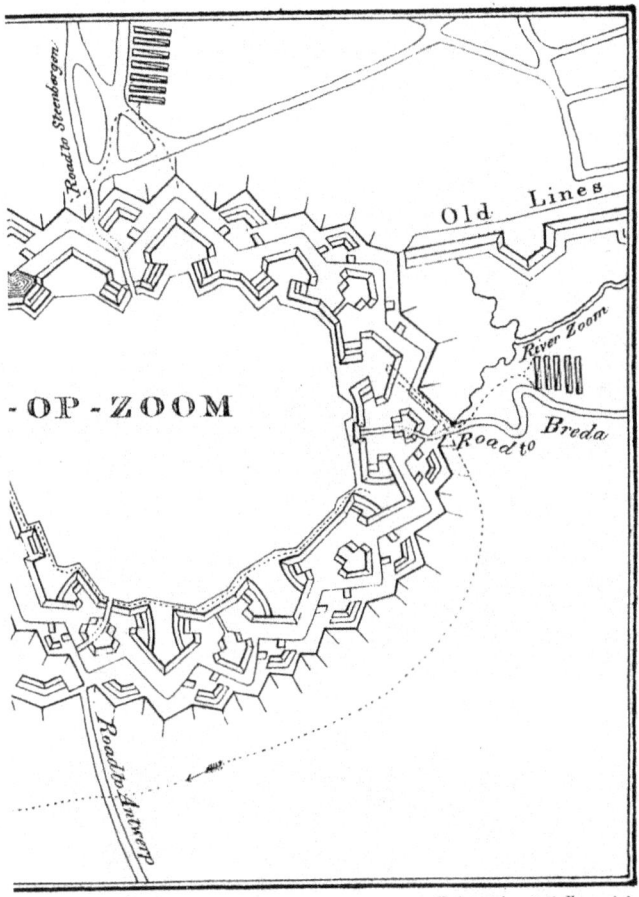

the troops was enabled to evacuate the place; thus the difficulties of an operation of this nature in the night; the impossibility of correcting the erroneous direction of the columns, which, surrounded by a garrison as powerful as themselves, were attacked while separated; the loss of the greater part of the commanding officers when their assistance alone could have extricated the troops from the unequal, but desperate, contest they were maintaining; these causes, after an action which lasted from nine o'clock at night till the following morning, reduced the British troops who still remained within the place, to a capitulation, by which (after the loss of 68 officers and 849 non-commissioned officers and privates, either killed or wounded,) 50 officers, 59 serjeants, and 1,526 rank and file laid down their arms *, and surrendered themselves prisoners of war. However unfortunate was the result of this enterprise, it is impossible not to admire both the boldness of the attempt, and the valour displayed by the troops throughout the operation. Buonaparte, in speaking of it to a British officer, and giving credit both to the original plan of the attack, and to the gallantry

* In this number are included all the detachments which in different parts of the town had surrendered to the enemy.

of its execution, admitted, in addition to the other difficulties which opposed its success, that the garrison was not surprised, the officer in command having been made aware of the attack which was meditated against him.

The army of the north, after the conclusion of the peace of Rendsbourg, moved into the Low Countries, (with the exception of the troops under General Benningsen, who continued the blockade of Hamburg,) and was assembled in the neighbourhood of Liege, where the Prince Royal of Sweden on the 27th of February established his head-quarters, and where he remained till the end of March, when he joined the Duke of Weimar at Brussels. This pause, in the operations of the large force he commanded, and the refusal to relieve the Duke of Weimar, so as to enable him to march to the assistance of Marshal Blucher, subjected him to the reproach of having, by his inactivity, clogged the great military combinations that had been agreed upon. The Prince Royal in his justification complained, that the corps of Generals Bulow and Winzingerode had been taken from him ; that the Saxon troops, who were to have formed a part of his army, had received a different destination; and that, in the high situation he occupied, it was not his business to relieve any other officer; that he would not consent to have the troops which belonged to him removed from his command; and that he should remain where he was until a new decision from the Emperor of Russia and King of Prussia could be received upon these questions. Towards the end of March, however, the corps of Count Walmoden and the Swedish troops were detached to the assistance of the Duke of Weimar, when they were employed in the operations which have been already described.

It has been stated, that, in consequence of the offensive movements undertaken by Marshal Augereau from Lyons, the Austrian army opposed to him was considerably reinforced, and placed under the orders of Prince Philip of Hesse Hombourg. The French force commanded by Marshal Augereau was collected about the middle of the month of February, and, including the garrisons of Lyons and of the other forts it was destined to cover, amounted to 27,000 men. Of these about 10,000 were troops detached from the force under Marshal Suchet. This army, being infinitely superior to that of Count Bubna, retook from that officer the positions he occupied at Macon, Bourg-en-Bresse, Nantua, Les Echelles, and Chambery; and in the early days of March, Marshal Augereau having directed the column of General Musnier from Nantua by Lons le Saulnier and Moret upon Nyon, the division of General Bardet upon the fort of L'Ecluse, which it was fortunate enough to gain possession of, and the corps of General Marchand upon St. Julien, which (after having been successfully defended by General Klebelsberg from the 27th of February to the 1st of March) was evacuated in consequence of the progress of the division of General Bardet, the Austrian troops were forced to retire into Geneva *. General Marchand,

* In the action which took place in advance of St. Julien, the French troops under General Marchand were divided into three columns, the right penetrated by Moissin to La Place in front of Collonge sous Saleve, where it was arrested by the Austrian left; the centre was repulsed in the assault made upon the town of St. Julien, while the left was only able to establish itself at Grache. On the morning after this action, the 1st of March, the corps of General Bardet having penetrated on the road from Lyons as far as Farges, General Bubna retired the whole force under General Klebelsberg to Geneva.

triumphing in these successes, advanced to the left bank of the Arve, while the division of General Bardet was established at the mill of St. Genis, and conceiving himself to be in a situation to summon the Austrians to surrender, sent an aid-de-camp into the town with a proposition to that effect. Count Bubna refused to return an answer to a proposal so little suited to the relative position of the troops opposed to each other; and menaced the officer with the utmost severity of the laws of war, if he dared to return upon such an errand.

While these operations were carried on upon the frontiers of Switzerland, and at the moment Marshal Augereau had recalled the division of General Musnier from Nyon for the purpose of attacking Prince Louis Liechtenstein, who was blockading Besançon, the force which had been detached from the army of Prince Schwarzenberg under General Bianchi on the 22d of February from Troyes was rapidly advancing upon the Saone; it reached Chalons, Mervans, and Louhans on the 4th of March; the corps under General Wimpffen arrived on the same day at Villette and Villers Robert, and on the 5th at Poligny,

The Prince of Hesse Hombourg was at the same time within a few days' march on the road from Basle through Besançon. The whole of this army amounted to 50,000 men and 130 pieces of cannon. Marshal Augereau, alarmed by the arrival of these troops, retired from Lons le Saulnier on the 5th, and concentrated the greater part of his army on the 9th in Lyons. On the 11th he moved to attack General Bianchi, who on the 10th had occupied Macon; the advance guard of this officer was driven in after a severe contest at St. Georges and La Maison Blanche, but from the attack of his main position between Vinzelles and the Saone, the French troops were repulsed with very considerable loss. Marshal Augereau, in consequence of this defeat, withdrew his army to a position near Arnas with its advanced guard at St. George's, where on the 18th he was attacked by the Prince Philip of Hesse Hombourg, who, having occupied Baye-le-Chatel on the 14th, had moved (together with the corps of General Wimpffen from Bourg en Bresse) to the right of the Saone, and on the 16th between Lancié and Crèche had concentrated his troops with those of General Bianchi. The Prince of Hesse directed the division of Prince Wiedrunkel to move from Beaujeu upon the French left, while the corps of Generals Bianchi and Wimpffen passing through Marsengue, attacked their centre at Lage Longsard; by these dispositions, after an action of some duration, the enemy was completely defeated and driven to the village of Limonest. The French army made another stand at this place, extending itself in a position from the Saone through Limonest and Dardilly to the Grange Blanche, situated in front of the Faubourg of St. Just, but its inferiority was too considerable to leave it any chance of success.

The Prince of Hesse having, on the 19th, established the corps of General Bianchi at La Tour de Salvagny and Dommartin, and General Wimpffen in support of him at Lozanne, directed these corps, on the 20th, to move along the road from Chatillon, through Dardilly, upon Lyons; while General Mumb, together with Colonel Haring, should advance from Chasselay upon the heights of Couzon and St. Romain. These operations were executed with great success. The heights above Dardilly were carried by General Bianchi, and the whole right of the French position forced by the column of

General Mumb. The French army, in consequence of these successes, was driven with considerable loss under the walls of Lyons. On the right of General Bianchi Prince Wiedrunkel was engaged in repelling an attack, which was directed by General Digeon from la Grange Blanche, upon the road to Salvagny, but which was entirely defeated. The immediate results of this action were the evacuation of the second city of the empire, and its capture on the following morning by the Allies.

In connexion with the movements here described, General Hardegg and the Prince Ferdinand of Cobourg, on the left of the Saone, co-operated with the corps of General Bianchi and Wimpffen, and drove back the division of General Boudet from Bourg-en-Bresse to Miribel and Calvire, from whence it retired, with the rest of the French army upon Valence.

On the frontiers of Switzerland General Bubna, being still observed by the force under General Marchand upon the Arve, remained in Geneva, without undertaking any material operation till the

PLAN OF L

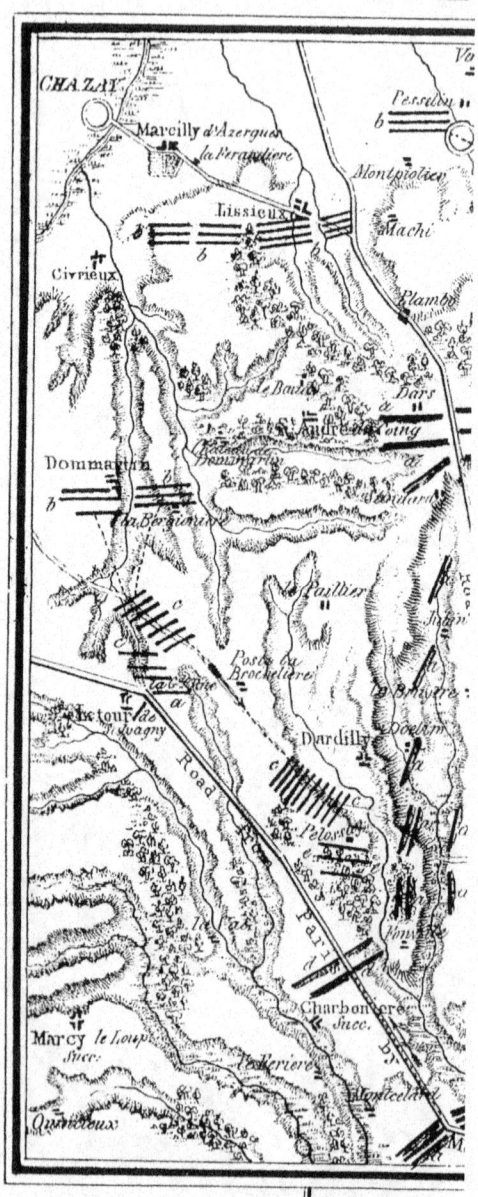

a a Position of the French Army.
b b Positions occupied by the Austrians.
d d Advance of the F
e e Movement of the

TTLE OF
S.

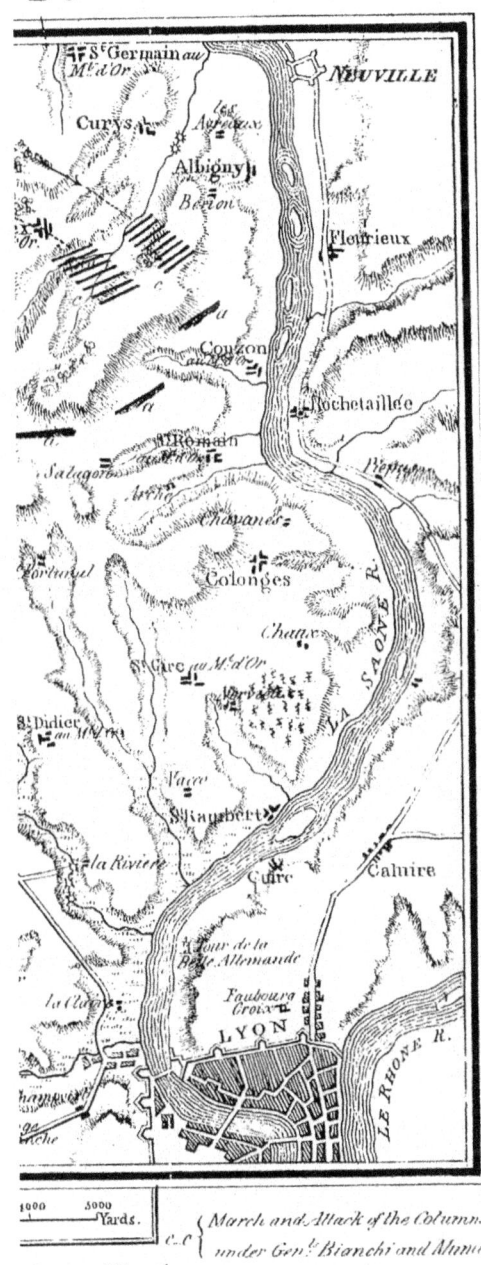

1000 5000
　　　Yards.

c c { *March and Attack of the Columns under Gen.ˡ Bianchi and Numb.*

Grange Blanche.
nkle to oppose it.

23d, when the French troops, in pursuance of the orders of Marshal Augereau, having fallen back, he followed them to Chambery, from whence, directing his force upon Conflans, he obliged the enemy to retire upon the fort of Barraux, and into the valley of the Maurienne, while the division of General Wimpffen being detached from Lyons upon La Tour du Pin, drove back the corps of General Marchand, on the 3d of April, from Les Echelles and Voiron, to a fortified position at Voreppe, where it remained forming the right of the French position along the Isere, till the termination of hostilities on the 13th. Marshal Augereau in the mean time had placed his head-quarters on the 23d at Valence, from whence he moved to his right towards General Marchand, breaking down the bridge of St. Romain; the Prince of Hesse pursued him, establishing his head-quarters on the 4th at St. Valier and on the 7th at Rives.

The object Marshal Augereau proposed to himself from the position he had taken up, was to prevent the junction of the Austrian army with the Marquis of Wellington, who (driving before him those eagles which were to have been planted on the towers of Lisbon), had unfurled the British ensigns triumphantly in the southern provinces of France, and after the victories of the Nivelle, of the Nive, and of Orthez, and the consequent capture of Bordeaux, was pursuing the army of Marshal Soult upon Toulouse; where, on the 10th of April, he closed his glorious and ever memorable campaign with the capture of that town, after the total defeat of the French army in advance of it.

With the view of effecting that operation which Marshal Augereau was so desirous of preventing, the Prince of Hesse had received orders to drive the French army from the Izere upon Avignon, and afterwards to detach General Bianchi, who was to be reinforced to 20,000 men, through the valley of the Upper Loire upon Clermont, and from thence, by making detachments upon Limoges, Tule, and Aurilac, to endeavour to open a communication with the British army. The rest of the Austrian army of the south (a corps being left to watch Marshal Augereau), was to move by Mont Brison and Moulins upon Chateauroux and Tours, and from thence on

Orleans, to which place General Bianchi was also to direct his march through Poitiers.

We must now return to the transactions in the vicinity of Paris.

Notwithstanding the Allied army had taken up a position in front of that capital, considerable doubts were entertained as to the propriety of accepting a general battle in such a situation. The immense population which would hang upon the rear of the Allies, and which might at any moment become hostile, was the chief ground upon which these doubts were founded; as soon, however, as the French authorities, who had taken a lead in the revolution, became aware of their existence, they hesitated not in declaring, that the French army would, in this instance, as it had on all former occasions, obey the constituted government of the country; and, consequently, when the orders were issued, that it would abstain from further hostilities. These assurances were received with considerable reserve; upon mature reflection, however, it was determined by the Allies not to withdraw their army from the ground it occupied.

The first step which was calculated to encourage a belief in the predictions of the French Authorities with respect to their army, was an application made to Prince Schwarzenberg, at his headquarters at Chevilly, on the evening of the 2d, by a friend of Marshal Marmont, for permission to proceed to Essonne; the declared object of his doing so, being to communicate to that Marshal the transactions which had taken place in Paris, the formation of the new government, and its directions to him to yield no further obedience to Buonaparte. This person entertained no doubt that he should be able to persuade the Marshal to submit to the orders he was conveying to him. Prince Schwarzenberg though less sanguine in his expectations, yet acceded to the wishes of this gentleman, and permitted him to pass. On the evening of the 3d, this person returned with the assurances from Marshal Marmont, that seeing the desperate situation into which his country was brought by Buonaparte; the obstinacy with which he still seemed determined to risk the remaining fortunes of France; the impossibility, after what had passed in the capital, of preventing a civil war, if hostilities continued; and, lastly, the danger with which Paris was again likely to be menaced, he had determined, in common with most of the distinguished general officers around him, to separate from the Chief, whom, since the declaration of the Senate and Legislative Assembly, he considered as no longer at the head of the French Empire; and that for this purpose he was ready to conclude a convention. The Marshal desired, however, to stipulate that his corps should move to a position where it would be entirely independent, and that the personal safety of Buonaparte, in case he should fall into the hands of the Allies, should be guaranteed to him.

Prince Schwarzenberg having acceded to these demands, a convention for carrying into effect the objects proposed was negotiated in the course of the day.

While these events were taking place at Chevilly, the French Marshals, who were in command of their respective corps at Fontainebleau, accompanied by Marshal Berthier and Monsieur de Caulincourt, presented themselves to Buonaparte, and communicating to him the decree of the Senate, by which he was deposed, requested to know from him by what means he expected to extricate the country from the situation in which it was placed; Marshal Ney intimating to him at the same time that his abdication alone seemed capable of effecting it. Buonaparte after some consideration consented to adopt this proposal, provided that it was in favour of his son; during whose minority the Empress Maria Louisa was to be at the head of the regency. He deputed Marshals Ney and Macdonald and Monsieur de Caulincourt to convey his decision to the Allied Sovereigns.

Marshal Marmont being at Essonne, when these officers passed on their way to Prince Schwarzenberg, after directing General Souham, to whom the command of his corps devolved, to make no movement during his absence, he followed them to Chevilly, where he explained to Prince Schwarzenberg the delay which must necessarily take place in the execution of the convention he had agreed to.

Marshals Ney, Macdonald, and Marmont, and

Monsieur de Caulincourt, accompanied by Prince Schwarzenberg, then continued their route to the capital; where, after some explanation with the Provisional Government, they were conducted to the Emperor of Russia, who, in company with the King of Prussia, received them.

A long and animated discussion took place at this meeting, to which, in addition to Prince Schwarzenberg, were invited the members of the new French Government, and General Dessolles. Marshal Ney and Mon. de Caulincourt pressed with the utmost vehemence the wishes of Buonaparte, in which they were supported by Marshals Macdonald and Marmont. The other French individuals who were present, with equal violence, insisted upon the restoration of the legitimate family, as the only means of saving their country from the dangers, both internal and external, with which it was menaced. The declaration of the Allied Sovereigns, pledging themselves no longer to treat with Buonaparte, or with his family, as having any authority in France, was appealed to, and the Emperor of Russia avowed his determination still to adhere to what had been promulgated. These discussions, however, led to no abatement of the firmness with which Marshal Ney and Mons. de Caulincourt maintained their propositions: and at near six in the morning, to which hour the meeting was protracted, nothing decisive had been settled. As the parties were separating, a courier announced that the corps of Marshal Marmont, in execution of the convention which had been agreed to, had passed within the lines of the Allied army. This intelligence, as little expected by Marshal Marmont as by the rest of the French officers in execution of Buonaparte's commission, at once decided Marshal Ney and Mons. de Caulincourt (who by that time were the only two who continued to hold out), to yield to the feelings of the rest of their countrymen; Marshal Marmont, withdrawing himself from all further participation in the negotiation. Marshals Ney and Macdonald and Mons. de Caulincourt, after a second meeting which was appointed at the Emperor of Russia's, and which took place in the course of the day, the 5th, returned to Fontainebleau, to apprize Buonaparte of the result of their mission, and to convey to him the resolution of the Allies, which was expressed in the following *Note Verbale*:

"Voulant prouver à l'Empereur Napoléon que toute animosité cesse de leur part, du moment où le besoin d'assurer le repos de l'Europe ne se fait plus entendre, et qu'elles ne peuvent ni ne veulent oublier la place qui appartient à l'Empereur Napoléon dans l'histoire de son siècle, les Puissances Alliées lui accordent en toute propriété pour lui et sa famille l'Isle d'Elbe. Elles lui assurent six millions par an, dont trois millions pour lui et l'Impératrice Marie Louise, et trois millions pour le reste de sa famille, savoir, ses frères Joseph, Louis, et Jérome; ses sœurs Elisa, et Pauline, et la Reine Hortense, qui sera considérée comme sœur, attendu sa situation avec son Mari."

Of the events here related, the most important was the unexpected defection of the corps of Marshal Marmont: this was brought about in consequence of a message sent by Buonaparte, in the night of the 4th, to General Souham, desiring his immediate attendance at Fontainebleau. Since this officer had been a party to the convention agreed to between Marshal Marmont and Prince Schwarzenberg, he is understood to have suspected that some report upon the subject had reached the head-quarters, for which reason he had been sent for. Communicating his suspicions to the other general officers, who, like himself, had been concerned in this transaction, it was agreed amongst them, that the stipulations of the convention should at once be fulfilled; and consequently, after taking precautions against any movement from the side of Fontainebleau, they formed their troops on the morning of the 5th, General Bordessoulle leading with his cavalry, the infantry and artillery following, and General Chastel with a brigade of cavalry in the rear; and in this order marched to Fresnes, and thence to Versailles.

Before Buonaparte was made acquainted with this defection, and while the French army, in ignorance of the real object of the mission of the Marshals to Paris, was in the greatest agitation, he held a language to those about him, from which it was apparent he had conditionally offered to abdicate, though he seemed to entertain but little belief that the proposition would be accepted. The knowledge of this fact was soon communicated to the army, which, still prepared for the movement upon the capital, that had been announced to it on the preceding day, awaited in anxious suspense for the result of the negotiations.

On the morning of the 5th, General Souham not appearing, Buonaparte despatched another messenger to require his attendance, from whom, upon his return, he learnt the measure which had been adopted by that officer, and by the troops under his orders; he immediately sent for General Belliard, and expressing the feelings of grief and indignation with which he was oppressed, desired him to proceed to the advanced posts, and to make those arrangements for the protection of his front which became necessary. At the same time, being persuaded that, with his army now so reduced as not to exceed from 30 to 35,000 men, he could no longer maintain the position he occupied, he gave directions for its retreat on the following morning, behind the Loire.

The corps under General Gerard was to open the march by Malesherbes upon Puiseaux; Marshals Macdonald and Oudinot, protected by the cavalry of Generals Defrance, Milhaud, and St. Germain, were to follow; the guards were to move in the same direction; while the corps of General Kellerman was to form at Pethiviers; and Marshal Mortier, forming the rear-guard, was on the 7th only to quit the Essonne, and fall back upon Fontainebleau.

As soon, however, as Buonaparte became acquainted with the result of the negotiations at Paris, after some discussion with Marshals Ney and Macdonald, and Monsieur de Caulincourt upon their return to Fontainebleau, he accepted the conditions offered to him, the communication of which was made to the Provisional Government by the following letter, from Marshal Ney to the Prince of Benevento:

" Monseigneur,

" Je me suis rendu hier à Paris avec M. le Maréchal Duc de Tarente et le Duc de Vicence, comme chargé de pleins pouvoirs pour défendre auprès de S. M. l' Empereur Alexandre, les intérêts de la dynastie de l' Empereur Napoléon. Un événement imprévu ayant tout-à-coup arrêté la négotiation, qui cependant semblait promettre les plus heureux résultats, je vis dès lors que pour éviter à notre chère patrie les maux affreux d'une guerre civile, il ne restait plus aux Français que d'embrasser entièrement la cause de nos anciens Rois ; et c'est pénetré de ce sentiment que je me suis rendu ce soir auprès de l'Empereur Napoléon pour lui manifester le vœu de la nation. L'Empereur convaincu de la position critique où il a placé la France, et de l'impossibilité où il se trouve de la sauver lui-même, a paru se résigner avec fermeté et consentir à l'abdication entière et sans aucune restriction. C'est demain matin que j'espère qu'il m'en remettra lui même l'acte formel et authentique. Aussitôt après j'aurai l'honneur d'aller chez V. A. Sérénissime.

"Je suis, avec respect,
"Monseigneur, &c.,
(Signé) "Le Marechal Ney.
"Fontainebleau, 5 Avril, 1814.
"A. S. A. Monseigneur le Prince de Benevento, Président de la Commission composant le Gouvernement Provisoire de la France."

On the day on which this letter was received, the Senate, having been assembled, decreed unanimously the new Constitution of France*, and recalled the Bourbons to the government of the country. This act was proposed to the Senate by the Prince of Benevento, who had previously obtained the assent to it of those members who had principally occupied

---

* See Appendix, No. XV.

themselves with questions of Constitutional Government, and above all, of those who were most opposed to the family of the Bourbons, that, by having the approbation of these persons, he might carry the measure unanimously. This object was attained, and every thing was transacted with a spirit of so much union and harmony, that even the Abbé Sieyes voted for the King's return, and voted without apprehension.

On the 7th, Marshals Ney and Macdonald and Monsieur de Caulincourt having returned to Paris, they concluded with Prince Schwarzenberg an armistice, the stipulations of which are here inserted, and by which hostilities were terminated:

" From the mouth of the Seine, the Allies were to occupy the right bank of that river, and in addition, the Southern limits of the Departments of

" the Lower Rhine,
" the Oise,
" the Seine and Oise,
" the Seine and Marne,
" the Yonne,

" the Côte d'Or,

" the Saone and Loire,

" the Rhone,

" and the Izere, as far as Mount Cenis.

" On the side of the Marquis of Wellington, the line of demarcation was to be fixed according to the ground occupied by his army and the one opposed to him, when the bearer of the above communications should reach the respective commanders in chief."

On the same day it was enacted, that all acts of sovereignty should in future be issued in the name and on behalf of the Provisional Government. On the 9th, the white cockade was assumed by the National Guard. On the 11th, the Comte d'Artois made his triumphal entry into Paris; and on the 14th, he received from the Provisional Government, as the King's Lieutenant, the sovereign authority of the country. On the same day on which the Comte d'Artois was received with universal acclamations in the capital, Buonaparte's Commissioners carried to him, at Fontainebleau, the treaty which they had signed in his behalf, with the ministers of the Allied Powers.

After it had been read to him, he dictated to the Duke of Bassano his abdication in the following words:—

" Les puissances Alliées ayant proclâmé que l'Empereur Napoléon était le seul obstacle au rétablissement de la paix en Europe, l'Empereur Napoléon, fidèle à son serment, déclare qu'il renonce pour lui et ses héritiers aux Trônes de France et d'Italie, parce qu'il n'est aucun sacrifice personnel, même celui de la vie, qu'il ne soit prêt à faire à l'intérêt de la France."

Having signed this instrument, he recommended to the officers about him to attach themselves to the dynasty which was now called to govern them. He spoke favourably of Louis XVIII., and believing him to be a person of considerable talent, augured well of the system of government he would pursue. Many of the difficulties he would have to contend against, however, he thought he would have some difficulty in overcoming. The intrigues of the Faubourg St. Germain, and the Imperial Guard, were amongst those which would cause him the greatest annoyance; yet, by firmness and prudence, they were to be got the better of. At the termination of this discourse, Buonaparte gave permission to those about him to proceed to Paris whenever they desired it, recommending those who remained to send in their adhesion to the new government.

In conformity with this permission, Marshal Berthier immediately transmitted the adhesion of the army, promising its fidelity to the Prince whom the French nation had recalled to the throne of his ancestors.

Such was the extraordinary termination of the French Revolution. Splendid as were many of the achievements by which it was marked, rivetted as it was considered to be in the feelings of the vast majority of the French people, yet it passed away, seemingly without a struggle. From the moment the French capital was occupied by the Allies, peace and good will seemed at once established among the various people, so singularly brought together, and so lately in violent hostility to each other. The spirit of conquest and oppression, from which had flowed such vast desolation throughout the world, seemed at once to be extinguished. Though vengeance and the desire of war were still the feelings by which the French armies were animated, yet at Paris these sentiments were absorbed in the general joy and satisfaction of every class of its inhabitants. Gratitude to the Allies, for the magnanimity of their conduct was the constant source of popular declamation; nor was the character of Prince Schwarzenberg ill suited to be the instrument by which those feelings should be perpetuated. At the gates of Paris, to which, under the most arduous circumstances, he had triumphantly conducted the allied armies, he laid aside the character of an enemy, to assume what was far more congenial to the kindness and benevolence of his nature—that of a friend and peace-maker. Whenever the best feelings of the human breast were necessary to the accomplishment of his objects, Prince Schwarzenberg was certain of success; no man possessed them in a more eminent degree. He has now, like his great companion in arms, Marshal Blucher, been taken from among us, regretted and admired by all who knew him, by all who were acquainted with the virtues which adorned his character, and who are able to appreciate the loss of so brave and excellent a soldier, and so good a man.

We have now conducted these memoirs to their termination. To recapitulate the events which succeeded to the cessation of hostilities, would only be to repeat what has already in so many shapes been related. For the glory of England, and to complete the renown already acquired by her armies, the spirit of the Revolution had not so completely subsided in France, as not to afford another opportunity of triumphing over the great military character, who at this period seemed for ever to have been deprived of the means of disturbing the tranquillity of the world. But to those, who were fortunate enough to have been actors in the memorable scene of Waterloo, devolves the task of transmitting its details. Be it permitted, however, here to remark, that when Buonaparte quitted Fontainebleau, unaccompanied by any escort, and conducted only by the four commissioners appointed by the Allies, with whom he traversed the greater part of the

French Empire, no human foresight could have predicted that he would again appear the uncontrolled ruler and governor of a people, who with so much indifference and unconcern allowed him to be taken from amongst them.

APPENDIX.

APPENDIX.

No. I.

Statement of the Allied Forces in the beginning of August.

Russians in Silesia	80,000	
Prussian troops of the line	40,000	
Landwehr picked and exercised	30,000	
In Silesia		150,000

Corps of the Prince Royal of Sweden.

Swedes	25,000	
Bulow	25,000	
Walmoden	11,000	
Woronzoff	4,000	85,000
Tauenzein	6,000	
German Legion	6,000	
Winzingerode	8,000	

Russian Reserves.

Tolstoy	60,000	
Docktoroff	14,000	
Labanoff	30,000	
		104,000

Austrians.

Troops of the line in Bohemia and other parts	150,000	150,000
Austrian Reserves	100,000	100,000
Rest of the Prussian Landwehr	90,000	90,000
To which should be added the Russian reinforcements already in march to join their army, amounting to	107,000	107,000
	Total	777,000

No. II.

Three different approximative Statements of the Force of the French Army, received at the head-quarters of the Allies.

		Aug. 17th.	Sept. 20th.	Sept. 24th.
Assembled in front of Dresden, and opposed to the Great Allied Army.	Old Guard	6,607	4,000	25,000
	Young Guard	32,000	24,000	3,000
	Cavalry of the Guard	10,500	6,000	
	Vandamme	25,000	4,000	6,000
	Victor	21,000	18,000	14,000
	Marmont	30,000	20,000	18,000
	Poniatowski	15,000	10,000	11,000
	St. Cyr	31,000	20,000	20,000
	Latour Maubourg Cavalry	10,000	6,000	7,000
		181,107	112,000	104,000
Opposed to the Northern Army under the Crown Prince of Sweden.	Bertrand	21,000	14,000	15,000
	Regnier	20,000	8,000	6,000
	Oudinot	24,000	10,000	18,000
	Arrighi and Kellerman } Cavalry	10,000	7,000	6,000
		75,000	39,000	45,000
Opposed to Marshal Blucher.	Souham	32,000	22,000	15,000
	Lauriston	35,000	10,000	7,000
	Macdonald	21,000	14,000	12,000
	Sebastiani and Milhaud } Cavalry	13,000	7,000	5,000
		101,000	53,000	39,000
		75,000	39,000	45,000
		181,107	112,000	104,000
	Grand Total	357,107	204,000	188,000

ORDER OF BATTLE OF THE GREAT FREN
17TH (

NAPOLEON

Marshal BE

Extreme Right, 4th Corps d'Armée, General

Right, under the orders of Marshal Murat
{ 8th Corps, Prince Poniatowsl
2d ,, Marshal Victor .
4th ,, (cavalry) Gen. Ke

Centre,
{ Infantry, under Marshal Aug
5th Corps, General Lauristor
11th ,, Marshal Macdone
1st ,, (cavalry) General L
2d ,, ,, General S
5th ,, ,, General M

Left, under the orders of Marshal Ney,
{ 6th Corps, Marshal Marmon
3d ,, General Souham
7th ,, General Regnier
3d ,, (cavalry) General /

Reserve,
{ Old Guard . . . . . .
Young Guard . . . .
Cavalry, General Nansouty

Not Comprised.

1st Corps of Infantry, General Mouton, a
10th ,, ,, General Rapp, shu
13th ,, ,, Marshal Davoust,
14th ,, ,, Marshal St. Cyr, a

No. III.—*Approximative Statement of the*

NCENTRATED NEAR LEIPZIG, ON THE
813.

n person,

of the Staff.

Effective Men.		Effective Men.	
Infantry.	Cavalry.	Infantry.	Cavalry.
15,000		15,000	
8,000		24,000	3,000
16,000			
	3,000		
39,000	3,000		
10,000			
9,000			
15,000		34,000	12,300
	4,500		
	4,800		
	3,000		
34,000	12,300		
18,000			
15,000		41,000	3,000
8,000			
	3,000		—
41,000	3,000		
4,000		20,000	4,800
16,000			
	4,800		
20,000	4,800	134,000	23,100
	Total	157,100 men.	

resden.

lbe.
resden.

Strength of the Contending Armies in the Battle of L...

ORDER OF BATTLE OF THE ALLIED ARMIE...

Their Majestie...

PRINCE SCHV...

Great Army,
- Austrians, Prince Schwarzenberg,
  - Advanced Guard, Prin...
  - 1st Corps d'Armée, Cou...
  - 2d ,, Cou...
  - 3d ,, Cou...
  - 4th ,, Cou...
  - Reserve, Prin...
- Principal Corps, Barclay de Tolly,
  - Russians { 1st Corps, C...
  -           { 2d ,, P...
  - Prussians 2d Corps, G...
- Reserve, Grand Duke Constantine,
  - Russians { 3d Corps of (...
  -          { 5th ,, of I...
  - Austrian, Russian, and ...
  - Gallitzin ...

Silesian Army, under Marshal Blucher,
- Russians, under Count Langeron,
  - 6th Corps d'Armée, Pri...
  - 8th ,, Ger...
  - 9th ,, Ger...
  - 10th ,, Ger...
  - Cavalry, Ger...
- Russians, under Baron Sacken,
  - 4th Corps d'Armée, Ger...
  - 7th ,, Ger...
  - Cavalry, Ger...
- Prussians, 1st Corps, under Ger...

Army of the North,
- Prussians, { 3d Corps d'Armée, Ger...
  -          { 4th ,, Gen...
- Swedes, Marshal Steding . .
- Russians, Corps of Winzingerode

Detachments from the Army of Poland, Russians and ...

Not C...

The Austro-Bavarian Army, marching on ...
The Army of Count Walmoden, opposed to ...
The Detachments of the Army of Poland, ...

UND LEIPZIG, ON THE 17TH OF OCTOBER, 1813.

ROR of RUSSIA,
ROR of AUSTRIA,
of PRUSSIA,
, General-in-Chief.

	Infantry.	Cavalry.	Infantry.	Cavalry.
chtenstein .	2,000	1,600		
. . . .	9,000	1,200		
. . . .	6,000	1,000	39,000	10,800
. . . .	7,000	1,500		
. . . .	9,000	2,000		
nbourg . .	6,000	3,500		
tein . . .	8,000		16,000	
Wurtemberg	8,000			
. . . .	24,000	5,000	24,000	5,000
unt Rayefsky	8,000			
unt Yermolow	10,000		18,000	8,000
alry, Prince				
. . . .		8,000		
	97,000	23,800		
. . . .	8,000			
. . . .	8,000			
. . . .	8,000		32,000	5,000
ch . . .	8,000			
. . . .		5,000		
. . . .	6,000			
ki	6,000		12,000	3,000
hichoff . .		3,000		
. . . .	25,000	5,000	25,000	5,000
	69,000	13,000		
. . . .	20,000	4,000	32,000	4,000
. . . .	12,000			
. . . .	18,000	2,000	18,000	2,000
. . . .	14,000	3,000	14,000	3,000
	64,000	9,000		
. Benningsen			20,000	4,000
			250,000	49,800

Total   299,800 men.

)ust.
olstoi, opposed to Marshal St. Cyr, before Dresden.

No. IV.

List of the Losses of the Enemy in Prisoners, Guns, and Ammunition Waggons, from the Month of April, 1813, to the end of October, in the same Year.

Date.	Names of Places.	Commanders.	Prisoners.	Guns.	Ammunition Waggons.
11 April	Mockern	Yorck	927	1	3
13	Langensalza	Hellwig	. . .	5	1
28	Halle	Bülow	428	3	3
2 May	Lunebourg	Dornberg	2,300	11 *2 of them were spiked and thrown into the river*	
2	Gross Greschen	Wittgenstein	100	10	
14	Königsbruck	Kowaisky	183		
12—15	. . . . .	Miloradovitsch	306		
18	Keinitz of Königsbruck	Kowaisky	226		
19—20	Bautzen & Königswarten	Barclay de Tolly	2,700	12	
20	Baruth	Bulow	300		
20	Zwickau	Colonel	. . .	21	40 destroyed.
24	Connern	Cossacks	380		
26	Haynau	Blucher	Considerable number of Prisoners has not been stated.		
31	Brinkenau	Russio-German Legion	500		
31	Mark Lissa ,	Kaisaroff	80	6	

APPENDIX.

No. IV.—continued.

Date.	Names of Places.	Commanders.	Prisoners.	Guns.	Ammunition Waggons.
4 June	Luckau . . .	Bulow . . .	500	3	
29	Halberstadt	Czerniczeff .	540	14	60
17 Aug.	{ Environs of Wittenberg	Borstel . .	152		
18	Leignitz . .	Sacken & Yorck	366		
19	Lahn . . -	Rudzewitsch .	300	8	
23	Gross Beeren .	{ Crown Prince of Sweden .	2,000	26	60
26	Katzbach . .	Blucher . . .	18,000	103	230
27	Beltzig . . .	Hirschfeld . .	3,500	8	
27	Lobenau . .	Blucher . .	305		
28	Luckau . .	Wobeser . .	800	9	Military Stores.
30	{ Culm and in the Mountains	{ Ostermau and Kleist . .	9,000	83	105 and Military Stores.
1 Sept.	Near Gorlitz .	Falkenhausen	. . .	1	
2	Wurschen . .	Prince Madatoff	711	. . .	100
9	{ Dresden and Bautzen .		1,200	.	200 destroyed.
6	Dennewitz .	{ Crown Prince of Sweden .	10,000	80	400
16	Queefurth . .	Fabeck .	442		
16	Dannenburg .	Walmoden .	3,300	8	52
17	Nollendorf . ·	Schwarzenberg	2,000	7	
18	Freyberg . .	Scheiter . .	648		
18	Weissenfels .	Thieleman . .	1,291		
19	Borack . r .	{ Kowaisky and Dobschnitz .	516		

No. IV.—continued.

Date.	Names of Places.	Commanders.	Prisoners.	Guns.	Ammunition Waggons.
23 Sept.	Beschofswerda	Katzler . . .	310		
25	Brunswick - .	Marwitz . .	323		
28	Altenburg . .	Platow . . .	1,000	5	
28	Cassel . . .	Czerniczeff .	650	41	
3 Oct.	Wartenburg .	Blucher . .	700	14	50
12	Neustadt . .	Colonel .	200		
14	Bremen . .	Tettenborn .	.	.	
11—14	Gross Hayn	Falkenhausen	. .	. . .	80 and a great deal of Ammunition in Boats.
16—19	Leipzig .	Allied Army	unhurt 30,000. Wounded and Sick 22,000	250	900
20	Lutzen . . .	Wasiltschichoff	2,100		
21	Freyburg . .	Yorck . . .	4,000	40	many
21	Buttersledt .	Bubna . . .	600	. . .	many
22	Gotha . . .	Chrapowitsky .	973	. . .	many
26	Keinitz of Gotha	Rudzewitsch .	2,000		
Near	Erfurth were	blown up by Buo	naparte's	Orders	600
		Total....	129,162	801	2,906

APPENDIX.

No. V.

Statement shewing the organization of the Army of Germany, Nov. 28, 1813.

First Corps.

Bavaria . . .	36,000	Wrede . . { With the Austrians.

Second Corps.

Hanover . .	20,000
Brunswick . .	6,000
Oldenburg . .	1,500
Hanseatic Towns .	3,500
Mecklenberg Schwerin	1,900

32,900 Walmoden—In the North.

Third Corps.

Kingdom of Saxony,	20,000
Saxe Weimar	800
Saxe Gotha	1,100
Schwartzburg .	650
Anhalt . . .	800

23,350 D. of Weimar—Ditto.

Fourth Corps.

Hesse Cassel . . .	12,000	P. El. of Hesse. { With Blucher.

Fifth Corps.

Berg . .	5,000
Waldeck .	400
Lippe . .	650
Nassau . . .	1,680
Cobourg .	400
Meinningen . .	300
Hildburghausen .	200
Mecklenburg Strelitz .	600

9,230 D. of Cobourg—Ditto.

APPENDIX. 323

SIXTH CORPS.

Wurtzburg	2,000
Darmstadt	4,000
Frankfort and Ysenburg	2,800
The Reuss	450
	9,250 { P. Philip of H. / Hombourg. } With the Austrians.

SEVENTH CORPS.

Wurtemburg . 12,000 { Pr. Royal of / Wurtemberg. } Ditto.

EIGHTH CORPS.

Baden	10,000
Hohenzollern	290
Liechtenstein	40
	10,380 { Pr. Eugene of / Wurtemberg. } With the Russians of the Great Army.

145,560
Landwehr . . 145,560

Total 291,120

Y

No. VI.

Account of the Revenue of the States of the Rhine, according to the most accurate Statistical Data.

	Florins.
Bavaria	30,000,000
Wurtemberg	11,000,000
Saxony	16,000,000
Hesse	4,000,000
Brunswick	1,200,000
Baden	4,000,000
Darmstadt	3,500,000
Franckfort	2,500,000
Wurtzburg	3,000,000
Houses of Nassau	1,700,000
Weymar	1,000,000
Gotha and Altenburg	1,500,000
Meinningen	350,000
Hilburghausen	150,000
Coburg	400,000
Anhalt Dessau	400,000
Anhalt Bernburg	300,000
Anhalt Cothen	220,000
Mecklenburg Schwerin	1,000,000
Mecklenburg Strelitz	500,000
Ysenburg	280,000
Schwartzburg Sonderhausen	250,000
Schwartzburg Rudolstadt	200,000
Lippe Detmold	250,000
Lippe Schaumberg	80,000
Waldeck	380,000
Hohenzollern Hochningen	80,000
Hohenzollern Sigmaringen	300,000
Principality of Lepan	40,000
Liechtenstein	40,000
Princes and Counts Reuss	350,000
	84,970,000

No. VII.

Copies of Letters from Prince Schwarzenberg, to Marshal Gouvion St. Cyr, upon the Capitulation of Dresden, &c.

Copie d'une Lettre du Maréchal Prince de Schwarzenberg au Maréchal Comte Gouvion St. Cyr; en date de Francfort S.M., 24 Novembre, 1813.

J'ai reçu la lettre que votre Ex. m'a fait l'honneur de m' adresser en date du 20 Nov. Le Général Comte de Klenau, avant que d'avoir signé une Capitulation à des conditions auxquelles il ne se trouvait pas autorisé, avait eu soin de vous en avertir, Monsieur le Maréchal, en ajoutant qu'il se flattait que la famille Royale de Saxe, entreprendrait de plaider sa cause auprès de son auguste Souverain. J'aurais désiré qu'étant informé de ce procédé illégal, au lieu de passer promtement à l'exécution, vous eussiez attendu que le Général Comte de Klenau fut investi de pouvoirs suffisans et qu'au moins, pour votre propre garantie, vous eussiez attendu ma ratification.

Le devoir que m'imposent les intérêts de tant de peuples réunis pour la même cause, ne me permêt pas d'admettre aucune vue secondaire. J'ai dû annuller cette Capitulation, comme illégale et aucunement analogue à votre position et à celle des armées Alliées.

J'ai ordonné qu'on vous, accorde, Monsieur le Maréchal, toutes les facilités pour rentrer à Dresde, et qu'on vous mette scrupuleusement en possession de tous les moyens de defense dont vous pouviez disposer avant votre sortie.

Je suis loin de méconnaître que cette complication peut vous offrir des inconvéniens mais je n'en suis pas moins convaincu qu'ils sont plus que compensés par ceux qui en résultent pour les armées Alliées. Des forces considérables se trouvent paralysées au lieu d'agir vivement à une époque aussi importante; la place de Dresde même, gêne essentiellement toutes nos communications ; les habitans ont eu le tems de se ravitailler, et ils ont profité du premier moment pour prendre tous les arràngemens propres à rendre la salubrité à leurs foyers.

Malgré toutes ces considérations importantes, je n'ai pas hésité un instant de vous inviter, Monsieur le Maréchal, à rentrer dans votre ancienne position. C'est à Dresde où l'on vous rendra vos armes, c'est là où je vous reconnaitrai entièrement libre. Hors de Dresde, je ne puis vous considérer que comme prisonnier de guerre ; et comme tel je dois vous donner les directions que je juge nécessaires.

Agréez., etc. etc. etc.

Copie d'une Lettre du Maréchal Prince de Schwarzenberg au Maréchal Gouvion St. Cyr.

Francfort, le 27 Nov., 1813.

Le Colonel Comte de Latour m'a remis la lettre que votre Ex. m'a fait l'honneur de m'écrire en date du 22.

Puisque vous déclarez, Monsieur le Maréchal, ne pas vouloir consentir aux propositions qui vous ont été faites, tendantes à vous replacer dans l'attitude que vous aviez avant la capitulation, il ne me reste qu'à vous inviter à suivre, comme prisonnier de guerre, la direction que les circonstances m'obligent à vous donner.

Veuillez être persuadé, Monsieur le Maréchal, que je m'occuperai du mode à établir pour l'échange des troupes qui formaient la garnison de Dresde.

Agréez., etc. etc. etc.

Copie d'un Ordre ouvert qui a été remis au Colonel Comte de Latour; en date de Francfort, le 27 Nov., 1813.

M. le Maréchel Comte Gouvion St. Cyr ayant déclaré qu'il n'acceptait pas, pour lui et pour la garnison, la proposition qui lui avait été faite de rentrer dans la ville de Dresde, où on s'était engagé à le remettre en possession de tous les moyens de défence dont il avait disposé avant la capitulation,—ils seront dirigés, en leur qualité de prisonniers de guerre, vers la Bohême dans les Etats Autrichiens où ils resteront jusqu'au moment où ils pourront être échangés d'après le mode qui sera établi.

Il est ordonné à tous les individus appartenant à la garnison de Dresde de suivre exactement les colonnes dont ils font partie.

Ceux qui s'en écarteraient arbitrairement se mettront dans la cas d'être arrêtés, et cesseront d'avoir droit à la protection spéciale accordée à tous les prisonniers de guerre.

M. le Général d'artillerie, Marquis de Chastêler, est chargé de faire exécuter cet ordre.

No. VIII.

Plan proposed at the Head-quarters at Frankfort, for the Operations of the Allies.

Against Marshal Davoust	{ Swedes	10,000	
	{ Walmoden	15,000	25,000

The Prince Royal of Sweden.

Destined to pass the Rhine near Cologne, and separate Holland from France.	{ Swedes	15,000	
	{ Winzingerode	30,000	
	{ Bulow	20,000	
	{ Saxons	15,000	80,000

Total . . . 105,000

Marshal Blücher.

Destined to cover the country on the two banks of the Mayn.	{ Yorck	12,000	
	{ Langeron	30,000	
	{ Sacken	10,000	52,000
	{ Hessians	10,000	
	{ Westphalians (new troops)	20,000	
	{ Reinforcements	15,000	
	{ Wurtembergers, Baden, and Darmstadt	10,000	
	{ Kleist	15,000	70,000

Total . . . 122,000

APPENDIX.

Great Army.

To act through Switzerland and penetrate by the Jura into France
{ Guards and Reserves 30,000
Wittgenstein . 10,000
Reinforcements . 15,000
Austrians 120,000
Bavarians . 30,000 }
——— 205,000

In Italy..

Destined to ascend towards the Var and to communicate with the army of Ld. Wellington. } Austrians 65,000

Different Corps for the Siege of the fortresses on the Elbe.

Benningsen	20,000
Tauenzein	. 28,000
Klenau .	18,000
Chasteler . .	9,000
Tolstoi . . .	25,000
	——— 100,000
Grand Total .	600,000

RECAPITULATION.

Austrians	. 215,000
Russians	147,000
Prussians .	. . 87,000
Bavarians .	30,000
Westphalians	. 20,000
Hessians	. 10,000
Carried over	509,000

APPENDIX.

Brought forward	509,000	
Saxons	15,000	
Swedes . .	25,000	
Walmoden	11,000	
Wurtemberg, Baden, and Darmstadt .	10,000	
Reinforcements	30,000	
		600,000

Upon this statement it should be remarked, that neither the Hessian troops put down as 10,000 men, nor the Westphalians as 20,000, were at that time raised; that the Russian reinforcements were merely said to be upon their march; that the Saxons, here estimated at 15,000, did not bring more than 7,000; that General Count Langeron's corps was considerably weaker than it here appears; and that the Austrian force, called 120,000 men, could not exceed 80,000. A deduction of 118,000 may fairly be made from the 600,000; leaving a total of 482,000 men.

No. IX.

Proposal for the Operations of the Allied Armies, transmitted from the Head-Quarters of the Prince of Sweden, November 2d, 1813.

It is proposed that the great army should place its left upon the Mein ; and its right upon the Sieg.

The Silesian army, its left on the Sieg, and its right towards Dusseldorf.

The northern army, after destroying that of Davoust, should undertake the siege of Wesel, and move upon Holland.

The whole of these armies, after being allowed the time necessary to recruit, should pass to the left of the Rhine.

No. X.

Number, disposition, and employment of the Forces of the Allies, proposed from the head-quarters of Marshal Blucher, Nov. 24, 1813.

Disposable at the present moment.

		Men.
A.	Russian guards and grenadier reserves	30,000
	Corps d'armée of Wittgenstein	10,000
	Austrian army	120,000
	Silesian army	52,000
	Bavarian army	30,000
		242,000

Disposable some weeks hence.

		Men.
B.	Corps d'armée of Kleist	15,000
	Troops of the Princes of the Ex-confederation of the Rhine (of the first formation)	20,000
		35,000

Reinforcements on their March.

		Men.
C.	To the corps of Wittgenstein	15,000
	To the corps of Langeron and Sacken	15,000
	To the corps of Yorck and Kleist	12,000
		42,000

Troops disposable hereafter.

				Men.
D.	All the troops which will become disposable after the reduction of the fortresses on the Elbe.			
	Klenau		18,000	
	Chasteler		9,000	
	Tolstoi		25,000	
				52,000
	Ulterior formations of the Princes of the confederation of the Rhine			150,000
	Troops which Bavaria has offered to furnish, besides those already in action			40,000
				242,000

Of these 242,000 men, half only shall be reckoned 121,000

1. The 30,000 Bavarians, or an equal number of Austrians, will remain on the right bank of the Rhine to observe Mayence. They will not go too near to it, but will take up a strong position some leagues from that fortress, and will confine themselves to forcing the neighbouring villages to evacuate whatever may be useful to the garrison.

2. 212,000 combatants will pass the Rhine on different points, leaving corps of observation before Landau and Strasbourg, and will take the direction of Metz and Nancy.

3. After the reduction of Erfurt, or of Dresden, the corps of Kleist, and all the troops of the ex-confederation of the Rhine which will then be disposable, will march towards the Upper Rhine, whence, according to circumstances, they will either relieve the corps of observation in Alsace, or invade Franche-Comté by Switzerland. In the first instance, the corps which will be relieved will form a reserve for the grand army.

4. All troops of the German Princes, which shall become disposable at a subsequent period, will form themselves into a grand reserve, and will take their position wherever the course of operations may render it advisable.

5. The corps of Walmoden, a part of the corps of Winzingerode, and that of Bülow, will be directed towards the Lower Rhine, will pass that river, and try to force their way by Liége and Givet.

6. The corps of Thieleman will pass the Rhine at Ehrenbreitstein, will take up the strong position of the Chartreuse near Coblentz, and will, according to circumstances, either support the operations of the corps directed upon Givet, or those of the grand army.

7. The Swedish corps d'armée, part of the corps of Winzingerode, and all the troops which will be disposable after the reduction of the fortresses on the Elbe, will be opposed to Davoust and to the Danes.

8. Supposing the grand army, while it marches on Metz and Nancy, to leave behind it 35,000 men to observe the fortresses in Alsace, it still brings 182,000 men to the field; from which, deducting 7,000 for sick, &c., there remains 175,000 effective men. These will be joined by 42,000 from the reinforcements

(C.), and will form an army of 217,000 men, with a reserve of 100,000*, and a second reserve of 121,000†. There is nothing to prevent the proposed operations from commencing immediately. They are independent of those in Italy, and of the army of Lord Wellington; and, whatever successes either of these may obtain, must be of advantage to the armies on the Rhine, and contribute to their success, without such being a necessary condition of them. By this operation, the enemy must place strong garrisons, munitions, artillery, and provisions of all kinds, in Mayence, Strasbourg, Luxembourg, Metz, Thionville, Landau, Brissac, Sarre-Louis, and all the small fortified towns of the Vosges, and on the Rhine. He will consequently have but very few troops, with which to form an army capable of resisting the allies, nor could he supply it with artillery and ammunition. If after the cómplete formation of the troops of the Germanic confederation we should not have dictated peace to France, our immense masses of troops would then give us the means of menacing the capital, and reducing it by taking away its subsistence. When the grand army shall be arrived before Metz and Nancy, the following will be the disposition of the forces:

Near Metz	212,000
In Alsace	35,000
Near Mayence	30,000
Near Coblentz	15,000
In Alsace and Switzerland	35,000
Near Liége	50,000
Grand reserve	121,000
	498,000

* Near Mayence	30,000
In Alsace	35,000
Troops mentioned under B.	35,000
	100,000

† Troops mentioned under D.

APPROXIMATIVE STATEMENT OF

Under th

Left Wing, } 3d Corps d'Armée,
Count Giulay,

{ We
  the
  acc
  the

Centre,
under
the orders of
Baron
Sacken.

⎧ Division Saz,
⎪   ,,   Stawitzky,
⎪ Brigade Seliwanow,
⎪
⎪ Division Tallisin,
⎪   ,,   Bernodossow,
⎨
⎪   ,,   Udom,
⎪   ,,   Karnielow,
⎪
⎪   ,,   Landskoy,
⎪   ,,   Pantschulidzew,
⎪
⎪ Brigade Karpow,
⎩   ,,   Biron de Courland,

{ Un
  alo
  Ro

{ Ur
  to
  of

{ Fo
  tw
  tw
  Al

{ Fo
  of
  Ge

{ Co
  wi
  Co
  wh

Right Wing, { 4th Corps d'Armée,   { M
                                          la

ExtremeRight, { Bavarian Corps,   { U
                                          tov

Russian Corps of Grena- { A
            diers,   th
Russian Cuirassiers,   { ce

Russian and Prussian { B
    Guards,   or

With 28

This Statement of the relative forces is taken from the V

COMPOSING THE ARMIES OF THE ALLIES AND OF
WITH AN APPROXIMATIVE STATEMENT

f Marshal BLUCHER.

	Infantry.	Cavalry.
ig the right bank of the Aube in Deinville, and merely, by an ence, detached a division on	12,000	1,500
of Count Lieven, were to move road of Bar, and attack la	8,000	
ons of Prince Scherbatow, were vith the foregoing, on the right	8,000	
nd line in conjunction with the 'isions of Cavalry, in rear of the , and under the orders of Count	6,000	
nd line, with the two divisions ified above, under the orders of schicow		8,000
column under Count Lieven, ice Scherbatow		1,800
olumn under Prince Scherbatow, Prince of Wurtemberg		1,500
clance into the wood towards iaumenil	12,000	2,500
s of Count Wrede, was to move ers and Chaumenil	18,000	3,600
ement of the action in position ossancourt, and in rear of the	8,000	4,000
al and Ailleville, waiting further	12,000	4,800
Totals	84,000	27,000
tillery.	106,700	

valier Koch. Whatever may be the precision of the numbers herein
60,000 men; with regard to the French force, it

FRANCE, IN THE BATTLE OF THE FIR
OF THEIR RELATIVE FORCES.

U₁

Right Wing, ⎧ Brigade Picquet,
General of   ⎨ Division Dufour,
Division,   ⎪
Count Ricard,⎩   ,,   Ricard,

Centre,   ⎧ ,,   Desnoettes,
             ⎪ ,,   Colbert,
             ⎪ ,,   Guyot,
             ⎨ ,,   Duhesme,
             ⎪ ,,   ,,
             ⎪ ,,   Piré,
             ⎪ ,,   Briche,
             ⎩ ,,   L'Heritier,

Left Wing,   ⎧ ,,   Doumere,
             ⎨
             ⎩ ,,   Lagrange,

             ,,   Rothembou

Reserves,   ⎧ ,,   Decouz,
             ⎨ ,,   Meunier,
             ⎩ ,,   Defrance,

With 1

given of the French corps, those of the Allies
was always rated, by the Allies at 50,000.

ARY, AT LA ROTHIÈRE AND BRIENNE,

and of NAPOLEON.

	Infantry.	Cavalry.
ed in front, and covering the in-between the Division Dufour Rothière		640
mns of battalions, resting upon ve of the Aube	3,400	
In second line, in rear of the	3,500	
ition in rear of la Rothière, to ght, and under the orders of Nansouty		850 880 750
ing la Rothière, Petit Mesgnil, aumeril	4,200	
ing la Gibrie	1,900	
ed in two lines, between la re and Chaumenil		870 1,250 1,000
yed on the plain ground of Mor- and Beauvais, in front of La		1,800
ying La Chaise and Morvilliers,	4,600	
ition to the left, and in line with ie la Vielle	4,900	
g from Lesmont upon the farm gné	1,800 3,000	
ing the bridge of Lesmont . .		800
Totals	27,300	8,840
tillery.	36,140	

ggerated; their numbers in the field that day not having exceeded

No. XII.

Chatillon, 9me Février, 1814.

Je me propose de demander aux Plénipotentiaires des Cours Alliées, si la France en consentant, ainsi qu'ils l'ont demande, à rester dans ses anciennes limites, obtiendra immédiatement un armistice. Si par un tel sacrifice un armistice peut être sur le champ obtenu je serai prêt à le faire.—Je serai prêt encore, dans cette supposition, à remettre sur le champ une partie des places que ce sacrifice devra nous faire perdre. J'ignore si les Plénipotentiaries des Cours Alliées sont autorisés à répondre affermativement à cette question et s'ils ont des pouvoirs pour conclure cet armistice, s'ils n'en ont pas, personne ne peut autant que votre Excellence contribuer à leur en faire donner. Les raisons qui me portent à l'en prier ne me semblent pas tellement particulières à la France, qu'elles ne doivent intéresser qu'elle seule. Je supplie Votre Excellence de mettre ma lettre sous les yeux du Père de l'Impératrice, qu' il voie les sacrifices que nous sommes prêts à faire, et qu' il décide.

(Signé) Le Duc de Vicence.

A son Excellence
Le Prince de Metternich,
etc. etc. etc.

No. XIII.

Translation of the letter from Prince Schwarzenberg to Marshal Berthier.

Dated Bray, 17th February, 1814.

Mon Seigneur,

I charge my aid-de-camp Count Paar to deliver to your Highness this letter.

Having received intelligence that the Plenipotentiaries were yesterday to sign the preliminaries of Peace on the conditions proposed by Monsieur de Caulincourt and accepted by the Allied Sovereigns, I have, in consequence of the orders I yesterday received, stopped offensive movements against the French army. I learn, Prince, that on your side they continue. I propose to you therefore, (with the view of putting a stop to the effusion of blood,) equally to cause them to cease. Otherwise I could not prevent the continuation of those operations, which a belief in the conclusion of a preliminary treaty, had induced me to suspend.

I authorize Count Paar to give you on the arrangements to be taken for this object, all the explanations your Highness may desire.

(*Signed*) SCHWARZENBERG.

No. XIV.

Intercepted Letter of Buonaparte.

Mon Amie,

J'ai été tous les jours à cheval ; le 20 j'ai pris Arcis sur Aube. L'ennemi m'y attaqua à 8 heures du soir ; le même soir je l'ai battu, et lui ai fait 4,000 morts ; je lui ai pris 2 piéces de canon et même repris 2 ; ayant quitté le 21, l'armée ennemie s'est mise en battaille pour protéger la marche de ses armées sur Brienne, et sur Bar sur Aube, j'ai décidé de me porter sur la Marne et ses environs afin de la pousser plus loin de Paris, en me rapprochant de mes *places*. Je serai ce soir à St. Dizier.

Adieu, mon amie, embrassez mon fils.

No. XV.

Extract of the new French Constitution of April 6th, 1814.

1. Le Gouvernement Français monarchique, héréditaire, &c
2. Le peuple Français appelle librement au trône de France, Louis Stanislas Xavier de France, frère du dernier Roi.
3. La Noblesse ancienne reprend ses titres, la nouvelle conserve les siens. La légion d'honneur est maintenue avec ses prérogatives. Le Roi déterminera les décorations.
4. Le pouvoir exécutif appartient au Roi.
5. Le Roi, le Sénat, et le Corps Législatif concourent à la formation des loix; les projets de loi peuvent également être proposés dans le Sénat et dans le Corps Législatif.
6. Il y a 150 Sénateurs au moins, et 200 au plus. Leur dignité est héréditaire et inamovible de mâle en mâle. Ils sont nommés par le Roi.

Les Sénateurs actuels restent Sénateurs, et ont les mêmes avantages. Les membres de la famille Royale sont Sénateurs de droit.

7. Le Corps Législatif a droit de discussion. Il s'assemble tous les ans de droit au 1er Octobre. Le Roi peut le convoquer ou le dissoudre.
8. Le Sénat, le Corps Législatif, et les Colléges Electoraux, et les Assemblées de Canton élisent leur Président.

Les Ministres peuvent être membres soit du Sénat, soit du Corps Législatif.

9. Egalité de proportion dans l'impôt. Il ne peut être etabli ni perçu s'il n'a été consenti par le Corps Législatif et le Sénat. L'impôt foncier ne peut être établi que pour un an.
10. Indépendance du pouvoir judiciaire.

APPENDIX. 341

11. Les Jurés maintenus
12. Les Militaires pennsionnés conservent leurs honoraires et leurs grades.
13. Inviolabilité du Roi. Responsabilité des Ministres.
14. Liberté des Cultes.
15. Liberté de la Presse.
16. Dette publique garantie.
17. Vente des domaines nationaux maintenue.
18. Aucun Français ne peut être recherché pour les opinions ou votes qu'il a pu emettre.
19. Quelques articles de détail.

En tout 29 articles dont le dernier est :
" La présente Constitution sera soumise au peuple Français
" dans la forme qui sera réglée. Louis Stanislas Xavier sera
" proclamé Roi des Français aussitôt qu'il aura juré et signé
" par un acte portant, 'J'accepte la Constitution, je jure de
" l'observer, et la faire observer.' Ce serment sera réitéré
" dans la solemnité où il recevra le serment de fidélité des
" Français."

ADDENDA.

ADDENDA.

No. I.

Lettre de S. M. Le Roi de Bavière à S. M. L'Empereur de Russie.

Monsieur mon frère et beau-frère,

La lettre que V. M. I. m'a fait l'amitié de m'écrire m'a procuré une satisfaction d'autant plus vive qu'elle contient des assurances si précises des sentimens pour ma personne et pour mes états qu'elle a bien voulu me répéter plus d'une fois, et auxquelles je n'ai cessé d'attacher le plus grand prix. C'est par une suite bien naturelle de la confiance entière, et de la juste reconnaissance qu'elles m'inspirent, que je ne fais aucune difficulté de m'en rapporter entièrement à elle pour tout ce qui concerne mes intérêts, et ceux de mes peuples.

Etranger, à tous les titres, à une guerre, qui en contrariant toutes mes inclinations personnelles ne pouvait m'offrir que des périls, des dépenses, je n'en ai pas moins rempli, avec une fidélité scrupuleuse, les engagemens que j'avais contractés dans d'autres tems, et sous d'autres auspices, et que j'avais partagés avec presque toute l'Europe. Aujourd'hui, que toutes les circonstances concourent à me dégager de ces obligations, je ne puis que me féliciter de pouvoir rétablir des rapports que j'aurais si sincèrement souhaité ne voir jamais interrompus. Je n'ai qu'un vœu à former, c'est le prompt rétablissement d'une paix solide et durable, dont mes sujets, autant et plus que d'autres, éprouvent le besoin pressant, et la conservation intacte des états que je possède. Je concourerai avec zèle, suite, et de tous mes moyens à tout ce qui pourra conduire à ce double but. J'ai déjà envoyé au corps du Général **Raglawich** l'ordre de revenir en Bavière. Il n'y a eu jusqu'ici aucune hostilité d'exercée entre mes troupes et l'armée Autrichienne du Prince de Reuss. Le Général Wrede a depuis longtems l'ordre précis de s'abstenir de tout mouvement offensif. Il serait facile de prolonger cet état de tranquillité tout naturellement établi jusqu'à ce qu'on puisse s'entendre ultérieurement au sujet des nouveaux rapports sur lesquels l'appui et l'intervention de V. M. I. auront une influence si puissante.

Veuillez, Monsieur, mon frère et beau-frère, être bien convaincu que j'irai au devant de ce moment heureux pour moi avec un empressement qui n'est que la suite bien naturelle de l'attachement sincère, et de la haute considération avec lesquels je suis, &c.

(Signé) MAXIMILIEN JOSEPH.

Nymphenbourg,
le 10 7bre, 1813.

A Monsieur mon frère et beau-frère,
S. M. I.
L'Empereur de toutes les Russies.

No. II.

Réponse de l'Empereur de Russie au Roi de Bavière.

Monsieur mon frère.

La réponse de V. M. vient de m'être remise. Les dispositions qu'elle m'annonce, la confiance précieuse qu'elle me témoigne, m'ont vivement touché. V. M. ne regrettera jamais de s'être livré avec un tel abandon aux sentimens que je lui porte. Uni avec l'Empereur d'Autriche par les liens les plus indissolubles je n'hésite pas à accéder à toutes les propositions qu'il va faire à V. M. et à donner ma garantie aux transactions qui en seront le résultat. Le retour d'un ordre de choses qui assure à l'Europe un long intervalle de paix et de bonheur, forme le but vers lequel tendent tous nos efforts. Je regarde la force et l'indépendance des puissances intermédiaires comme le premier moyen de l'atteindre. Cette importante considération rend indispensable que les frontières de l'Autriche soyent mieux établies sous le rapport militaire, ce qui ne sauroit être obtenu que par des arrangemens à prendre avec V. M. Elle envisage sans doute, l'état actuel des choses d'un point de vue trop élevé pour ne pas en être convaincu, et moi je suis trop franc pour ne pas m'expliquer envers elle sans la moindre reserve sur un objet aussi délicat. Mais l'indemnisation la plus complette, calculée sur les proportions géographiques, statistiques, et financières du pays cédé, sera formellement garantie à V. M. afin qu'un pareil échange ne puisse même que tourner à son avantage, car elle ne se désaisiroit que de celle de ses provinces qui ne s'amalgame guères avec les autres parties de ses états, et où le vœu de retourner à leurs anciens maîtres est trop fortement nourri dans le cœur de chaque habitant pour que l'esprit d'insurrection ne suscite des embarras continuels au gouvernement.

Loin de vouloir que par là la puissance de la Bavière éprouve la moindre diminution, mon attachement pour V. M. me fera plutôt trouver un moyen d'aggrandissement pour elle dans les changemens que les circonstances pourraient réclamer. Il serait difficile que je lui fournisse dans ce moment des preuves plus prononcées, combien j'ai ses intérêts à cœur, et aussitôt que les arrangemens préliminaires avec l'Autriche auront été signés, je suis prêt à faire conclure avec toute personne qu'elle voudra envoyer à mon quartier général, des engagemens basées sur les principes que je viens de développer. J'attends en revanche une coopération active et immédiate de la part de V. M. Les momens sont précieux, les assurances positives qu'elle m'a données m'autorisent à compter sur son empressement à les faire. Dans le cas contraire, et si la plus belle chance pour la délivrance de l'Europe devait être perdue, V. M. sentirais que je ne serai plus le maître de réaliser à son égard les vues dictées par l'amitié, et confirmées par la politique liberale de tous mes alliés. Les arrangemens militaires qui vont être proposés à V. M. doivent lui inspirer toute confiance et ajouter une nouvelle preuve en faveur des principes qui nous guident.

Je réitère à V. M. l'assurance, &c. &c.

(Signé) ALEXANDRE.

Töplitz, le $\frac{11}{23}$ *Sept^{re}.* 1813.

A Monsieur mon frère,
 S. M. le Roi de Bavière.

No. III.

Précis d'un Entretien du Général Comte de Meerveldt avec l'Empereur Napoléon, au Camp près de Leipzig, le 17 Octobre, 1813.

———

L'Empereur Napoléon me fit appeller le 17 à 2 heures après midi, et après un compliment sur les efforts que j'avais fait pour passer sur le derrière de son armée, et l'attaquer sur ses communications, me dit qu'il voulait, comme un témoignage de son estime me renvoyer sur parole. Après quelques questions sur la force des armées alliées qu'il assura ne pas avoir supposé aussi considérables, il me demanda si sa présence à l'armée nous avait été connue ; ce dont je l'assurais. Vous aviez donc le projet de me livrer bataille ? Oui, Sire. Vous êtes dans l'erreur sur les forces que j'ai rassemblées ici ; quelles forces me supposez-vous ? Au plus 120,000 hommes. J'en ai plus que 200,000. Je crois que je vous ai taxé moins fort que vous n'êtes, quelle est votre force ? Plus de 350,000 Sire. M'attaquerez vous demain ? Je n'en doute pas, Sire ; les armées alliées en confiant sur la supériorité de leurs moyens attaqueront V. M. journellement, et espéreront par là amener le résultat d'une bataille décisive, et la retraite de l'armée Française, que ses talens prouvés pourraient nous enlever les premiers jours. Cette guerre durera-t-elle toujours ? il sera bien tems de la finir une fois. Sire, c'est le vœu général, et la paix est dans les mains de V. M. ; il eut dépendu d'elle de la conclure au Congrès de Prague. On n'était pas de bonne foi, on a finassé, on m'a fixé une terme péremptoire ; une aussi grande affaire ne peut pas se finir en dix jours ; l'Autriche a manqué le moment de se mettre à la tête des affaires de l'Europe, j'aurais fait tout ce qu'elle eut voulu ; et nous aurions dicté la loi. Je ne puis cacher à V. M. qu'on pense en Autriche qu'à la suite de votre dictature vous auriez fini par dicter la loi à l'Autriche. Mais enfin, il faut que quelqu'un porte la parole, que ce soit l'Autriche ! si vous écoutez la Russie elle est sous l'influence de l'Angleterre, et celle-ci ne veut pas la paix. Je ne suis nullement instruit des idées de mon gouvernement Sire, tout ce que je puis avoir l'honneur de dire à S. M. je le supplie de ne considérer que comme mes idées à moi, mais je sais avec certitude que l'Empereur mon maître est décidé à ne jamais se départer dans les négociations de l'accord le plus étroit avec les cours alliées, que c'est à cet accord qu'il est convaincu devoir la position heureuse de ses affaires, et l'espoir fondé d'une paix durable. V. M. connait combien les cours alliées partagent le désir de pouvoir amener cette paix le plutôt possible. Eh bien, pourquoi n'accepte-t-on pas mes propositions de négocier ? Vous voyez bien, que l'Angleterre ne veut pas la paix. Sire, je sais avec certitude qu'on attendait journellement une réponse del 'Angleterre à laquelle on a transmis les propositions de V. M. d'entamer des négociations, et on se croit assuré de son consentement. Vous verrez qu'elle ne voudra pas. L'Angleterre a trop besoin de la paix, Sire, pour ne pas la désirer avec ardeur, mais elle désire une paix, et non une armistice ; une paix qui porte dans ses conditions la garantie de sa stabilité. Et en quoi supposez vous que cette garantie pourrait se trouver ? Dans une équilibre de puissance en Europe, qui mettra des bornes à la prépondérance de la France. Eh bien ! que l'Angleterre me rende mes iles, et je lui rendrai le Hanovre ; je rétablirai les départemens réunis et les villes Anséatiques. Je crois, Sire, qu'ils tiendront au rétablissement de la Hollande. Oh elle n'existera pas, elle ne respecterait pas les pavillons ; la Hollande, isolée, serait sous la dépendance de l'Angleterre. Je crois, Sire, que les principes maritimes établis par l'Angleterre sont occasionnels, et une conséquence de la guerre, et cesseront avec elle ; en suite de cela les raisons que V. M. dit avoir pour vouloir conserver la Hollande disparaitront. Eh bien il faudrait s'entendre sur cette indépendance, mais cela ne sera pas facile avec les principes de l'Angleterre. Ce serait une résolution généreuse et un grand pas vers la paix. Je la désire ardemment ; je ferai des sacrifices, de grands sacrifices même, mais il y a des choses auxquelles mon honneur tient, et dont surtout dans ma position je ne saurais me départir ; par exemple, le Protectorat de l'Allemagne. V. M. connait trop combien son influence en Allemagne est contraire au rétablissement de l'équilibre de force en Europe pour supposer qu'on puisse la consolider encore par une Paix ; notre alliance avec la Bavière et plusieurs autres Confédérés de la Ligue du Rhin, la possession que nous espérons obtenir de la Saxe, enlèvent au reste à V. M. de fait une partie de ses alliés, et nous comptons que le reste tombera par la suite des succès que notre grande supériorité nous promêt. Oh, ceux qui ne veulent pas de ma protection, je les abandonne. Ils s'en repentiront, mais l'honneur ne me permet pas de me départir de la qualité de protecteur pour les restants. Je me rappelle que V. M. anciennement m'a dit elle-même, qu'il était necessaire pour le repos de l'Europe que la France soit séparée par une ceinture de petits etats indépendans des autres grandes puissances de l'Europe. Que V. M. revienne à ces justes principes qu'elle avait conçue dans sa sagesse dans des momens de calme et de réflexion, et elle assurera le bonheur de l'Europe. L'Empereur ne répondit point négativement à cette observation, et il s'en suivit un instant de silence qu'il interrompit par l'exclamation : Eh bien, nous verrons : mais tout cela ne nous amenera à la paix ; comment négocier avec l'Angleterre qui veut m'imposer la loi de ne pas construire plus de 30 vaisseaux de ligne dans mes ports ; les Anglais sentent eux-mêmes tellement combien cette condition est inadmissible qu'ils n'ont pas osé l'articuler jusqu'à-present, mais je leur en connais l'intention. Sire, j'ai supposé dès le commencement de cette conversation que le but de cette guerre pour les puissances alliées était le rétablissement de l'équilibre de l'Europe ; l'Angleterre ne peut pas se cacher qu'avec l'étendue des côtes que V. M. possède depuis l'Adriatique jusqu'à la Mer du Nord, dans quelques années elle aurait une marine double et triple de celle de la Grande Bretagne, et avec les talens et l'activité de V. M. les résultats seraient faciles à calculer ; comment obvier à cette supériorité prochaine, qu'en fixant le nombre des vaisseaux que pourront se construire dans les ports de la France, à moins que V. M. ne revienne aux stipulations qu'elle a établie elle-même en se plaçant à la tête du gouvernement du Royaume d'Italie ; savoir, de vouloir rendre l'indépendance à ce pays, à la paix continentale et générale. Je ne sache pas que V. M. ait jamais rien publié qui revoquât cette loi, qu'elle s'était imposée à elle-même, il serait beau de porter à la tranquillité de l'Europe, ce que l'Europe considérerait comme une sacrifice généreuse, au lieu du déshonneur que V. M. attache avec justice à la loi qui bornerait le nombre des vaisseaux de la France ; elle aurait toute la gloire de cette paix, et après avoir acquis le plus haut degré de gloire militaire, la paix lui donnerait le tems d'achever tous les superbes établissemens qu'elle a commencés en France, et de faire le bonheur de son empire, auquel sa gloire ne laisse pas de conter un peu cher. L'Empereur convint que cette condition serait plus admissible. Dans tous les cas, ajoutait-il, je ne m'entendrai au rétablissement de l'ancien ordre de choses en Italie. Ce pays, réuni sous un même souverain, conviendrait à un système général de politique en Europe. Quant au Duché de Varsovie, V. M. y a renoncé je suppose! Oh oui, je l'ai offert et on n'a pas trouvé bon de l'accepter. L'Espagne pourrait encore être une pomme de discorde. Non, répondit l'Empereur, l'Espagne est un objet de dynastie. Oui, Sire, mais je pense que les puissances belligérantes n'ont pas toutes le même intérêt pour la même dynastie. J'ai été obligé d'abandonner l'Espagne, cette question est donc décidée par là. Il semble, donc, répliqua-je, que la paix devrait être possible. Eh bien, envoyez moi quelqu'un en qui je puisse avoir confiance, et nous pourrons nous arranger. On m'accuse de proposer toujours des armistices; je n'en propose donc pas; mais vous conviendrez que l'humanité y gagnerait beaucoup: si l'on veut, je me placerai derrière la Saale; les Russes et les Prussiens derrière l'Elbe; vous en Bohême, et la pauvre Saxe, qui a tant souffert, restera neutre. Nous ne pourrions guères nous passer de la Saxe pour vivre; si même nous ne portions nos espérances (vu la supériorité de nos moyens) à voir V. M. passer le Rhin cet automne encore, il ne pourrait donc jamais, je pense, être de la convenance des armées alliées de voir V. M. par une armistice établie en deça. Pour cela il faudrait que je perde une bataille, cela peut arriver,—mais cela n'est pas.

No. IV.

Copie d'une Note minutée par Monsieur St. Aignan.

Franckfort-sur-Maine le 10 *Nov.* 1813.

M. le Prince de Metternich m'a fait l'honneur de me dire que la circonstance, qui m'a amené au quartier général de S. M. L'Empereur d'Autriche, pouvait rendre convenable de me charger de porter la réponse aux propositions que S. M. l'Empereur des Français a fait faire par M. le Comte de Meerfeldt.

En conséquence, M. le Prince de Metternich et M. le Comte de Nesselrode m'ont chargé de rapporter à S. M. :

Que les souverains coalisés étaient engagés par des liens indissolubles qui faisaient leur force, et dont ils ne dévieraient jamais. Que les engagemens réciproques qu'ils avaient contractés leur avait fait prendre la résolution de ne faire qu'une paix générale ; que, lors du Congrès de Prague, on n'avait pu penser à une paix continentale, parce que les circonstances n'auraient pas donné le tems de s'entendre pour une paix générale, mais que depuis, les intentions de toutes les puissances, et celles de l'Angleterre étaient connues ; qu'ainsi il était inutile de penser, soit à un armistice, soit à une négociation qui n'eût pas, pour premier principe, une paix générale. Que les puissances coalisées étaient unanimement d'accord sur la puissance et la prépondérance que la France doit conserver dans son intégrité, et en se renfermant dans ses limites naturelles, qui sont les Alpes, le Rhin et les Pyrénées.

Que le principe de l'indépendance de l'Allemagne était une condition *sine quâ non* ; qu'ainsi la France devait renoncer, non pas à l'influence que tout grand état exerce nécessairement sur un état de force inférieure, mais à toute souveraineté sur l'Allemagne ; que d'ailleurs c'était un principe que S. M. avait posé elle-même ; en disant qu'il était convenable que les grandes puissances fussent séparées par des états plus faibles.

Que, du côté des Pyrénées, l'indépendance de l'Espagne et le rétablissement de l'ancienne dynastie étaient également une condition *sine quâ non*.

Qu'en Italie, l'Autriche devait avoir une frontière qui serait un objet de négociation, que le Piémont offrait plusieurs lignes que l'on pourrait discuter, ainsi que l'état de l'Italie, pourvu toutefois qu'elle fût, comme l'Allemagne, gouvernée d'une manière indépendante de la France, ou de toute autre puissance prépondérante.

Que de même l'état de Hollande serait un objet de négociation, en partant toujours du principe qu'elle devait être indépendante.

Que l'Angleterre était prête à faire les plus grands sacrifices pour la paix fondée sur ces bases, et à reconnaître la liberté du commerce et de la navigation, à laquelle la France a droit de prétendre.

Que si ces principes d'une pacification générale étaient agréés par S. M. on pourrait neutraliser, sur la rive droite du Rhin, tel lieu qu'on jugerait convenable, où les plénipotentiaires de toutes les puissances belligérantes se rendraient sur-le-champ, sans cependant que les négociations suspendissent le cours des opérations militaires.

(Signé)   Saint-Aignan.

No. V.

Lettre de l'Empereur Napoléon à l'Empereur d'Autriche.

Monsieur mon frère et très-cher beau-père,

JE désire rendre la place de Zamose et conclure à cet effet une petite convention avec V. M. Je verrais avec plaisir qu'elle voulut charger le Comte de Bubna de recevoir des ouvertures à cet égard. Le général Comte de Bubna me paraissant destiné à commander une division d'observation, je désirerais que V. M. voulût l'autoriser à être le canal de la correspondance qu'elle et moi avons voulu conserver malgré l'état de guerre.

J'ai fait connaître par l'officier porteur de ma lettre au Comte de Bubna que j'étais dans des sentimens très-pacifiques.

Je ne saurais me persuader que V. M. puisse trouver de l'intérêt à la continuation d'une guerre, dont le résultat, si elle se prolongeait, serait le malheur de la France, de l'Allemagne, et de l'Autriche, et qui ne peut tourner qu'au profit de l'Angleterre et de la Russie.

Les dernières nouvelles que j'ai reçues de l'Impératrice sont du 18. Elle était de retour à St. Cloud, et jouissait d'une bonne santé, mais, comme V. M. peut le concevoir, elle était fort peinée d'une pareille lutte.

De V. M. Imp. et Royale
Le bon frère et gendre,
(Signé) NAPOLEON.

à *Dresde, le 25 Sept.* 1813.

No. VI.

Réponse de l'Empereur d'Autriche à l'Empereur Napoléon.

J'ai reçu la lettre de V. M. Impériale en date du 25 Septembre.

La Place de Zamosc n'étant point assiégée par mes troupes, je ne puis me mêler de sa capitulation, et cet objet ne pourra être réglé que par les commandans respectifs. V. M. I. ne saurait douter des vœux que je forme pour la paix. Sur 21 années de règne 10 ont été perdues pour le bonheur de mes peuples.

L'office que le Duc de Bassano a adressé le 18 Août dernier au Comte de Metternich semble prouver que V. M. partage ma conviction, qui n'est pas moins celle de mes alliés, que l'Europe ne peut plus être particllement pacifiée, et que mieux vaudrait couler à fond les chances d'une guerre entamée, que la terminer en conservant la crainte de nouveaux et immanquables bouleversemens.

J'ai fait passer en Angleterre simultanément avec l'Empereur de Russie et le Roi de Prusse, les ouvertures de V. M. J'attends sous peu la réponse du Prince Régent, et je m'empresserai de la communiquer à V. M. I.

De votre Majesté Impériale
Le bon frère et beau-père,
(Signé)   François.

Töplitz, le 29 Septembre, 1813.

No. VII.

Paper drawn up by the King of Prussia, and presented by him to the Emperor of Russia.

Dec. 7th, 1813.

———

LA Suisse se déclare neutre, mais l'acte de médiation subsiste, et les troupes de cette république combattent dans les rangs de l'armée Française, donc cette neutralité n'est qu'illusoire ; elle ne peut, fut-elle reconnue par Napoléon, offrir aucune sûreté aux Puissances Alliées, car sans doute la violera-t-il sous quelque prétexte facile à trouver, dès qu'il verra son profit. Ne nous y trompons pas, sa marche par le territoire neutre d'Ansbach en 1805, nous a fait voir à quoi l'on doit s'attendre de sa part.

On se propose de passer le Rhin, soit à Basle, soit un peu plus bas, hors du territoire Suisse, et de pousser les opérations dans l'intérieur de la France. Ce plan ne présente-il pas les plus grands dangers, aussi longtems que nous ne serons pas maîtres de la Suisse, ou qu'elle ne se sera pas déclarée pour nous ? Si nos armées passent par son territoire, en reconnaissant d'ailleurs la neutralité, les Français useront de la même liberté, et quand même nos armées les respecteraient ne risquerions-nous pas d'y voir entrer l'ennemi par les routes qui lui resteraient ouvertes, par celle de Génève, &c., et de le voir s'y placer sur nos derrières ? Quelles difficultés n'offrirait pas une retraite sous de telles circonstances ; surtout si elle était la suite de quelque revers, et si le Rhin chariait des glaces, ce qui d'un jour à l'autre peut arriver dans cette saison ? Une saine politique pourrait d'ailleurs nous défendre pour le moment la poursuite de ce plan, car si nous entrons dans l'intérieur de l'ancienne France tandis que Napoléon se prête à des négociations de paix, nous lui donnons des forces morales ; nous paraissons en contradiction avec nos offres et nos déclarations nous lui facilitons la réunion de tous les moyens de résistance.

Ne vaudrait-il pas mieux donc ajourner le plan en question jusqu'à ce que le résultat des négociations actuelles fut connu, et qu'il nous fournisse des argumens propres à prouver au peuple Français que c'est à son souverain qu'il doit s'en prendre s'il voit le théâtre de la guerre porté dans ses foyers, malgré le désir qu'avaient les alliés de lui donner la paix ?

Ne conviendrait-il pas d'attendre que la Suisse fut gagnée pour nos intérêts que le printems favorisa les opérations que les armées soyent recrutées, augmentées par les levées Allemandes, et suffisamment fournies de munitions et de tous les nécessaires pour une aussi grande entreprise ? Supposons que nous réussissons à pénétrer dans le cœur de la France, pourrions nous esperer d'aller planter nos étendarts à Paris, d'opérer quelque chose de décisif, sans nous être préalablement assurés de ces moyens ? Et qu'aurions-nous fait si nous étions obligés de nous arrêter à moitié chemin, quelle serait notre situation si nous étions forcés de revenir sur nos pas ? Un échec en France nous rejetterait bien en arrière de ce que nous avons atteints ; releverait l'opinion en faveur de Napoléon, lui ferait bien hausser le ton, et serait le plus grand de tous les malheurs. Ce n'est point qu'on veuille se ralentir le moins du monde à l'égard des opérations de guerre en général. La manière dont Napoléon a accepté les bases de la paix nous prescrit au contraire d'y mettre la plus grand énergie, mais il semble que nous sommes appelés à pousser ces opérations avec toute la vigueur imaginable, d'abord sur notre droite, par le vœu des peuples d'Allemagne transrhenane, de la Belgique, et de la Hollande, et par les mesures déjà prises pour celle-ci. Là, la saison loin de nous être contraire, pourra même faciliter nos efforts ; là, Napoléon ne trouvera point les puissans arguments capables de provoquer les Français à leur propre défense, car nous n'entrons point dans l'ancienne France ; là, nous nous rapprochons des secours de l'Angleterre, et de nos communications avec elle, des munitions, des subsistances ; là, nous pouvons espérer des succès rapides, et en cas de malheur nous ménager une retraite assurée.

D'après tout ceci.

Une défensive forte sur notre gauche et au centre ; une offensive prompte, vigoureuse, et bien calculée, sur notre droite.

Ne serait-ce pas ce qui conviendrait le mieux dans les circonstances présentes ?

Nous ne sommes guère sûrs de ce que fera le Prince Royal de Suède pour les opérations en Hollande. C'est une raison de plus pour nous en occuper nous-mêmes, ainsi que leur grande importance exige. Les négociations avec le Danemarck ne semblent offrir que bien peu d'espoir. Si elles manquent il paraît utile d'abandonner la guerre contre cette puissance au Prince Royal, en lui laissant des troupes auxiliaires. L'on ne peut pas mettre trop de promptitude aux opérations sur-mentionnés, et dans tous les cas on ne doit pas l'attendre du Prince Royal maintenant occupé à agir contre Davoust.

Francfort-sur-Maine. 7 *Déc.* 1813

No. VIII.

Note on the Battle of Toulouse.

A CURIOUS pretension that the French gained the victory of Toulouse, has lately been set up by the partisans of Marshal Soult; it is so stated in several of the French military publications; and in the *Annuaire de France* it is asserted, that the British in that action lost 18,000 men. As authority for this statement, the letter of the Duke of Wellington published in the London Gazette of the 26th of April is referred to. From the official return enclosed in that letter the following numbers are copied :—

	Killed.	Wounded.
British	312	1812
Portuguese	78	529
Spanish	205	1723
	595	4064

The mis-statement thus made in the French publication would be no bad standard by which to appreciate the value of the other assertions contained in this work, of which the enumeration of the forces of the contending armies in this battle is not amongst the least erroneous. But we will pass by all discussion on this point to meet the question of the victory; and we state upon that point, that the French had intrenched themselves outside the town of Toulouse, and along the heights extending from Borde de la Pajade to near Montandran. They had five redoubts upon this ground, besides other field fortifications. This part alone of the French position was seriously attacked by the British troops, and the whole of it was carried from one end to the other, all the redoubts taken, and the enemy, in the evening, driven behind the canal of Languedoc, and within the walls of Toulouse. In the other parts of the field of battle, General Hill, on the left of the Garonne, drove the French from their outer line of works into the faubourg of St. Ciprien, and General Picton, whose part was limited to the defence of the right of the canal of Languedoc, prevented the enemy from passing, by the attacks he repeatedly made upon the tête-de-pont at Jumiare. Such was the result of the action; but in answer to it, and as the grounds on which the victory is claimed, it is stated, that the French were not attacked in the position into which they been driven behind the canal of Languedoc, or in the town of Toulouse. The reason for this is, that the Duke of Wellington, instead of attacking an army as brave and intelligent as the one opposed to him, protected by so formidable a line of defence, determined to cut off its retreat. To carry an operation of such a nature into effect, it was necessary that he should attack the canal with his left, and extend that left to the Garonne, to do which, it was of essential consequence that he should remove the bridge he had established over that river nearer to Toulouse, that he might have a shorter communication with General Hill, and that he might make a fresh distribution of his forces by concentrating them towards his left. The movements necessary for the attainment of these objects, together with the accurate reconnaissance of the positions gained on the preceding day which was required for carrying them into effect, were not completed till late in the day after the battle. The Duke therefore determined to postpone his operations till the following morning; but Marshal Soult, in the course of that night, evacuated Toulouse, leaving in it three generals, 1600 prisoners, and a great quantity of guns and military stores. Now, where is the victory? Did Marshal Soult fight to retain possession of the heights which he had fortified, and which commanded the town, and to the defence of which he sacrificed 3600 men*?—if so, he lost them. Did he fight to keep possession of Toulouse?—if so, he lost that.

The French have but one success to boast of in this battle, which is the having repulsed the Spaniards, who were twice driven back from the attack of the redoubts of la Pajade, and pursued till they were supported by a part of the light division of the British and Portuguese reserve under Sir Andrew Barnard. The momentary disorder of the Spaniards was soon repaired, and they afterwards co-operated in the general attack of the position. But of what value is this to the claim of the victory? The simple fact is, that the Duke of Wellington fought to possess himself of Toulouse, and to drive Marshal Soult from his communications with Paris.

In these objects he completely succeeded, which, according to the general understanding of the word, was to gain a victory, and a splendid victory; for it was gained over the finest army the French at that time possessed; it was gained, notwithstanding the discomfiture of the Spaniards, and it was gained by a manœuvre along the front and

---

* Vide Annuaire de France.

round the flank of the fortified position of the enemy, by only two divisions of the British army, and under circumstances which will ever render this battle one of the most brilliant achievements of the genius of the Duke of Wellington, and of the skill and valour of his troops.

No. IX.

Note referred to in page 89.

In pages 20 and 21 of Baron Fain's Memoir of the Operations of 1814, it is stated that the English had agents in different parts of France, endeavouring to revive the hopes of the old partisans of the House of Bourbon. If this had been the case, it is singular that M. de Beauchamp's work, which Baron Fain cites as his authority for the details of the conspiracy formed for this purpose, should make no mention of it whatever; this gentleman is equally mistaken as to the force of the Duke of Wellington's army which he reckons at 200,000 men, when, in fact, it did not amount to 100,000. In page 43, he speaks of the resistance which the peasantry of the Vosges and of Alsace opposed to the allied armies; and in page 102 he mentions the defeat of a corps of 25,000 Bavarians after the battle of Brienne by the corps under Marshal Marmont. Both these statements appear to be totally incorrect.

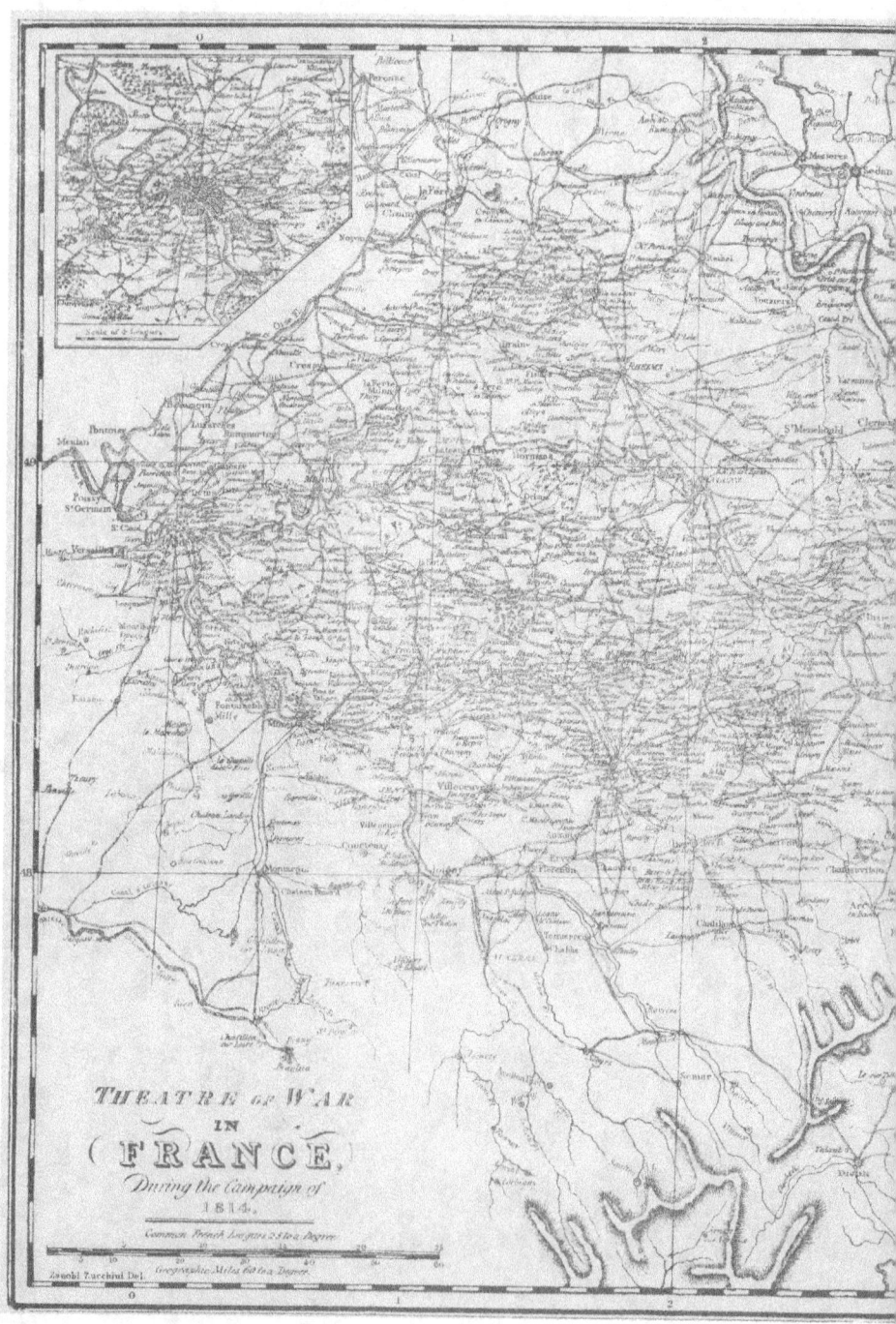

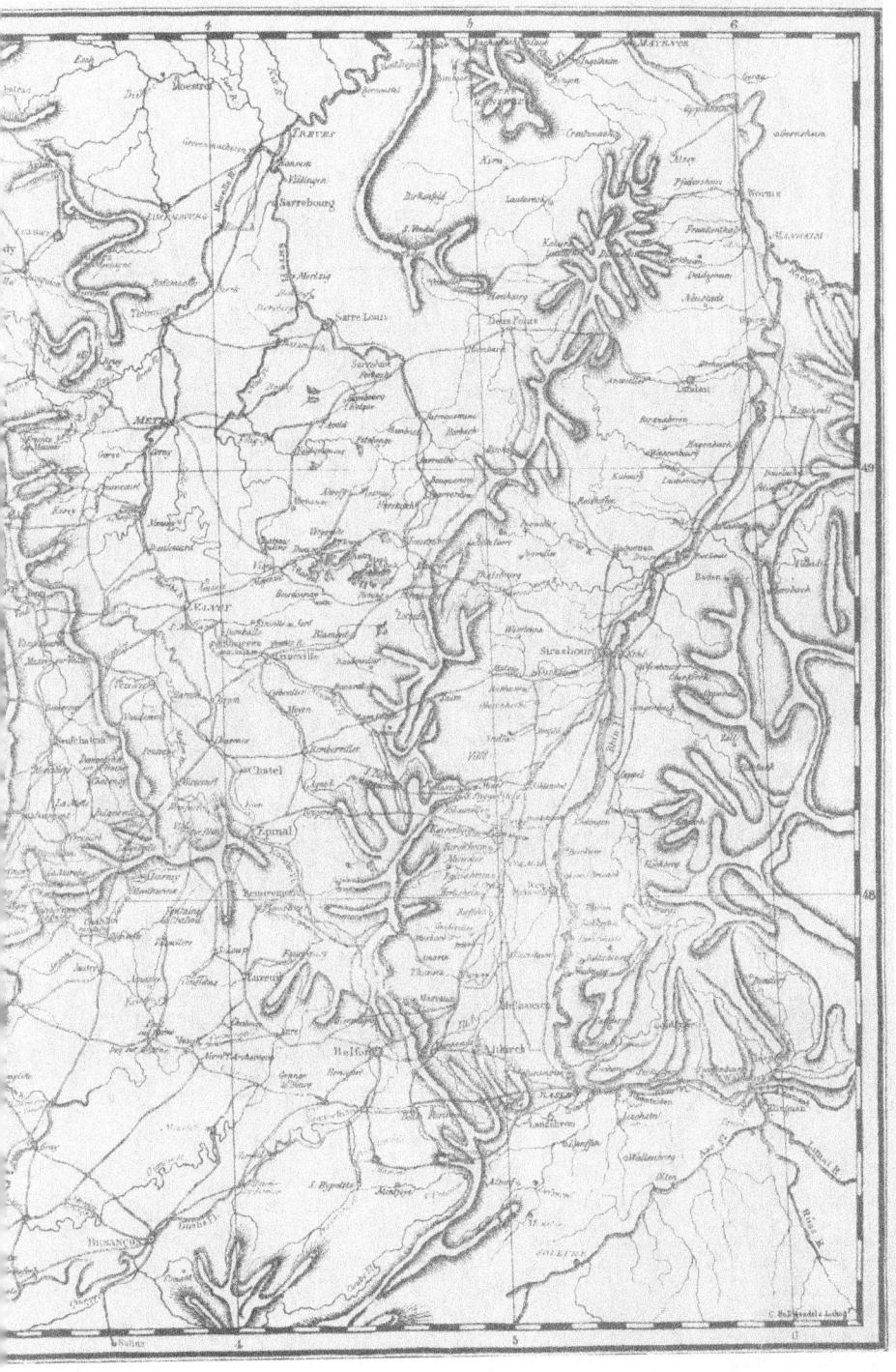

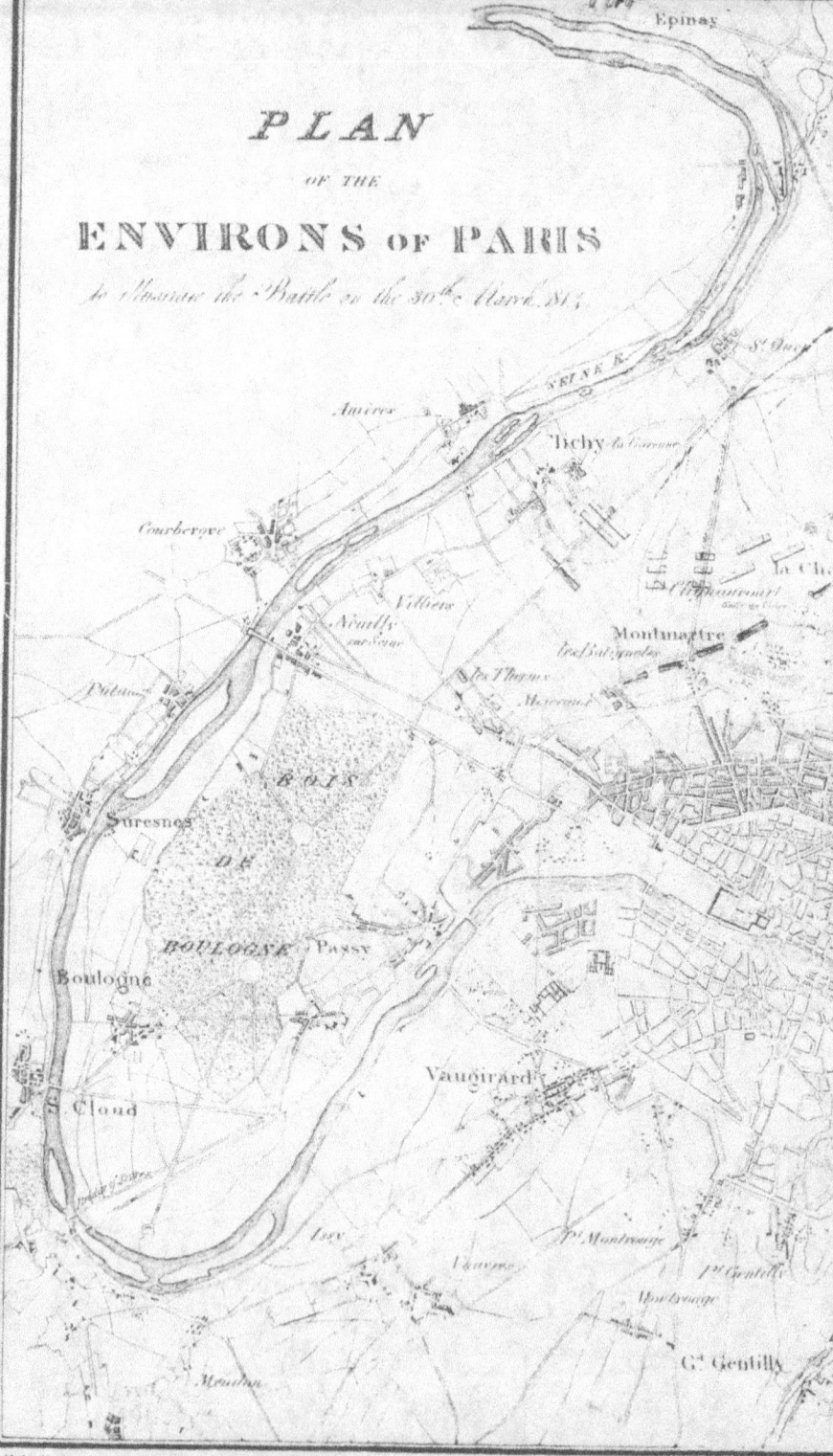

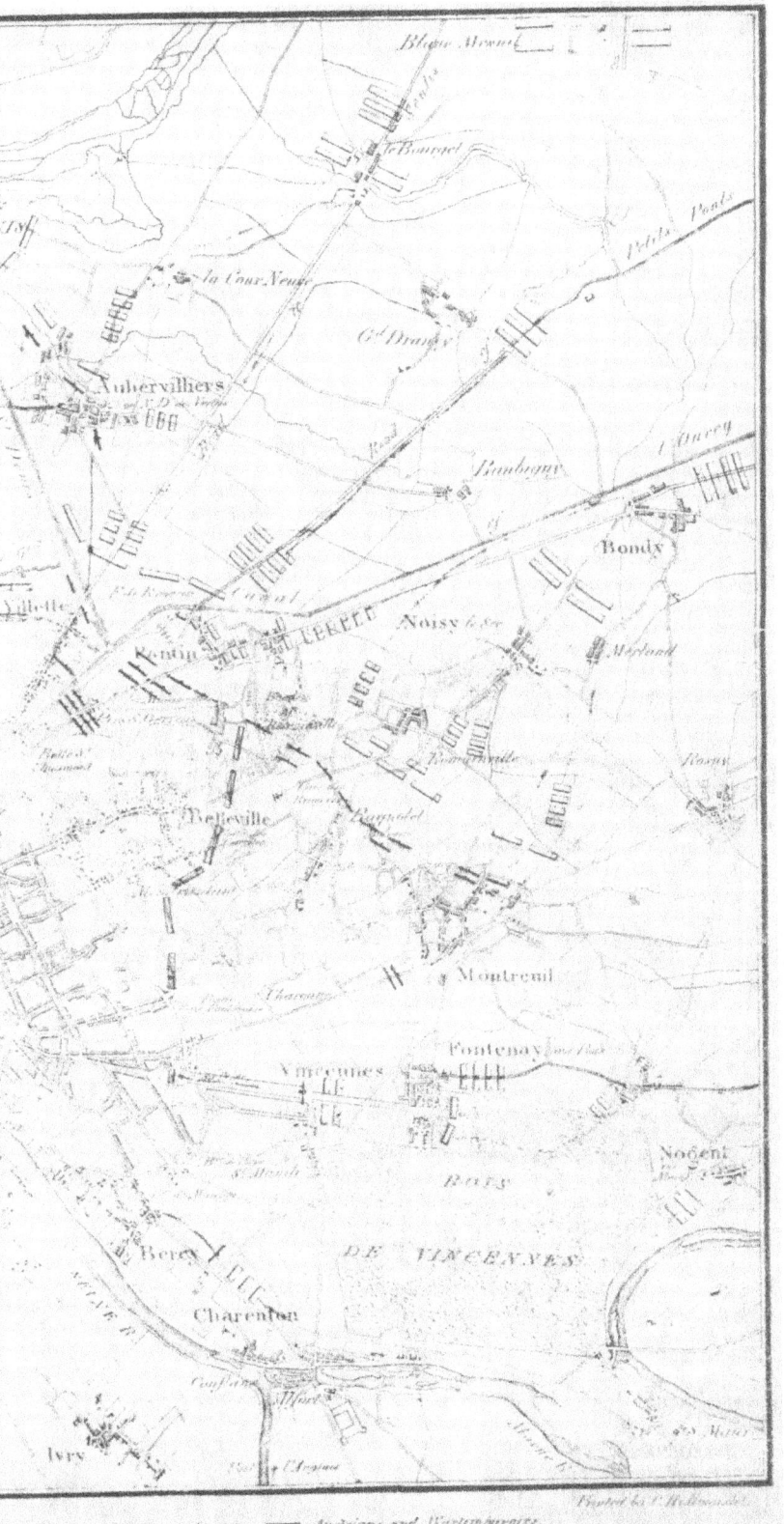

www.ingramcontent.com/pod-product-compliance
Lightning Source LLC
Chambersburg PA
CBHW071356300426
44114CB00016B/2084